To Whom Shall I Go?

Sermons of a Country Parson

William R. Boyd, Sr.

Parson's Porch Books

To Whom Shall I Go? Sermons of a Country Parson
ISBN: Softcover 978-1-960326-91-1
Copyright © 2024 by William R. Boyd, Sr.

Parson's Porch Books is an imprint of Parson's Porch *&* Company (PP*&*C) in Cleveland, Tennessee. PP*&*C is a self-funded charity which earns money by publishing books of noted authors, representing all genres. Its face and voice is **David Russell Tullock** (dtullock@parsonsporch.com).

Parson's Porch *&* Company *turns books into bread & milk* by sharing its profits with the poor.

www.parsonsporch.com

To Whom Shall I Go?

Contents

Some New Year's Resolutions

Scripture lesson: Romans: 33-36; 12:1-21
Text: Romans 12:1

It was a stormy, wintry night. Snow was falling with gale-like intensity. The wind was fierce and terrifying in its savage velocity and a young girl, staring out of her bedroom window in fear exclaimed, "God must have lost grip of his winds tonight."

This is the way we sometimes feel when things go very wrong, but it is comforting to remember the words of Jesus who said, "Take heart, I have overcome the world." And to Paul, nothing is ever out of God's control.

However, situations sometimes come up that are beyond our control and beyond our understanding. What can we do? We pray, asking for wisdom and strength to go on. And we are able to press on through prayer and accepting God's will after we have done all we can do. The bottom line is that it comes down to a matter of faith, faith in Christ and his promises. It is up to us to choose whether or not we will live by faith. If we do, we will gain an insight into the power of God and insight into the power of spiritual resolve. So, at this point we begin a quest and a spiritual journey where, as a Spirit-filled believer, we would do well to resolve to grow in the faith and make the following New Year's resolutions:

Resolve to Apply Christian (Christ-like) values including morals and ethics Often this is difficult when it comes to money, power, or personal relationships. May we:

Resolve to live our daily lives (even our routines) unto God, to present our bodies as a Living sacrifice, saying, "God use me according to your will." And accepting the body God gave us. We are much more than our physical body. We that we are body soul and spirit - created for eternity.

Resolve to live according to Christ-like standards and values. Resolve to not allow the world to dictate their values to us because their values are materialistic are made with the capacity to be much more than this. Resolve to not let secular thought with its subtle communication skills dictate to us how to spend our time, our talents or our money. Christ-like standards have their basis in Living a spiritual existence not weighed down by what is material and temporary. Jesus said, "Be anxious for nothing." This should be our goal, especially when, at times, it is difficult to achieve.

Resolve to live our lives as being a part of something bigger than ourselves. To reach out more to our family, our community, our country, and to the world because what we believe concerning Jesus Christ and the gospel is bigger, better and beyond this world. It is the best, most satisfying way to le!

Resolve to Really Demonstrate Christ-Like Virtues in a world that laughs at virtue and celebrates winning at any cost. Virtue takes a back seat.

Resolve to live a life that is genuine. Away with the masks that lead to hypocrisy. Away with the masks that cause us to deny who we really are. Away with the masks that mislead others into thinking we are something we are not. Follow the axiom, "To thine own self be true." And, yes, we should all do this, but it must be our redeemed self. Slipping into the behavior of our past, unredeemed self is to be guarded against. A problem we all have at times. The writer of Hebrews warns us about this when he wrote in chapter two verse one, "We must pay more careful attention, therefore, to what we have heard, so that we do not drift away."

Anyway, it is frustrating and futile to go it alone. It is the transformed self of which we speak here. It is the self, changed through the saving work of Jesus Christ. The masked, artificial self carries with it a lot of burdensome psychological baggage anyhow. So, let's resolve that, through Christ, in the year 2017, we will live the overcoming life leaning on the everlasting arms of Christ.

Resolve to serve the Lord with zeal This is an outflow of true inner joy. It is the joy of the Lord that is our strength. Zeal is akin to devotion which comes through Divine relationship. And zest is akin to enthusiasm which is better caught than taught. In point of fact, zest for the spiritual life (Which makes no sense at all to an unbeliever) when coupled with the power of God's Word, has a life of its own. It penetrates into the darkness where we begin to see the unseen. "Faith comes by hearing and hearing by the Word of God."

Resolve to associate with people of all stations of life even the lowly and to live at peace with all persons.

Resolve to Adopt a Christ-Like Attitude A Christ-like attitude is never rude.

There was an athletic coach who once said, "Attitude is everything." Well, maybe it isn't everything, but it's close. I believe our attitude can make or break us. Adopting a Christ-like attitude means how we approach and face life's situations. So,

Let us resolve to accept God's justice. In this very advanced age of technology and psychology, it is often very difficult for us to finally come to grips with the concept that in the end, God's ways are "past finding out."

We seem determined in our notion that we can somehow resolve all of our problems if we just work at it with enough push and technological know-how. Of course we should try, but in matters of justice some situations are truly beyond our reach. So, rather than tearing ourselves apart at the seams because of some situation we can't seem to resolve, it is better to leave such situations with God, at the foot of the cross. I have to do that often. It is better to leave them in God's hands. That old gospel song, "Take your burdens to the Lord and leave them there," is very good advice.

Just as Jesus yielded his will to that of his Father's as he prayed in the garden of Gethsemane, so we will only find God's eternal peace by leaving ultimate justice in the hands of a just and holy God. And understanding often comes with faith and seeing the outcome.

Resolve to adopt a Survival Code-of-the-Road attitude in personal relations which is, "Do unto others as you would have them do unto you." After all, when we sum it up, the end of God's grace in our lives is graciousness - a very precious commodity.

Resolve to refuse to allow evil to win even one battle. Remember, as time plays out history, Satan and all evil will be shown to have lost the war.

We all know that many New Year's resolutions are not kept simply because people do not really want to change. They want the desired outcome without the pain of change.

In simple matters, for example, like going to bed earlier in order to get enough sleep, we may have to miss a favorite television program, so we rationalize and stay up only to pay the consequences of lost sleep the next morning. These are things we can easily do if we really want to.

However, on a spiritual level, the matter is not so simple. Applying Christian ethics in a hostile, greedy world, demonstrating Godly virtues when evil abounds and others laugh at your efforts, determining to follow Christ when the world follows its own selfish desires should be our resolve and our goal for 2017.

Recognizing that adopting a Christ-like attitude when injustice comes close to our own lives, is only possible through God's holy presence within us. Sometimes life is tough.

Essential is his Holy Spirit that guides, comforts and sustains when it seems that the bottom has fallen out.

May we in this year of our Lord, resolve to learn in greater measure to lean on Jesus Christ who is the source of our spiritual strength and use this power of resolve - to know and to do his will.

Pressing On

Scripture lesson: Philippians 3: 12-21; 4:1

One evening, while listening to a performance by the New York Philharmonic Symphony Orchestra, I was surprised to hear the conductor tell the audience that the celeste keyboard player was 86 years old. She had continued with her career all those years and true to her form and to the delight of the audience, her last performance was flawless. A hearty round of applause quickly followed, and she certainly deserved it. She had pressed on with precision and grace to the very end of her career. Inspiring? Yes, and she was also fortunate to have good health.

And for a further example, there was a bookkeeper in Red Lion, Pennsylvania with a sterling reputation for accuracy and I was told that he wouldn't leave his work and go home at the end of the day until he had balanced his books. At junior high school, where I taught, word got out that he had balanced his books for the last time and went home retired. There was much admiration for his honesty, his accuracy and supremely successful career. This, dedicated man had quietly pressed on, but his reputation gave a message that was loud and clear.

After undergraduate college I took four years of lives on with the symphony hornist, Harry Reber, and after my third year of lives on I was invited, to play French horn with the Spring Garden Band of York, Pennsylvania. Harry, my teacher, played principal first chair. The second hornist was Earl Hart, in his eighties and played much better than I did. We admired him for his excellent playing, for his performance being kept at such a high level and for his continued loyalty to the band. Earl pressed on.

Then, we think of former president, the senior George H. W. Bush who, on June 12, 2014, jumped out of a plane, parachuting safely to the ground at ninety years of age. The eighth time he had done this. He did it at 80, 85 and then at 90. A most impressive example of keeping a promise and pressing on.

Now you're probably thinking of people you know who have pressed on. Family, neighbors, friends, so inspiring because as long as they are able, they just don't quit. Here's another favorite one of mine.

While watching a telecast of a Billy Graham evangelistic service, George Beverly Shea came up to the microphone and sang a favorite hymn. He sang beautifully, as usual, and he was 90 years old at the time. I heard him sing that evening. What an inspiration!

But even more amazing is the story I am about to relate to you. I will begin by telling you that while living in Jackson, Louisiana I was asked to preach at the Dixon Correctional Institute just outside of Jackson. There I met, and got to know, Warden Burl Cain. His daughter, a very attracted and talented young lady, was in the band and was selected to be the drum major. Years later after we had left Jackson, Warden Cain was transferred as Warden to the Louisiana State Penitentiary (aka Angola), a prison for lifers. This is where the story gets even more interesting. When I looked up George Beverly Shea's life on the internet, I found to my surprise, that he sang a 45-minute concert for the prisoners in Angola at the age of 100. Astounding! He lived to be 104 and was buried in a coffin lovingly built by the inmates, by prior arrangement for the inmates to build coffins for the Billy Graham Association.

At George Beverly Shea's funeral, Warden Cain, not used to crying, couldn't stop the tears from flowing. "I thought it was the most incredible funeral," Cain said. "It was just a celebration of someone's life." Cain had interviewed Shea shortly before he died. "He was brilliant," Cain said. "He was so witty and had such a great sense of humor. You would have thought he was 20."

Two days after that interview with Cain, George Beverly Shea died. The world lost a great singer and hymn writer. He had pressed on, and with a sense of humor, to the very end of his life. We too, should determine, as best we can, to press on.

And I believe that it is important for us to keep pressing on regardless of our age. Some folks give up on their dreams when they are relatively young and could have a great life of satisfaction from their accomplishments. And at a time when they could be of help to others, who are battling problems they may have already solved.

Youthful energy and determination along with maturity and experience are the most valuable resources we have at any age. And it makes me wonder; could it be that the real motivation behind some of the gossip we hear in barbershops, beauty salons, restaurants and other public places, is the result of a negative view of life? A negative attitude often defended as being realistic What it really is, is perceiving life through a lens devoid of salvation and Christian values. Christians really do look at things differently. Our world view is seen through the lens of someone who is redeemed. It is, in spite of difficulties and disappointments, a life of joy and hope, cradled in love.

There are some folks, who call themselves Christians are really, what I call, cultural Christians, who have not benefited much from the nurture of the Church. And their negative view of life gains reinforcement through negative talk that, over time, becomes ingrained in their thought patterns.

I have been amused more than once, hearing someone stop talking abruptly when they ran out of negate things to say. I believe it is important to look at the positive things and let these be our motivation. This is the way to press on.

After all, we are exceedingly blessed because of our Christian faith, its teachings, the communion of saints and where we are privileged to live - whether among beautiful mountains, plateaus, plains or valleys. These certainly are important reasons to appreciate the goodness of God and press on.

And we should never take for granted how blest we are to live in the United States of America, especially in this section of the United States called the Bible Belt. Some people use the term Bible Belt as a derogatory term, focusing on a fanatical fringe.

They're wrong. The term Bible Belt is a badge of honor that recognizes the Bible as the great collection of sacred writings that it is.

1, personally, am proud of the designation, Bible Belt. It is a statement of our Christian heritage and what it means to us. I believe our entire nation should be a Bible Belt! Without question, our emphasis on the importance of scriptures is a great testimony to the world. And I say to those who criticize; it's really their problem. Deal with it.

We should always keep in mind that we are part of the largest religion in the world. It is truly great, and it is truly worldwide. It proclaims truth, the good news. Yes, the gospel.

The gospel message is what motivated the apostle Paul to evangelize, plant churches and write inspiring letters to his fellow Christians. And he was thankful for their help and support. Travelling, as he did, to bring Jesus Christ to so many places, required additional help and support beyond what he could earn as a tentmaker. So, he thanks the church at Phillipi for their help and while encouraging them in the faith, places important responsibility on the Christians there. He exhorts them saying, and I paraphrase here:

Let us, as Believers, live Up to the Revelation Gen to Us He says this knowing those who are new to the Christian faith still have worldly understandings of life and are in special need of the nurture of the Church. They have come to the Christian faith with a background where some of their values would be detrimental to their progress as new Christians. So, Paul says: Many desire the destruction of Christianity and so, it is today in the twentieth-first century. People refuse to believe and doom themselves to seeing the world through a glass very darkly with no hope. And they seek to destroy the very thing that would make life truly meaningful for them and ge them inner peace.

Natural food is not a substitute for spiritual nourishment Where did the term comfort food come from? It sounds so innocent, but could it, for some, take on meaning beyond merely eating a meal? Natural things can never substitute for spiritual nourishment. It could become a kind of idolatry, worshipping creation, food, rather than the Creator. And drinking alcohol to excess is no exception to this.

Some People seem to glory in wrongdoing. They take pleasure in getting away with things. Such a dangerous path is this, a downward spiral that leads to apostasy. At first, it may seem more easily travelled, but it leads to despair and will destroy an otherwise happy life.

Having our mind taken up with earthly things squeezes out spiritual development. To live as though material things are what is most important, stunts our spiritual growth. Quite simply, people who live by secular values are not spiritual persons. They never feel fulfilled because they exclude the most important aspect of Living - a relationship with the Lord. This relationship has no substitute!

Let Us Now and Always Remember Who We are We know that the Bible says, "Know thyself." One of the greatest things that Jesus taught us is that he was unshakable in his knowledge of himself. He knew who he was and why he was on the earth. And that took precedence over everything else. It is vital for us, too, to know ourselves, how we should occupy our lives and know it is well with our soul. Paul tells us that, as Christians,

Our citizenship is in heaven. So, we should press on, sharing our Christian testimony while we are still here on the earth.

We eagerly await the Savior's return. And we should continue to press on, living a useful, meaningful life knowing it is a source of strength and encouragement to others knowing that:

We will be transformed from a temporal physical existence to an eternal existence So, it is important to continue to press on toward the mark of the high calling in Christ Jesus, who is the ger of eternal life.

Let Us Stand Firm in the Lord! - That false values will not deter us, declaring:

We will press on to take hold of what Christ has already acquired for us.

We will forget what is behind knowing what is in the past cannot be changed. So, let us press ahead by saying,

"Today, really is the first day of the rest of my life and I am going to make the most of it no matter what." Remember, Jesus said, "I am the way, the truth and the life."

It is good to embrace the future as we look to the Lord to help us press on. So, applying the admonition of the apostle Paul,

We will press on, "toward the mark of the high calling in Jesus Christ."

Since Jesus Christ has revealed himself to us through his Word, through the Spirit's inner witness and through increased strength within us we are changed. We know it is so very true, "The Lord is our strength."

May God through the power of his Holy Spirit help us to live up to our own personal spiritual experiences. May we keep the spiritual flame burning within ourselves, in our prate devotions, in our family unit, in our community and through our faithfulness to Christ's Church that has been established forever.

May we never neglect the spiritual aspect of our lives. May we never, even for an instant, ever forget who we are! We are the redeemed of the Lord! And May we then, as God's grace flows through us, continue to stand firm in the faith!

In the name of the Father and of the Son and of the Holy Spirit, let us continue to press on! And all the people said, Amen!

The Hope Within Us

Scripture lesson: Hebrews 10: 1-25 Text: Hebrews 10: 23

The writings in the New Testament are full of hope for those who believe. In Romans 1: 16 Paul says,

"For I am not ashamed of the gospel, because it is the power of God for the salvation of everyone who believes: first for the Jew. then for the Gentile. For in the gospel a righteousness from God is revealed, a righteousness that is by faith from first to last, just as it is written: "the righteous will live by faith."

The apostle Paul knows power. There was a time in his life when he thought he could by his own efforts destroy the Christians, the people of the Way. At the time when he felt so powerful, while traveling to Damascus to continue his persecution, "Suddenly a light from heaven flashed around him. He fell to the ground and heard a voice say to him. 'Saul, Saul, why do you persecute me?" "Who are you Lord, Saul asked." "I am Jesus who you are persecuting," he replied." "Now get up and go into the city, and you will be told what you must do." Well, Paul was converted, went to Damascus and the rest is history. Paul went on to become a great Christian and a great writer emphasizing the hope of the gospel and giving much important instruction to the churches.

In verse 20 Paul gives us some insight into the faith principle. Philosophers, scientists and deep thinkers of all walks of life have wracked their brains trying to understand, using their systems of logic, creation and why we are here. No matter what approach they take, without the faith principle, they are always at a loss to definitely explain what is right in front of them, creation itself. It is to be experienced, enjoyed and marveled at. The complexities and beauty of creation are ample proof. Paul writes concerning this,

"For since the creation of the world God's invisible qualities - his eternal power and Divine nature - have been clearly seen, being understood from what has been made, so that men are without excuse."

People sensitive to the arts often have a better grasp of this than others because a true work of art makes a statement. And the statement of a work of art often goes beyond the ability to craft a verbal understanding of it.

I've often been amused at reading some explanation of a masterpiece in a music history book or an art book. It is not very meaningful without experience. First experience the music, the painting, the photograph, the sculpture. Then, writing or talking about it will make more sense. It is like trying to describe a baby's smile to someone else. When we mutually experience the smile then we can talk about it. This explains why we like to share photographs! So, to understand the gospel. First, experience it!

Expanding on the faith principle, in 2nd Corinthians chapter 13, Paul writes,

> "Examine yourselves to see whether you are in faith: test yourselves. Do you not realize that Christ Jesus is in you...?"

This alludes to the fact that our bodies are the temple of the Holy Spirit. It hints at why Christians are so sensitive to the importance of Living a holy life and become more so as they mature in the faith. Paul further explains this in Ephesians 2:8 by saying:

"For it is by grace you have been saved, through faith - and this not from us, it the gift of God - not by works, so that no one can boast. For we are God's workmanship, created in Christ Jesus to do good works, which God prepared in advance for us to do."

Ephesians 2:8 is a passage full of hope that recognizes God's workmanship within us as we climb higher spiritually in our lives. We rejoice, not because of something we have done, but what Christ has done for us.

In Philippians, 1:3, Paul writes another passage full of hope. In his greeting to the Philippian Church, he beautifully describes his fellow Christians as partners with him in the gospel and shows confidence in them to carry on the work. He begins the passage by affirming them as people and their worth, a most important thing to remember in interpersonal relations. Paul is a fine example of servant leadership as he writes:

"I thank God every time I remember you. In all my prayers for all of you, I always pray with joy because of your partnership in the Gospel from the first day until now, being confident of this, that he who began a good work in you will carry it on to completion until the day of Christ Jesus."

In Colossians, 1:3-6a, Paul greets the Church at Colosse and gives them hope. He praises the Colossian Christians for their faith and love and encourages them informing them that the gospel is producing fruit all over the world just as it is doing among them.

"We always thank God, the Father of our Lord Jesus Christ, when we pray for you, because we have heard of your faith in Christ Jesus and of the love you have for all the saints - the faith and love that spring from the hope that is stored up for you in heaven and that you have already heard about in the word of truth, the Gospel that has come to you. All over the world this Gospel is producing fruit and growing, just as it has been doing among you since the day you heard it and understood God's grace in all its truth."

In the illuminating light of New Testament scripture, do you think that it possible for Christians, who, in spite of their church-going and good deeds, are still Living under the law of the Old Testament? We know that the answer to that question is yes. Many Christians, unfortunately, do just that. Do they believe in Jesus as their Savior? Yes, of course they do, but an inner battle is still going on inside of them where they need to take the final leap of faith and accept the fact that Jesus really has paid it all.

Consciously or unconsciously Living under the bondage of the law, merely exposes their imperfections, offering no solutions; they miss out on experiencing the great truths of the Christian faith that reveal God's love and his grace through Jesus Christ. The gospel song has it right, "Jesus Paid it all."

Ling under the law, made obsolete through Christ's atoning work at Calvary, we learn from today's scripture that:

God's Saving Grace Transforms Us From within Hebrews 10:16 says, "I will put my laws in their hearts, and I will write them on their minds." - "Their sins and lawless acts I will remember no more." -

That's the love of God. That's the atoning work of Christ.

It is written on our hearts not only the symbolic seat of our emotions but inextricably connects our emotions and intellect through our entire nervous system.

It is written on our minds the seat of our intellect, the sum total of who we are.

It is woven into the fabric of our lifestyle as an expression of who we are.

God's Grace Can save Us from Our Sinful State How? Through the forgiveness of sins and the freedom it gives enabling us to live our lives meaningfully and with real fulfillment that expresses a life well led, holy and acceptable before the Lord, our interceding High Priest.

All of humanity needs salvation However, by believing in Christ we are saved.

Salvation involves total, not partial, forgiveness God by his grace, through his Son, blots out all our sins forever Sacrifices for sin are no longer needed. In fact, all the sacrifices made until the time of Christ needed to be authenticated by Divine act. Thank God this has been done through Jesus Christ. We serve a risen Savior.

We all need healing. Everyone is hurting in some way. Christ will heal our hurts. It is for us to pray and believe.

God's Promise gives us a Life of Hope - Scripture teaches, "For he who

19

promised is faithful."

We are cleansed "Having a pure conscience." Ah, the joy of a pure conscience! There are many people who do not sleep well because of sin, and they carry a guilty conscience that follows them in their dreams. Momentary pleasure can bring much lasting pain.

We are baptized - having a pure testimony in Christ Baptism, the outward confession of an inward possession.

We can all experience inner healing. Love is a great healer of the soul and spirit.

Knowing all these great truths concerning salvation, faith and hope, it is important for us to live according to what has been revealed to us. The writer of Hebrews exhorts us to,

"...hold unswerving to the hope we profess for he who promised is faithful.," and further we are exhorted, "Let us spur one another on toward love and good deeds."

When someone does something good, commend them for it. It affirms their self-worth and spurs them on to even greater things. And it makes them feel warm inside.

As Christians, God's law is now within our hearts (the seat of all our feelings), and within our minds (the seat of all human understanding). It is Jesus Christ within us the hope of glory. It is Jesus Christ our law of liberty. This is the reason for great rejoicing.

God's grace through Jesus Christ saves and forges and his promise are secure. We are, through Christ, free from the bondage of sin and fear. We are free to receive eternal life.

Through Jesus Christ, we are truly made spiritually free. So, let us rejoice in our freedom as the redeemed of the Lord.

There are many placards and signs that begin with, "Happiness is." Let's make our own sign and finish it by saying, "Happiness is a right relationship with God through Jesus Christ" or "Happiness is being born again." For as John's gospel tells us, "Whom the Son has set free is free indeed."

This is something to be truly thankful for. We have been bought with a price, by grace that has superseded the law. Grace that cleanses and sets us free. Now, that's real hope!

Sharing the Transforming Power of the Gospel

Scripture lesson: Timothy 1:1-14 Text: Tim. 1:12

We know there are many ways to share the gospel. For example, someone observing your lifestyle may be an encouraging testimony to them. You may not even think about it, but other folks, seeing that you are a sincere Christian may be inspired by your life, especially when they see your faith in difficult times. Often, what we see as little things may count the most to other folks.

Some time ago, Josephine and I decided to do a bit of shopping in Crossville. It's a lovely drive up the mountain and so off we went. Since it was lunch time, we went to a restaurant for a home-cooked type meal. After we ordered our meal, as is my custom, I removed my hat, and said grace. Upon opening our eyes, when we looked up, we saw a gentleman and his wife come close to our table. His voice was unsteady. Almost trembling he said, "I saw you remove your hat and say grace; Would you pray for my wife and me? She just lost her mother a few days ago and she and I need prayer." Naturally I was honored to do this. So, again, removing my hat, Josephine and I prayed that the Lord would comfort them by the presence of his Holy Spirit in their grief. Immediately there was a sense of calm. They thanked us several times and, after a brief, but lovely conversation, they went on their way. I never ever thought that a hat could minister to people, but it did. It was just a hat and a short prayer over our meal, but it became an opportunity to pray a prayer of comfort to a couple who were distraught by the loss of their mother. Often what seem to be little things are what count the most.

The gospel may be shared in many ways; and, as individuals, we each have to find our own way of doing it. A good beginning is reminding ourselves that we are social beings, and we need each other. Opportunities arise, not just in hard times, when we can be of comfort and support, but in happy times as well, where we can rejoice with friends and loved ones.

Sometimes, the most important is to just be there with them, showing support and that we care.

And concerning our own happiness and the happiness of others, there may be friends, even relatives, who secretly wish they were as happy as you are? You may not think much about this; just going about your business, but others will see joy in your life, and may wish that they, too, knew the joy that you know. So, as opportunities arise, we can share our sense of peace and joy because of Jesus, who is the ground of our being.

And there may be those who just admire your good attitude and wonder. How can you have such a positive outlook on life, handling life's difficulties so well, taking them in your stride? They see you are a problem solver and wonder how you are able to do this? Where do you get your strength? And how are you able to move on with your life when they are stuck in their problems?

You seem to manage the cares of this world with a certain strength when other folks become dispirited so easily? They wonder how you do it. To you, it's not a secret. You know the answer. It resides in the depth of your soul giving you a different world view because of your spiritual experience with the Lord. You are truly born again! Down deep within you is the source of your joy and strength even in difficult times. It is a beautiful, precious thing. It is Jesus and his Holy Spirit within you. So, share it.

y our gifts and graces, prompted by the Holy Spirit, urge you to share your faith. Do it. You may be able to lead someone to Christ or help someone in their time of need. How do you get started to do this? Launch out in faith. And simply share God's love and caring.

You may not feel special and wonder why someone would look to you for help. It is because they see something different in you and they desire that quality in their own lives. It is because you have encountered Jesus. You are born again, a changed person led by spiritual values and that is what guides your life. It is Christ within us, the hope of the ages. It is this that others see in you and that is why they are drawn to you. There is a genuineness about you that is winsome; your life is not a false statement. You are authentic in a world full of false images. It is refreshing for folks to see the authentic in you. Yes, they know you aren't perfect. Nobody is, but they see goodness in you and see the spiritual values you live by. Your very life is a powerful way to share the gospel.

People today are looking for what is real, what is genuine, and it is beautifully refreshing to see a person who is truly authentic in a world with so many fakes. They see the genuine person you are, and this is what draws them to you. They see Jesus in your life, though they may not, at the time, realize it, and they sense something is missing in their own lives. They feel a void. This is your opportunity! Share your joy and love for them as a Christian. Remember, the gospel really has great power. Billy Graham said it well, "I don't understand everything in the Bible, but 1 know it has the power to change men's lives."

The gospel has changed your life. So, share it! Share it from your own personal spiritual journey. The proof is in you and is being seen in Christians everywhere who have been truly saved.

So, as we walk with Jesus, as the disciples did, following Jesus along the shore of the Sea of Galilee, our lives, too, by God's grace, are moving onward and upward.

However, just as a large lake needs fresh streams or springs flowing into it, the lake also needs an outlet for the water to flow out from it to maintain the lake's level, balance. So, it is with our own lives. By sharing the gospel, we can be continually renewed and refreshed telling what Jesus Christ has done in our lives, and doing this also helps maintain our own spiritual balance. Here, in today's scripture, Paul gives Timothy some sound advice. It concerns Timothy's own spiritual balance and the importance of being affected in his ministry. And his advice really applies to every Christian.

As Christians, We Are All Called Our calling is unique, personal and real.

The gifts within each of us are of God, making us unique in the world. Jesus said, "You are the salt of the earth." It really is true; Christians are unique Not only are we all unique as creations of God, but Christians also have a unique, spiritually enlightened, world view because of revelations in God's Word and God's presence in our lives.

The Holy Spirit enables and empowers us to live a victorious, overcoming life in a world that still struggles with the meaning of its own existence.

We receive spiritual enrichment through reading God's Word and grow as we share the gospel The apostle Paul said,

"'For I am not ashamed of the gospel for it is the power of Cod that brings salvation to everyone who believes."

And we should not be timid about sharing our spiritual journey either. When we share the gospel, through our own spiritual journey, we are also blest and we become a part of history, Christians proclaiming the gospel all over the world sharing the greatest story ever told. Jesus Christ has saved us, is leading our lives, and has called us with a holy calling, the way to a spiritually guided way of ling. We have peace in our souls that enables us to deal with difficulties beyond our own strength. And through it all we can bond closer to our Lord, indeed, called with a holy calling to reach out to those misguided travelers who have lost their way.

We Know We Are Called by Christ into a New Relationship.

Jesus Christ conquered sin and death that we might live forever in his eternal light. The universal fear of death has been conquered by Jesus the Christ.

Jesus Christ has provided salvation and the means to live an abundant life in this present world. How is this possible in a world with so many people eaten up with hate and the determination to destroy? It is possible because Jesus has conquered all and gives wisdom and eternal life to everyone who believes in him. This is good news! Yes, there is forgiveness and salvation for everyone, for everyone who believes. This is the gospel! It is universal and it is good news, indeed! Considering suffering.

The apostle Paul also suffered but says he is not ashamed because he knows Jesus Christ and knows he is saved. (Note: There was an ancient belief, think of Job, which persisted into Paul's day that if you suffered you should be ashamed because you deserved it. Paul knew better. Besides, he had a genuine experience with it. Jesus Christ and therein lay his strength.) As we reflect on this,

May we be ever mindful that, in spite of life's struggles, the Christian life is an upward movement toward God In our trials God's love and presence is always there for us. And as Paul wrote that we can be joyful in our sufferings for the gospel. And:

We Can Really Know the Truth of God The agnostics of our day who claim a person can't really know anything will never understand spiritual knowing. And the agnostic will have to say in the end that he can't even know that he doesn't know. A ridiculous kind of circular reasoning.

We learn to know God through Jesus Christ who said, HJ am the way, the truth and the life." Jesus also said, "No one comes to the Father, but by me." Ultimate truth, then, is a person. And, make no mistake, that person is Jesus Christ who is the embodiment of truth. We are prone to think of truth as facts or merely correct information, but at its highest level, truth is a person, and that person is Jesus Christ.

This explains the scripture, "'You will know the truth and the truth will set you free."

So, when we witness holy ministry, we see Jesus. And Jesus said, "He who has seen me has seen the Father." Christ manifests himself through holy witness and through holy ling. This is why we want others to see Christ in us. This is, in itself, a witness. Christ manifests himself through holy witness and holy ling.

We know Jesus will guard our trust until the day of the Lord that day when God will judge the world. Then, Jesus Christ, our heavenly high priest will intercede for us.

We know we are called to salvation called to holy Living and called to witness - called to holy sharing of the gospel.

So, let us go forth bringing the good news to those spiritually misguided souls in the world who are bound up with greed, eaten up with anger, submerged in power struggles and embracing distorted, destructive moral values. In short, let us witness, knowing there are souls lost in sin and in need of redemption.

Thankfully, we, as Christians, can say with the apostle Paul,

"I know whom I have believed and am persuaded that he is able to keep that which I have committed unto him against that day."

This is the power of the gospel and the comforting sense of a settled faith. Faith that should be shared because we live in a world with many misguided people with misguided values who are travelling down a road that leads to their own destruction. And there are often sincere people looking for answers in the wrong places because they don't know where to look. And we do.

The apostle Paul wisely advises,

"Guard through the Holy Spirit who dwells in us, the treasure which has been entrusted to us, the treasure of spiritual knowledge and the knowledge of our salvation."

We know the right path. It begins with salvation through Jesus Christ. Then, as we continue to grow in faith, we are enabled to share our faith with others. We are all called to do this.

It is absolutely true. What the world needs is Jesus, with the life-changing insights revealed in God's word, the life changing, positive energy contained in the gospel, the life-changing power of Divine presence - God's Holy Spirit!

Salvation itself is truly life-changing! The Christian Walk, like the disciples' walk to Emmaus with Jesus is truly transforming and sharing the gospel is very rewarding! This, my dear friends, is the glory of the gospel! - what we are called to embrace and share! -The marvelous, good news of Jesus Christ! There is no greater joy than the Christian life and sharing the gospel! This is God's will for us all!

The Signs of a Healthy Church

Scripture lesson: Acts 2: 38-47 Text: Acts 2: 42

There is something very refreshing and inspiring in the scriptural passage,

"They broke bread in their homes and ate together with glad and sincere hearts, praising God and enjoying the favor of all the people. And the Lord added to their number daily those who were being saved. "

Here, the Church is new and like a newborn baby is a-glow with a wonderful power. The Holy Spirit has been with and within the believers since the Day of Pentecost. People are hearing the good news. Their lives are being changed and the move is on to bring the gospel to the whole world. There is a new work happening among them. Hope and anticipation are everywhere the gospel is presented. People are embracing the good news.

The presence and power of the Holy Spirit is being experienced within the Church and the message of salvation through Jesus Christ is bearing fruit. People are being saved and filled with the Holy Spirit. Their lives are being transformed in wonderful ways because of the gospel. Through the eyes of the redeemed, their view of the world has changed.

They realize that Jesus, The Desire of Ages, is with them. He is manifesting himself among them, through his Holy Spirit, just as he promised while he was still with them. They know that the Holy 'Spirit entered the world on the Day of Pentecost and is forever with them as Comforter and Guide.

Salvation is wonderful and life is good! The infant Church is off to a good start. How is this happening? For one thing, the Church is getting organized as it launches its great mission and most important, the Church is keeping its message pure, untainted by outside influences. There is much to learn here.

So, let's take a look at some important elements that could be classified as the elements of a model church. Certainly not perfect, but the Church of Jesus Christ, still in its infancy, is thriving and is off to a good start.

There are many attributes of the early Church that provide excellent examples for us today and we should be keenly aware of outside influences that could dilute the message. First, after the gospel is shared, those who believe are now a part of the Church. Another way of saying it is, those who are saved are now part of the family of God. Ceremonies don't accomplish this; salvation does it.

The most important task then, for the body of believers, is to continue to share the gospel and model Jesus for the world, a tall expectation, indeed!

But we know how important it is. We know that those who are not saved, often view the Church critically as a model for society. And, though they might not like to admit it, the Church is a kind of model for them personally. This leads us to say:

A healthy Church Teaches and Preaches the Whole Gospel The whole gospel for the whole person, not just a part that seems most appealing to attract a crowd. The gospel is not a popularity contest. It is a vital, spiritual message for a world that needs the Savior. Where does it begin? It begins with what is the most difficult decision for some.

The whole gospel begins with recognizing and accepting Jesus as the Savior of the entire world and it means me. What is the next step, then? It is repentance. What is true repentance? It is recognizing that we are sinners and need to turn our lives completely over to God. It is turning our lives away from a life of sin. And, let's face it, every one of us has fallen from grace. This means that it is impossible for anyone who says they have never repented to rightly call themselves a Christian. Why is this so? It is because salvation begins with a glimpse of the holiness of God and the inevitable contrast of our fallen nature with that holiness. At this moment of spiritual insight, we realize we are in need of cleansing; in the presence of a high and holy God, we see ourselves as sinners in need of redemption. We realize that we need to be saved and Jesus is the answer. So, we repent; we believe in Christ and are saved. But there is more to consider. Our first step in fulfilling the great commission might well be making a public confession of our faith. This may be one reason why.

The whole gospel includes the rite of baptism. Adults who become believers are baptized as a public confession of their faith; infants who are baptized become the responsibility of the church for their nurture until they can make the decision for Christ for themselves.

And we are not baptized in just any name. Baptism, itself, is not new. Pagan religions practiced strange baptisms during this same time period of the early Church's history. No, we are baptized in the name of Jesus Christ. This is a spiritual work of God within us. It is more than the physical act of baptism. It is the work of the Holy Spirit within us. This is why it is not necessary to be baptized a second time. We are not baptized into a denomination. A lot of people are confused about this. Scripture is very clear. We are baptized into the Church of Jesus Christ.

The whole gospel recognizes the Holy Spirit within us as believers It recognizes that the gift of the Spirit is within every believer. And this gift needs to be recognized and nurtured through prayer, God's Word and the assembling of ourselves together. Another sign of a healthy church is that:

A Healthy Church Has Continuity. Continuity means responsible people who carry on the work of the Church and community.

This means continuity in its educational program where we are constantly learning and constantly growing in faith.

This means continuity in social development. Where we are constantly reaching out to others because we care.

This means sharing communion - where we are constantly remembering what our Lord did for us and where all believers are welcome to participate. Closed communions are not scriptural.

This means in the Church's prayer life Where we are constantly seeking God's guidance and presence and purpose for our lives knowing that God is constantly drawing us closer to himself It is important for us to draw close to God through our prayer life. Sadly, some people never pray.

A healthy Church has Outreach. This shows that we care. A healthy Church is constantly seeking others and is inviting. It may shock you to hear this, but many years ago, when I taught at Bryan College, they hired someone who went to a church in Chattanooga and who said his church never reached out to the community. He said, "They know where we are." That person, by the way, didn't stay but one year.

A healthy Church is one that really worships. We exist to reach the lost for Christ and to nurture all who come through our open doors. The United Methodist slogan, "Open doors, Open hearts and Open minds" is serious business. We exist to reach the lost for Christ and to nurture all who come through our open doors to find open hearts and open minds.

A healthy Church is of one spiritual mind, and it should be the mind of Christ. This cannot be emphasized enough. We do not exist for entertainment or to involve ourselves in social trends or to take up secular causes. Being involved in legitimate causes is fine on an individual basis. For example, I belong to Trout Unlimited, which is a worthy effort to care for the environment. But the Church is different; it exists to reach the lost for Christ, nurture the saints and reach out in ministry to the community. Worthy causes are fine, but we do well to not confuse them with the purpose of the Church.

A healthy Church experiences stability and growth. It has consistency.

I know an opera singer, Wendy White, who won first prize at the Metropolitan Opera competition one year, who told me that her vocal coach emphasized that she must attain consistency in order to maintain a professional standing. The same is true for anyone attaining a professional degree. The assumption in attaining that degree is that the person will be able to function at that professional level in his or her chosen career. Consistency is the ticket! A healthy church has consistency in dependability in its mission and outreach. A church that has these qualities is on the march for Jesus Christ!

At the moment of true repentance when we turn our lives over to God, we are, at that moment, saved. In our scriptural example, baptism followed as an outward sign of an inward salvation experience and was, indeed, part of the experience.

And all of these spiritual events are accompanied by the Holy Spirit who enters to abide within us forever and to empower us to live a truly spiritual existence.

As we grow in faith and learn to apply our spiritual knowledge, we learn to care and share, praise and pray. In praying we tap into that great source of power that sustains us all. Our goal is to be of one spiritual mind, having the mind of Christ which is to do God's will.

There was a naval officer who had always dreamed of commanding a battleship. He was finally given the commission and of the newest, proudest ship in the fleet. One foggy night as the ship plowed through the seas, the captain, on duty on the bridge, spotted off to the port side, a strange light rapidly closing in on his vessel.

Immediately he signaled, "Alter your course 10 degrees to the south." A quick reply came, "Order your course 10 degrees to the north." Immediately the Captain snapped back, "Order your course ten degrees. I am the captain." Another quick reply, "I am Seaman Third Class, Alter your course 10 degrees." Now infuriated, the captain signaled, "Alter your course, I am a battleship." Instantly, came the reply, "Alter your course, I am a lighthouse."

This is what the Church of Jesus Christ is. It is a lighthouse.

May God, through Jesus Christ and the power of his Holy Spirit, help us to continue to be that light house.

An Attitude of Prayer

Scripture lesson: Luke 18; 9-14Text: Luke 18: 13c

The disciples came to Jesus and said, "Teach us to pray" and Jesus gave us the marvelous prayer that we just prayed this morning. But did you know that Jesus did not include the doxology we use at the end of the prayer. The doxology begins with "For thine is" and continues with "the kingdom and the power and the glory forever, Amen." If Jesus didn't say this as recorded in Matthew chapter 6:9-13, then where did it come from? Who added this doxology to what we know as the Lord's prayer? Who added, "For thine is the kingdom and the power and the glory forever. Amen.

Don't be shocked to learn this. Jesus never designated the prayer that he taught the disciples that we call, "The Lord's prayer" for obvious reasons. This is the designation the early Christians gave to it. And the added beautiful doxology is not a statement of petition, but an affirmation of praise to God bringing everything to a beautiful conclusion. You might say that's all good and well, but where did this doxology come from? Does it possibly have biblical roots? The answer is yes. Here, we do a bit of research and trace this doxology back several hundred years before New Testament times to an interesting account found in, I Chronicles chapter 29, of the Old Testament. The scene is with King David gathering gifts for the building of the temple. Here is what the record tells us:

"Then, King David said to the whole assembly: "My son Solomon, the one whom God has chosen, is young and inexperienced. The task is great, because this palatial structure is not for man but for the Lord God. With all my resources I have provided for the temple of my God - -I now ge my personal treasures of Gold and silver for the temple of my God, over and above everything I have provided for this holy temple. Now, who is willing to consecrate himself today to the Lord?

Then the leaders of families, the officers of the tribes of Israel, the commanders of thousands and commanders of hundreds, and the officials in charge of the king's work gave willingly.

The people rejoiced at the willing response of their leaders, for they had gen freely and wholeheartedly to the Lord. King David rejoiced greatly.

David praised the Lord in the presence of the whole assembly saying:

'Praise be to you, O Lord, God of our father Israel, from everlasting to everlasting. Yours, O Lord, is greatness and power and glory and majesty and splendor, for everything in heaven and earth is yours. Yours, O Lord, is the kingdom and you are exalted as head overall. Wealth and honor come from you; you are the ruler of all things. In your hands are strength and power to exalt and ge strength to all.' 'Now, our God, we give you thanks, and praise your glorious name.'- - -

"Then they acknowledged Solomon, son of David, as king a second time, anointing him before the Lord to be ruler and Zadok to be priest.

So, Solomon sat on the throne of the Lord as king in place of his father David. David ruled over Israel forty years - He died at a good old age, having enjoyed long life, wealth and honor. His son Solomon succeeded him as king."

There you have it. In the Early Church, Christians Living in the eastern half of the Roman Empire added the doxology "for thine ... "Evidence of this practice is also found in the "Didache" (Teaching of the Twelve Apostles) a first century document. Also, when copying the scriptures, Greek scribes sometime took the liberty of adding the doxology onto the original Gospel text of the Lord's Prayer.

So, the prayer was lovingly preserved in the scriptures and the doxology was then added, early on, as a statement of adoration and praise.

Prayer is vital to our Christian faith and is effectual. James 5:16 affirms this, "The effectual prayer of a righteous man availeth much." The New International Version translates it, "The prayer of a righteous man is powerful and effective."

However, as we all know, just saying the words of a prayer without really meaning what we say is of little use.

As an illustration of this, I once read where a newspaper columnist once described a certain preacher's prayer as, "The most eloquent prayer ever offered to a Boston audience." The prayer should have been described as being offered to God in the presence of a worshiping congregation. If this description was correct, that prayer was not effectual because the intent was not pure.

It is of great interest to me that some medical doctors pray daily for Divine help and pray with their patients; and some surgeons pray before and even after an operation. When my wife Josephine had her knee surgery, Dr. Ballard prayed before and after the surgery. Unfortunately, some other persons in the medical and other professions scorn prayer.

Several years ago, while ministering in Louisiana, I received an urgent phone call that Bobby Smith, our Lay Leader at the Prospect United Methodist Church had had a heart attack. Josephine and I rushed to the emergency room at the medical center where Bobby lay unconscious on a gurney. After trying to comfort his wife Ina, we prayed for him and the medical personnel. As the prayer was finished, one of the doctors, of eastern descent, quipped condescendingly, "It'll make you feel better." We were shocked by his inappropriate remark; and to this day, I wish I would have had the presence of mind to have said, "Doctor, we were also praying for you so you wouldn't screw up."

When the med- vac came and whisked Bobby away to a hospital in Shreveport, our prayers went with him. Everything went fine. Bobby recovered completely and we considered that our prayers were answered. Sure, the fine medical care he received was vital, but doctors and nurses are only human, and they need prayer as well as the patients.

Jesus instructed us to pray and so we pray; but the key to real prayer lies within each of us. We might now describe:

A Poor Example of Praying is found in Luke 18:9-14:

Jesus describes two different approaches to prayer. He begins by saying:

"To some who were confident of their own righteousness and looked down on everyone else, Jesus told this parable: "Two men went up to the temple to pray, one a Pharisee and the other a tax collector. The pharisee stood by himself and prayed: "God, I thank you that I am not like other people - robbers, evildoers, adulterers - or even like this tax collector. I fast twice a week and ge a tenth of all I get.'

"But the tax collector stood at a distance. He would not even look up to heaven, but beat his breast and said, "God, have mercy on me, a sinner.'

"I tell you that this man, rather than the other, went home justified before God. For all those who exalt themselves will be humbled, and those who humble themselves will be exalted."

Praying just to hear ourselves or to make an impression on others is not real prayer. It is a performance.

Praying with an attitude of pride or a sense of entitlement- as though God had some kind of obligation to us. This is why praying for God's will, though sometimes difficult, is effective prayer.

Praying with an argument of self-justification - true justification is of Divine origin. How so? God reaches down to us because of Jesus Christ's work on the cross of Calvary and his atoning work justifies us, before God, which is as though we had never sinned.

A friend of ours Dr. Don Hill told us of a relate who, with an air of arrogance, actually said that in the end he thought that he and God would come out about 50-50. Such an attitude has no place in the life of a true Christian. There is much we will never understand. It is truly a walk of faith - a faith journey. It is only God who knows the beginning from the end. It is only God who knows our hearts. We are to walk humbly before our God and that includes prayer.

A Good Example of Praying - would be:

Praying with humility - and of course, through Jesus our heavenly High Priest.

Praying with an attitude of praise - In spite of our difficulties, we have much to be thankful for, as we recognize and lay bare before God our personal shortcomings and needs.

Praying with faith - as we call on God realizing that it is only God's grace that can offer us salvation, Divine justification and strength for our journey. It is only God who really knows us and knows our needs. God hears the prayers of the sincere, penitent heart. God hears the prayer of faith. God hears our thankful praise.

Jesus said, describing the tax collector who prayed with penitence and faith:

"I tell you this man went down to his house accepted by God rather than the other because everyone who exalts himself will be humbled, but he who humbles himself will be exalted."

May we pray often. May we truly pray to God, recognizing, with humility, how we all compare in presence of Divine holiness. Yes, we know we are saved and are Christians; but let us never forget that at one time, we were all sinners; but now as Christians, being born again, we are saved by God's grace.

Whatever we are and whatever we become, may we grow in the faith, and be always mindful that our salvation is a gift, a gift from God, "not of ourselves, livest anyone should boast, "through our blessed Savior.

So, when we pray, let us be mindful to really pray; and God will hear us and answer our prayers. The scriptures tell us, "The fervent prayer of a righteous person is powerful and effective." There is power in prayer. So, may we continue to tap into that power and pray, pray, pray!

Lessons in Spiritual Ling

Scripture lesson: I Thessalonians 4:1-18; 5:1-24 Text: I Thess. 4:18

Ministers in our district meet on a regular basis to take care of business, but before this we have church. We begin with a hymn, then, prayer requests, a prayer, then, a sermon from the district superintendent or another designated speaker. At the end of the church service, we have communion.

It is a special time for us. And there are many reasons for this protocol. One of them is that, as Pastors, we need to participate in communion as a regular worshipper with someone else officiating. Why? It reminds us that we are all the same in the eyes of the Lord. And we all need encouragement as we live our lives, especially the spiritual aspect of it. And the apostle Paul, in a pastoral letter, writing to the Church at Thessalonica, includes many important reminders as to how we should view our situation as Christians on our faith journey.

In today's scriptural passage we learn that the Church at Thessalonica was much in need of encouraging words and spiritual direction from the apostle Paul. The times were crucial for the emerging Church partly because the evangelists, as well as the Church at large, were attempting to bring the gospel to the entire world. And it was at this period of time, especially crucial for the Thessalonians. Why? Well, one challenge was that it was the location of the church. Thessalonica was a harbor city. This involved trade and commerce of many kinds. In fact, its main street was part of the very road that linked Rome with the East! Talk about crucial! Yes, it was crucial, especially to the development of the Church at Thessalonica. And further, the congregation had a great responsibility to support Paul's effort in bringing Christ to the East.

So, when the young Timothy, the new evangelist, joined Paul at Athens, Greece, the information he gave about the state of the Church was vital. Happily, he brought some good news, but there were also some problems with the Church. True the Thessalonian Church was thriving, but they had stopped working. Perhaps feeling entitled, they had a tendency to despise authority and sadly, they were in danger of relapsing into immorality. Someone had to steady the course. So, Paul writes this letter reminding them of certain prophecies to take place and stresses the importance of Christian ling. And he declares hope! This, to dispel any doubt they might have Paul declares:

We Have Hope in the Day of the Lord. Always an important reminder! And just as important for us today that Jesus is coming back to earth again. We don't know when, but we need to be ready, and we need to remind ourselves that:

Our faith is bound up in the work of Jesus Christ (4:14). How so? Jesus is the embodiment of truth and thus, he is the Living Word of God.

Our faith is in the life of and in the very words of Jesus. (His spoken Word is life.)

Our faith is in the work of Jesus (his wisdom, his miracles, his death and resurrection).

Let Us live According: to Our Great Hope. (It begins with our salvation and the presence of the Holy Spirit within us. It continues with the promise that Jesus is coming back to earth again. And we should be ready through spiritual ling. It is wise for us:

To live with an awareness of the time in which we le. (We live in a crucial time in history and at a crucial time in our country's history.) So, it is wise for us:

To live as children of light, and with true spiritual enlightenment. Being born again awakens us to spiritual enlightenment. Experiencing the light of God within us is a wonderful experience. We know within our innermost being that it is the light of the gospel that brings light to the world.

In 1991, after taking hundreds of slides and photos, I decided to take a course in professional photography from the New York Institute of Photography. It was a lot of work, but also a lot of fun and after graduating in 1993 I began to do weddings, baseball pictures, basketball pictures and family reunions.

During an early part of the course, they had a section on light. It was titled, "It's all in the light." Donald Sheff and Charles De Laney, the instructors, taught, through the books and video tapes, how to use light for portraiture, for dramatic effect, how to avoid unwanted shadows, they strongly emphasized this, by saying, "It's all in the light!" Wow! What a life on! Excited, I took my camera outside and began seeing everything through the camera differently. Using the light at different angles was great fun.

The sun backlighting common Pompous Grass was exciting, catching the light in the Azalea bush in front of our house gave me a rush. Even capturing wildflowers by the side of the road with side or back lighting seemed to set them on fire. And using a white umbrella over the flowers, softening the sunlight gave them a special glow. 0 how they were right! "It is all in the light!"

Applying this insight to the salvation message and to spiritual enlightenment, we can say with the utmost confidence, yes, "It is all in the light because Jesus Christ is the light of the world."- For us, as Christians, this is the great insight! The power of the Holy Spirit, enables spiritual Living to become our reality, enabling us to live our lives in the light of eternity. Remember, "It is all in the light and Jesus Christ is that light." So, the apostle Paul tells the Thessalonian Church and us. We are to:

Live our lives with dignity with self-control and with the heightened awareness of who we are in Christ. We are a people redeemed! We know that Spiritual Living is Living our faith with love and consistency, and it is very much within our reach. Then, Paul, with the true heart of a pastor, says:

Encourage one another. Why is this so important? Encouraging someone affirms their worth. It is telling them that you have confidence in them and confidence in the effectiveness of prayer.

It is important for us to remember. Talk is never cheap unless we cheapen it. And we can cheapen our talk by gossiping. What do we mean by gossip? It is not just talking about someone. We all do that. No. Gossip is spreading unconfirmed, negate information, often with a bad mote, tearing a person down. So, Paul enjoins us:

A Build each other up and respect good leadership And not with cheap flattery. It is sincerely affirming the value and worth of the other person. Respect, of course, must be earned, but if earned, it should never be denied. There is no substitute for respect. In fact, it is scriptural that a woman can't love a man unless she respects him first. Here is an interesting account along the lines of respect:

Back in the 1960's there was a social scientist doing a study on the family. She was interested in what makes a family tick, what makes a good or bad family environment. As part of her research, she was invited into various homes to observe the dynamics of family interaction.

One particular family piqued her interest. The husband and wife had several children and their mother, toward the end of the day, looked longingly for their father's return. She would say to them. "Just wait 'til daddy gets home!" The children loved their dad and were anxious for his arrival from work. And their mother's remark made them more anxious than ever. Because of this dynamic, the social scientist expected to see a tall, very handsome specimen of a man walk through the door. Instead, what she saw was a small rather diminutive ordinary looking man smiling broadly as the children ran up to meet him. What was the important dynamic here? What was happening in this seemingly ordinary situation? What was the important insight the researcher learned? The children's respect for their father was directly linked with the mother's respect for him. She modeled respect and the children followed her example. An important lesson for all of us!

So, Paul, continuing his instruction to the Thessalonian Church, says:

Le in peace with each other. This requires maturity. How many sit-corns have we watched laughing at the immature behavior of family members who just don't get it. They don't know how to be problem solvers or how to live peaceful lives.

It's fun to watch shows like, "Everybody Loves Raymond," but not so funny in real life.

There is much pain and sorrow in families who don't know how to get along with each other. Paul enjoins, "Live at peace with each other." This is very doable if everyone is willing to work at it.

Let us be joyful always - pray continually- ge thanks in all circumstances. (That's a hard one, but nevertheless, we should try to see what good can come out of a difficult situation!)

We should test everything. It is immature to accept a new trend or religious idea without a litmus test. (An example is the basic chemical test for an acid or a base. It is one or the other). We should test everything.

We should make every effort to hold on to the good and avoid every kind of evil. (This means for us to live a positive life, recognize evil for what it is and make every effort to avoid it.)

We learn great lives on in spiritual Living in the Bible. They sometimes live on what to avoid, not only what we should do. Many thoughts and ideas spring from the misguided lives of corrupt individuals. When they are public figures, their negate influence is incalculable. They may be improperly influencing, even corrupting millions!

They are certainly not a standard to live by, nor are they, our standards. Our standards, as Christians, come from Divine revelation through God's Word and the leading of his Holy Spirit.

May we, through the presence of the Holy Spirit and by the power of God, become sanctified through and through. May our whole spirit, soul and body be kept blameless at the coming of our Lord and Savior Jesus Christ. For we know that "The One who calls us is faithful and he will do it."

For all of God's blessings on our lives, let us be thankful. For all of life's difficulties and challenges, let us be prayerful. For every event we meet along life's path of life may we determine to live a walk of faith! And by God's help we can so live our lives that we are in tune with God's Spirit.

The Day of the Lord for us, as Christians, is a day of joy! So, let us rejoice in the hope and assurance of our salvation through our blessed Savior who is Jesus Christ. Living by this faith is real spiritual living!

John the Baptist Heralds a New Age

Scripture lesson: Luke 3:1-20 Text: Luke 3: 16-17

John the Baptizer (which is what his name means) leaves his life in the desert to enter the public arena with a message of warning to the people of Israel and all others, against the sinful lives they were ling. The people had reverted back from Mosaic law to heathen practices. They had forsaken their mission to bring God's revelation of himself to the world. Though many undoubtedly knew of the Old Testament prophesies concerning the Messiah who was to come, they were Living as though it wouldn't happen, at least not in their lifetime. So, John preaches a hard-hitting prophetical message. He cuts through their religious facade and tells them they need to repent. They need to abandon their sinful lifestyle and move on as people cleansed of their sins. He doesn't speak in weak general terms. He addresses the root of the problem. He preaches the need for individual repentance; however, he doesn't leave them in a quandary as to what is in the future for them. John leaves them with a message of hope - He proclaims, with the rush of anticipation and excitement - the Messiah is about to reveal himself.

I can almost hear him now. Jesus makes his appearance and John, with a loud cry of authority, calls out as one who has survived the stress of desert life - "Behold! The Lamb of God who takes away the sins of the world." His message is clear, plain and unmistakable. Here is Jesus, your Messiah!

John was a remarkable man. He knew his calling, knew what his message was and was not deterred by it. His preaching was successful, attracting a large following to the point where some were thinking he was the Messiah, but he made his message very clear:

"After me comes he who is mightier than I, and thong of whose sandals I am not worthy to stoop down and untie. I have baptized you with water, but he will baptize you with the Holy Spirit and with fire."

John knew he was not the Messiah, but the Messiah's actual identity was apparently not revealed to him until Jesus appeared at John's baptismal service. Here, Jesus asked to be baptized by John, and was baptized.

John's prophetic Messianic message is remarkable. It went beyond repentance and included the Day of Pentecost when he said the Messiah would baptize them with the Holy Spirit and with the visual evidence accompanying it, flames of fire. John, with these remarks, is setting the stage for the new Age of Grace.

And Jesus much admired John. He told the multitudes as recorded in

Matthew: "I tell you the truth: among those born of women, there has not risen anyone greater than John the Baptist: yet he who is least in the kingdom of heaven is greater than he."

It should be pointed out, many people during this time led with a double sense of fear, the fear of the Roman government and fear of God's wrath. Why was this? Rome had, by military might, conquered the, then known, world and it was because they knew that they and their nation were Living in sin. They were not right with God.

The Jews were not ignorant of these matters. They knew of the exceeding sinfulness of sin from the Old Testament writings, especially from the prophets and the Psalms. And they also knew of the importance of God's forgiveness from the sacrificial system that was practiced, set up as a constant reminder of their need for forgiveness.

The time was ripe for a spiritual awakening and now the people were open to John's message. He came down hard on them when he made it so clear:

Israel Has Failed in Her National and Spiritual Purpose - under the law.

Israel has utterly failed to bring God's message to the world and so has failed to meet God's expectations of them through Divine law.

John calls for the fruits of repentance, not just remorse. He demands a turnaround in their ling.

John warns Israel against claiming their covenant relationship unearned - that is, through their heritage, the founder of their nation - Abraham.

Israel Is Soon to be Cut Down and Replaced What did this mean? It meant that their time was up to be the spiritual leader of the world as was their duty. As it turned out the gentiles were the replacement. John teaches this with an illustration:

The ax is already laid at the foot of the tree Just what did this mean? It meant that Israel, as a nation, was in grave danger of being cut off from God forever. Why?

Israel did not bear the spiritual fruit she should have borne She was to take the message of the love of God to the world. Sadly, the state of Israel is still in spiritual turmoil to this day.

Israel has lost her status as spiritual messenger - But repentance could still change all this.

Individuals Should Repent! -John, as the last of the Old Testament prophets is in a transitional role when he gives the last call under the old order. Their ways should change.

John tells them they should care for the lives of others They should live the scripture, "Love thy neighbor as thyself." They should help others with the basic necessities such as clothing and food.

John tells them they should live honestly Again, if you love your neighbor as yourself you won't cheat. You won't use power wrongly to gain possessions. You won't accuse falsely. You will be content with your wages in the sense of fair wages for the work done, not greedy for more than the job is worth.

A New Age Is Dawning! John tells them to prepare their hearts and minds for a radical change.

John declares the Messiah is coming! He says,

"He will baptize you with the Holy Spirit and with fire."

A great spiritual harvest is also coming. It is the gathering of those who repent and the separating of the evil ones from the righteous.

John the Baptizer, seeing that Israel has so far, failed in her national purpose, calls for individual repentance; he preaches the demands of the law, repentance and he prophesies concerning the coming Age of Grace. How fortunate we are today to be able to receive this grace and to benefit from the wonderful works of God through our Messiah Jesus Christ who has secured our salvation!

We are people of the Age of Grace. We are no longer under the bondage of the law that expects perfection without the spiritual help to rise toward perfection in love and righteousness. How is this possible? We are made perfect in Christ.

We are people of the Age of Grace. We have Jesus our Savior, our heavenly High Priest who intercedes for us before God and justifies us through his blood. We are enabled to stand before God, perfect in his sight, because of Jesus Christ. This is the wonderful New Age of which John the Baptist heralded.

We are people of this new Age of Grace and happy on our faith journey because we are redeemed by the blood of the Lamb!

When God Calls Us

Scripture lesson: I Samuel 3:1-10 Text: I Sam. 3: 10b

There are many people in our country, and in other places in the world, who are Living lives that are unfulfilled. Wandering aimlessly without a plan or direction, with low values, and with low self-esteem, they will likely never be able to reach the God-gen potential that lies within the1n. However, there are ways to reach a person's potential and live lives that are life fulfilling.

Not being able to embrace personal fulfillment, life-long satisfactions, or making a lasting, positive difference in their own lives or in other people's lives, is one of the most unfortunate outcomes of an unspiritual, often self - centered life that I know.

Young children have dreams. Dreams of doing and being something special when they grow up. They look for people to respect that they can look up to and model.

Sometimes, they look to people in public life like athletes, teachers, doctors, business executives, ministers, military persons, etc. This is usually a good thing; but when something goes wrong between the futuristic dreams of childhood and youth, as they become adults; when hopes and dreams are dashed, disillusionment and bitterness result in a broken life. We ask just what has happened to them in the interim of their complex, litany of dreams? Bad decisions? Perhaps. Traveling with the wrong crowd?

This is never good.

And what about their spiritual lives? Have they neglected the most important, vital ingredient? Likely they have, and may have never addressed a sense of calling, or of purpose? That spiritual rudder of our ship that helps steer our lives in the right direction.

Make no mistake. A sense of calling is foundational. A sense of calling helps us realize who we are. We all need a sense of calling, of purpose, the sense that our life's decisions and direction are right for us. How is this grasped and attained? It begins when we self-evaluate. We need to ask, what have I done with my life? And what do I do with my life now, important questions no matter what our age?

It is beneficial to prayerfully consider opportunities and options. Pray with careful thought until down deep, you know something is right for you; its sense of rightness will bring great personal satisfaction. And, of course, always pray for God's will. The sense of direction that emerges is personal, just for you, and may be a calling or lead you to a calling. Very personal? Yes. But it will bring you genuine spiritual fulfillment and satisfaction. It is like saying, "Now, I know why I'm here.

On a personal note, when I was in my teens, I had the feeling that I would someday work with young people. Why I felt this way I don't really know except to say that, looking back, I realize that God was leading me though I didn't know it at the time. Be assured. When we are open to God's call, his Holy Spirit will lead us even when we are not totally aware of it. I wanted to follow God's leading, but I didn't know where he would lead me. I was just a kid. I had no idea that I had teaching ability. I didn't even think about it, but an interesting development occurred at the ages of thirteen and fourteen.

While in junior high and during my freshman year in high school, the neighborhood kids, knowing I was interested in science, were curious about it and they liked to gather in my little lab on the third floor of our home and have me show them my experiments. It was simply fun for me. I did chemical experiments and showed them what I saw under my microscope. Many years passed before I realized that my friends, without realizing it, by asking me to show them my experiments, were recognizing my inborn aptitude for teaching and really asking me to teach them. I had a teaching ability that I didn't know I had. And later, in my adult life taught my entire career. As a boy, I was just having fun sharing what I knew. And teaching has always been about sharing.

And yes, we were kids, and some of it was mischievous; like the time I took iron filings and Sulphur, an experiment from the chemistry set, heated them over a flame and wow! - rotten eggs - with the smell travelling all through the house by way of the vents. I thought it was funny. My parents did not. There were missionary guests in the house at the time. It certainly was not funny. Even though later they laughed about it, I never did that again.

And the time I made gun powder, took a tiny bit of it, placed it on paper, lit a match to it and poof! That really scared me never again! Maybe it was that incident that jarred me so much that I finally got some common sense. At that young age I certainly had a more natural aptitude for exploring and experimenting than common sense. I was a risk taker. Common sense finally came later.

I believe we all are born with certain inclinations, aptitudes and abilities and it is our duty to discern what they are and put them to good use. Our God-gen abilities are a precious commodity. When used properly they ge us great satisfaction in life fulfillment. And we answer a very important question about ourselves Why we are here; and we are all here for a purpose.

When we sense God calling us, whether to a career or an individual task, we must not miss the opportunities he provides; they may not come by us again.

Trying to each some ethics to my son Mark, when he was a young boy, I said, "It's not whether you win or lose, it's how you play the game." Quickly Mark sputtered back, "But dad, it not just whether you win or lose, it's if you are in the game.

He was right. Some people never really get into the game of life. They never experience that special fulfillment in life that God desires of them. What to do?

Listen for the call, that inclination. Notice when things come easy for you. Don't take this for granted. These are your aptitudes. They are special gifts. Be aware of those things that are of natural interest to you. Your curiosity about them is really a gift. Your ability to do is a gift, whatever it is. These things are part of who you are. They are genetic. They are inborn abilities for us to identify and use for God's glory.

Everyone is different; so, constantly comparing ourselves with others is not a good idea.

We must simply be who we are, accept our bodies, be grateful for our mind with its gifts and graces, and not constantly compare ourselves with someone else.

If we do, we will always find someone who we think is better and that person may not be better at all, only different from us. It is good to be comfortable in our own skin and the body type we are endowed with. It is good to be happy with who we are and just be our own best self. And discerning God's call is not that difficult if we listen to the inner prompting of the Holy Spirit. And his call isn't always mysterious. It's often plain to see.

The French composer, Saint-Saens who composed exquisitely beautiful music with little effort, compared with the struggles of others, said, "I produce music like an apple tree produces apples."

This statement of his ability is an excellent example of someone discovering their gifts, knowing who they are, why they are here and fulfilling their life using those God gen gifts. This is a most important part of human fulfillment.

There are many voices in the world calling us with their demands. And, at times, we may wonder as to what purpose. Some demands may actually be unfair, but as Christians, Living our lives in the light of eternity. We have a different world view. We see meaning as God's purpose manifested in our lives. It's good to think of meaning in our lives that way; true meaning is God's purpose manifested in our lives.

Yes, there are many voices in the world; we need answer to but one, the voice of God. God calls us all to a knowledge of himself. He calls us to action where it is needed. He calls us to know the joy of life fulfillment. So, now, we will consider that like Samuel:

There Was a Time Before We Even Recognized God's voice Samuel thought the voice was that of Eli, the priest, until he was taught how to respond to it.

Like Samuel, we did not know God's voice. Perhaps it was simply before God chose to reveal himself to us, or our own self-centeredness or rebellion that got in the way.

It reminds me of a student I met, who, so taken up with his intelligence, declared that he was not going to listen to anyone. He didn't and failed miserably.

Like Samuel, we did not know how to listen or even try to listen to God's voice. Nor did we know how to respond. Samuel, at the advice of his mentor, Eli, the priest, learned to do this so he answered, "Speak Lord for I am your servant, and I am listening." With this response Samuel invited God into his life, and that he would do what God told him to do.

Like Samuel, there was a time when we simply did not know how to recognize or respond to the voice of God. Scripture teaches us,

"Faith comes by hearing and hearing by the word of God." - What does this mean?

First, we have to really listen to the Word of Truth and reflect on it. Second, we should allow God to speak to us through the prompting of his Holy Spirit and through his Word (a great benefit of prate devotions). Third, we should

act on it. Just as Samuel needed instruction, so did we. Just as Samuel needed a genuine spiritual experience, so did we. (The Bible is full of examples of God calling people, e.g. Daniel, Moses, Joshua, Paul.) And then,

There is a Time When God Calls, and God's call is always timely.

The call may come unexpectedly, Yet we should welcome it as the beginning of a spiritual journey. Unmistakably,

The call will be definite. It will be a call with purpose and to purpose. God always calls us to good purpose - his purpose. This, in part, is the meaning of the scripture that says we can go, "from glory unto glory and we are being changed into the likeness of "Christ."

The call will have a wonderful outcome. Why? Because through our deepening spiritual experience, we will grow. As we draw closer to the Lord, for his help strength and guidance, he draws closer to us. This is taught clearly in the scriptures. Here, we put our personal agenda aside and wait for the

Lord to reveal his will.

The call will be heard, if we really listen, amidst all the competing voices in the world. We may find that his call is heard in that still small voice that rises above the storms of life. Situations may fail us. God will still lead. People may fail us. God will still lead. We may even fail ourselves, but the most vital lives on of all is, no matter what, God will still lead. Jesus, who is God incarnate, never fails! He will take us through the most difficult times. God's voice rings clearly as the voice of hope for the future, the voice that leads in our daily walk and the voice that calms the storm within our spirit. We only need to truly listen as the young Samuel did.

There is a Time to Respond to God's Call as Samuel did.

Prayerfully, say, "Lord, I am listening." Listening is a skill. Most of us can improve our listening skills.

Prayerfully, say, "Lord, I am open to your call., whatever it is" Here we need to keep an open mind. Life is full of surprises. This may be one of them.

Prayerfully, say, "Lord, I will do your bidding as your Holy Spirit leads me." - I will not do as Moses did and tell God "I can't do it." Instead, I will say, "Help me Lord, for though I don't know how yet, I know you will enable me."

God chose Samuel to do his work. He called and Samuel listened. God led and Samuel followed. The result? God blessed Samuel and as a result, he had a most useful life and most useful ministry as a prophet.

May we search our hearts and minds, seeking earnestly to hear God's voice, that inner prompting, bidding us to do his will. To us, they may seem like small things, but in God's eyes they are all important.

So, as we sense his hand on our lives, may we respond, "Speak Lord, for your servant is listening." And pray, "Lead me Lord, for I know you want what is best for me. Help me Lord to do your will, for you always enable those on whom you call."

In the name of the Father and of the Son and of the Holy Spirit. Amen!

The Call for Cleansing

Scripture lesson: Mark 1-1-8; Hebrews 4:12-14

Just imagine that in our country there would be no churches or religious leadership for even one generation. The spiritual chaos that would ensue would be unimaginable. Even when we consider the results on the general population, when prayer and Bible reading were taken out of the public schools. It has left its mark on millions of children, some of whom all the religious exposure they experienced were those few minutes of Bible verses and prayer at the start of the school day. Those few moments taught respect and that there is someone out there bigger than them. So, what would be the effect on populations, largely illiterate, who, for 300 years, were without proper spiritual leadership.

It is shocking, that, after the prophet Malachi, the children of Israel had no prophet for 300 years. What did this mean? During that time the people looked for spiritual leadership through a prophet and were wandering spiritually all this time. If we consider a generation at about 33 years, as suggested by Don Devine, retired attorney and archivist, there are, approximately, three generations per 100 years, this meant that nine generations had passed without a prophet as spiritual leader for the people of Israel. Folks, that's a long time, a very long time.

It follows, then, that religious teachings and practices became perfunctory for many Jews personally and for the nation, in general. The oppressed nation of Israel had been on a downward spiral path for a long time. Where was the proclaiming voice of prophecy?

Where was the voice of hope for the future since the people were under the severe domination of the Roman government?

What happened to the spiritual direction of Israel, the nation, which originated with Abraham and whose very existence was under Divine covenant? What could stop their downward spiral?

Without proper spiritual leadership they became increasingly legalistic and hopelessly entangled in endless details, fastidiously interpreting mosaic law. This left them struggling to normalize their law burdened lives and trying to figure ways to sidestep the laws they had falsely interpreted.

This reached a point of Israel nearly losing its purpose for existing, which was to lead other nations away from idol worship and evil practices, to know the true and Living God. They became so legally entangled that they went far beyond the intended meaning of God's law, originally gen to them by Moses

47

to improve their lives. These laws with their overreaching interpretation became the object of their religion, instead of a Wholesome relationship with God. The result? They were a people who walked in spiritual darkness.

Then, came John! - a voice - the last of the Old Testament prophets who was the voice of transition to the new Age of Grace! - with one penetrating message. Repent! The nation and its people must repent! John proclaimed his message, "to make straight paths for him," the coming Messiah. He preached,

Repent, be Baptized and recognize the Dinity of Jesus Christ These are the elements of the gospel. John was very clear in recognizing Christ's Dinity. He actually placed himself below the lowest servant of the household by saying he was not even worthy to untie Jesus' shoes. Then he prophesied, "I baptize you with water, but he will baptize you with the Holy Spirit and with fire." This fire is the impetus and energy for a renewed spiritual awakening. In fact, flames of fire did rest on everyone in the Upper Room, and they were "filled with the Holy Spirit and began to speak in other tongues as the Spirit enabled them." This is the marvelous power within all Christians that enables us to live productive holy lives. Further, by illustration, John taught the people to,

Recognize the Power of the Scriptures The writer of Hebrews instructs us with these penetrating words:

"The Word of God is Living and active. Sharper than any double-edged sword, it penetrates even to dividing soul and spirit. joints and marrow; it judges the thoughts and attitudes of the heart. Nothing in all creation is hidden from God's sight. Everything is uncovered and laid bare before the eyes of Him to whom we must ge account."

Take heart, these words were not written to inspire fear without hope. No! They are to be instructed. These scriptures lead us to realize the vital importance of knowing Jesus Christ our eternal Prophet, Priest, and King-our Lord and Savior. This leads and encourages us to experience the refreshing experience of cleansing:

Rejoice in the Hope We have in Christ Jesus. Hebrews 6: 19-20 gives us these encouraging and inspiring words:

"We have this hope as an anchor for the soul, firm and secure. It enters the inner sanctuary behind the curtain, where Jesus, who went before us, has entered on our behalf. He has become a high priest forever, in the order of Melchizedek."

The inner sanctuary was located, first in the tabernacle in the wilderness and later placed in the temple. Entrance was forbidden except for the High Priest who entered the Holy of Holies once a year, until Jesus was crucified. Then, mysteriously, the veil separating the Holy of Holies from the rest of the temple, was rent from top to bottom making access to God open forever to all believers.

We conclude our message today with Hebrews 10: 19-25,

"Therefore, brothers, since we have confidence to enter the Most Holy Place by the blood of Jesus, by a new Living way opened for us through the curtain, that is his body, and since we have a great priest over the house of God, let us draw near to God with a sincere heart in full assurance of faith, having our hearts sprinkled to cleanse us from a guilty conscience and having our bodies washed with pure water. Let us hold unswervingly to the hope we profess, for he who promised is faithful.

And let us consider how we may spur one another on toward love and good deeds. Let us not gave up meeting together, as some are in the habit of doing, but let us encourage one another - and all the more as you see the Day approaching."

May we continue to pray for God's leading and cleansing daily!

The Power of Resolve

Scripture: Joshua 24:13-15; Romans 8:35-38

Joshua, chapter 23, describes the current peaceful state of Israel and that Joshua, now advanced in years, wishes to leave them with some final words of wisdom: "After a long time had passed and the Lord had gen Israel rest from all their enemies around them, Joshua, by then old and well advanced in years, summoned all Israel - their elders, leaders, judges, and officials - and said to them: 'I am old and well advanced in years.'

Realistic about his age, Joshua recognizes that his time on earth is short and wants to ge his fellow Israelites some important parting words. He begins by reminding them that their victories are a result of God's help, so, Joshua reminds them of the source of their victories He declares,

"It was the Lord who fought for you ... 'Be very strong, be careful to obey all that is written in the Book of the Law of Moses. So, be careful to love the Lord, your God ... Now I am about to go the way of all the earth. You know with all your heart and soul that not one of the good promises the Lord your God gave you has failed. Every promise has been fulfilled; not one has failed. But just as all the good things that the Lord your god promised have been fulfilled for you, so the Lord will bring upon you all the bad things, until he has destroyed you from this good land that the Lord your God has gen you. If you transgress the covenant of the Lord our God, which he enjoined on you, and go and serve other gods and bow down to them, then the anger of the Lord will be kindled against you, and you shall perish quickly from the good land he has gen o you.".. "Then Joshua, assembling all the tribes of Israel at Shechem and reminding them again of God's works among them, declared, "Now fear the Lord and serve him with all faithfulness. Throw away the gods your forefathers worshipped beyond the river and in Egypt and serve the Lord....

Joshua requires them to make a vital, spiritual decision - It would involve the future spiritual direction of their nation, placing the responsibility on them. He continues,

"But if serving the Lord seems undesirable to you, then choose for yourselves this day whom you will serve, whether the gods your forefathers served beyond the river, or the gods of the Amorites, in whose land you are ling. But as for me and my household, we will serve the Lord." Then the people answered, "Far be it from us to forsake the Lord to serve other gods....

This was the answer Joshua wanted to hear so:

Joshua Challenged them to make a public declaration of their Faith-And what was their response? Happily, the people said, "No, we will serve the Lord." At that point, Joshua, pleased with their declaration, still wanted more than a verbal commitment. So, he challenged them to act on their decision, "Now then," said Joshua, "Throw away your foreign gods that are among you and yield your hearts to the Lord, the God of Israel."

Why this challenge? He wanted them to make a public commitment of their faith. So,

The People Made a Public Declaration of Commitment - at the level of resolve. The people said, "We will serve the Lord our God and obey him."

Now we have a Public Record of their Commitment - Scripture tells us,

"On that day Joshua made a covenant for the people there at Shechem; he drew up for them decrees and laws. And Joshua recorded these things in the Book of the Law of God."

Brilliantly, Joshua led the people to the level of resolve. They needed this direction. And they needed to make this commitment, especially with idolatry all around them.

Joshua's excellent leadership reminds us that there is great power in resolve!

This situation may prompt us to ask, "Just what was the situation like during Abraham and Joshua's time period?" A partial answer is, archeologists have, fairly recently, unearthed many artifacts and ancient texts that help us better understand the culture of these ancient peoples.

Some discoveries occurred during a most fascinating archeological expedition that began in 1925 by Leonart Wooley. The finds were rich, yielding many valuable artifacts and texts from ancient life in the Near East, especially during Abraham's time. These explorers found harbors along the river, storehouses, prate houses, palaces and a huge temple to the moon god Nanna. And archeologists found tombs containing fully outfitted soldiers, charioteers, musicians, grooms, dressers, courtiers, and cooks, giving gruesome evidence that some people were buried ale.

It was from this large, influential city that Abraham and his family left, rejecting idolatry and astrology, the religions of this culture, looking for a city whose builder and maker was the true and Living God Abraham was a man of resolve!

Do you know of anyone who left their family upbringing to become a Christian? It is often very difficult! Resolve can have long-lasting consequences, hopefully, good ones!

There is nothing quite like the power of resolve. When, after careful consideration, a decision is made, it may take on the dimensions and impact of resolve. At this point things may begin to happen, now you are not to be dissuaded from your decision or from its resultant action. At this point, your decision has reached the level of resolve.

There is great power for our life's direction in resolve. Good resolute decisions can cause good things to happen, even life changing things. As an example:

The patriarch Noah was a man of great resolve. Responding to God's direction, Noah built a giant Ark with dry land all around him, and in an arid area with no possibility of bringing his great raft to water to even test its seaworthiness. But as, we all know, the Ark's maiden voyage, and its only voyage, was a life-saving journey over raging seas. There was great positive power when Noah made the decision to build the Ark, a good, faith based, decision with resolve. Are you a person who constantly vacillates, or do you, when appropriate, elevate your decision to the level of resolve?

Here, in today's, Old Testament, narrate, Joshua recounted to the Israelites Abraham's far-reaching decision to leave his hometown, Ur, reminding them and us, that God can lead a person in their life-choices. Joshua proclaims,

God Kept His Promise - God led his people.

God led his people God led Abraham out of Ur - promising to make a great nation of him. God sent Israel, Moses, and Aaron, - and they led the Israelites out of Egypt. God led them to victory over hostile nations, like the Amorites.

Now, through Joshua, God gave the Israelites the responsibility to make a decision of resolve - whether or not to serve YHWH, only true God. Joshua says: Fear the Lord recognize that YHWH is the only true and Living God. And do this with resolve. Destroy all the false gods. They are only a pathetic illusion of reality anyway. (What a wasted lie is that life is guided by illusions.) God says, through Joshua, "Get them out of your sight and your mind so that you will be ready to serve YHWH, the Lord, the only true a Living God." But Joshua does not impose his ideas on Israelites; it is their decision.

Joshua says, "Choose for yourselves this day whom you will serve." Then, Joshua makes his own declaration.

"But as for me and my household, we will serve the Lord." The apostle Paul made such a choice, declaring in Romans 8:35-38 that nothing could separate us from the love of God. Paul was a man of resolve, a great leader and a consistent follower of Christ to his last breath. What a wonderful statement when he proclaimed, "For me to live is Christ and to die is gain."

The choice is ours. So, let us affirm or reaffirm our covenant with God through Jesus the Christ that, no matter what, we will say with resolve, "As for me and my household, we will serve the lord."

Mary Anoints Jesus

Scripture: John 12:1-8 Text: John 12:7-8

It was six days before Passover. A special event that commemorates Israel's release from Egyptian slavery, about 1400 years B.C. which also includes the time the Israelites were spared the punishment of the destroying angel. They had been enslaved by the Egyptians over 130 years and now they were under Roman rule.

During Passover, Jesus was staying in the home of Martha and Mary in Bethany, a town located outside the city of Jerusalem; also, where Lazarus was staying, ale and well, a constant testimony to the resurrecting power of Jesus Christ.

Here was a home filled with love. And Mary, overflowing with love and respect for Jesus, felt she had to express that love and respect. What could she do? Not spoken of in the scriptures, as a woman of means, what could she do? She possessed something very precious, something the equivalent of a year's wages. Undoubtedly, she had been saving for years in order to purchase it. What was this special possession? It was Spikenard, a precious ointment, extracted from Nardostachys jatamansia, a flowering plant of the honeysuckle family that grows in the Himalayas of Nepal, China, and India, and used to make a type of perfume. And Mary, after carefully saving it for herself, was about to ge it away, anointing Jesus' feet.

Mary showed her love and respect for Jesus with an act of great sacrifice A beautiful example of seizing the moment to do something very special. And this moment for Mary was not to occur again. Thankfully, she acted, seizing the moment before it passed.

But we may ask, aside from doing this for Jesus, why was her loving act so special? Of course, it was about the situation, but also, it was about the special ointment she used:

This precious Spikenard could have been used for her own burial, the practice of the day. It was one of her most precious possessions and she gave it away to Jesus.

And her hair, the Bible describes a woman's hair as her crowning glory. Mary surrendered her crowning glory, along with her dignity, to Jesus as she wiped his feet with her hair.

The house was now filled with a beautiful fragrance, allowing her experience to be shared by everyone in the house.

However, someone was there who misunderstood her beautiful gesture, Judas Iscariot, and instead of trying to understand her beautiful gesture:

Judas Criticizes. He missed completely the magnitude of this humble, unselfish act of Mary. What was the root of his problem?

He saw dollar signs. He didn't appreciate the real meaning of her selfless act. He criticized that the Spikenard should have been sold for profit. To Judas, it was all about the profit mode. He hadn't learned the important life lives on about caring for others. He sounded like he cared about the poor, very doubtful, because he was willing to sell the life of Jesus for 30 pieces of silver.

It is so unfortunate, but Judas missed totally the spiritual implications of what Mary did. In fact, he ignored what was obvious to everyone else. What she did was done out of love and care. In fact, this very personal act was none of Judas' business. Yet he interfered.

Judas said that the profit could have been given to the poor. At face value, this seemed plausible, but his motes were not pure. Why?

Judas had already decided to betray Jesus. There was no way he could have been on the proper spiritual wavelength to understand what had just happened. He didn't believe in Jesus anyway or he would not have planned to betray him. And, of course, Jesus would not allow Judas' remarks to go uncorrected. So,

Jesus Explains Mary's mote to Judas and To the Other People Present Here is Jesus, in a very critical moment, taking time to explain Mary's act to Judas who he already knew was going to betray him. It was like Jesus was giving Judas one last chance to repent even though the evil decision was already made, and the plans were already in motion. In a direct and proper way, Jesus defends and clarifies Mary's beautiful action. He makes it very clear that Mary did the right and proper thing. So,

Jesus clarifies Mary's mote for everyone who was there, especially Judas. It was a beautiful teaching moment for Jesus as he explained:

She anointed me for my burial Jesus knew his future here on earth was coming to an end and here was an opportune time to make it known. It was prophetic in nature, but also a futuristic look at his atoning for all who would believe in him. Impossible, at this time, for them to see it, but Jesus, by implication, was quietly announcing his determination to die on the cross as the final sacrifice for sin and save all those who would believe in him as their Messiah.

From Mary's point of view, she seized this singular opportunity to express her deep love for her Messiah. Down deep she may have known that this opportunity would not come again. So, she acted on her desire to anoint

Jesus's feet and wipe them with her hair, her crowning glory.

True love has no bounds. Mary showed her love and devotion to Jesus, her Messiah in a unique way that none of the men who were present could do. As a woman, this was her special moment, so special that over two thousand years later we still remember and regard it for the loving act that it was.

Mary anointed Jesus' feet with Spikenard and wiped his feet with her hair, her crowning glory.

May we, this day, rededicate our lives to the Lord, remembering Mary's beautiful, deeply spiritual act of selfless love, and remember that Jesus gave his all for us as his ultimate act of love. True love has no bounds.

And may we continue to learn the meaning of such sacrificial love and seize those special moments of opportunity as God leads us.

Jerusalem's Last Chance

Scripture lesson: Luke 19:28-30 Text Luke 19: 44b.

Luke's scriptural account shows Jesus as an assassination target. How could this be? This wise teacher, this Rabbi who went around teaching love and caring, who taught his followers righteous ling, who healed the sick and bound up the broken hearted, who was so in touch with his feelings that at Lazarus' tomb he wept. And later, overlooking Jerusalem, he wept again. This Jesus, who taught his disciples how to pray, who had the power to forge sins, was now the target of a plot designed to kill him. We question why? Why would anyone even think to do such a thing to this wise, caring, kind, loving man?

Jesus' words of wisdom had such power that they moved thousands toward believing in him. The result? He came to be perceived as a threat to established religion. In short, the power structure of the religious community wanted him gone. You may ask. What about the Roman government? At this time, it could care lives. But this was not the case with some people in the religious community.

Along with this bias, Jesus knew that after all the healing miracles he had done and after all the things he had taught his disciples about the kingdom of God, one of his chosen twelve disciples was going to betray him. Yet, Jesus showed such supreme love that even at the last supper he invited Judas, the devious betrayer to participate in the meal.

In spite of his personal example of grace and love, and his very existence in jeopardy, Jesus continued to move toward his destiny with deliberate intent. How could he do this? Totally contrary to what a natural reaction would be, but he moved forward because he knew he was following his father's will. And this knowledge did not make his mission any easier. However, Jesus continued to move forward with unwavering assurance.

At such a critical time it was necessary for Jesus to have a crystal-clear conception of who he was and an awareness of the magnitude of his mission. Just what was his mission? Jesus was to carry the sins of the entire human race, past, present and future on the cross.

And strangely, after this singular event, the sacrificial system of the Jewish nation was abolished after his death. And this happened after the emperor Titus conquered Jerusalem and sacked the temple in A.D. 70, just as Jesus had predicted. And it is worth noting that this temple has not been rebuilt after over 2,000 years, with the evidence of piles of stones at the temple's base still in a heap like trash. We saw the piles of stones on our trip to the Holy Land.

Further, Jesus' own identity could not be derived from anyone else's conception of who he was. He realized that many of his followers did not really know who he was, and some allowed their own religious prejudices to keep them spiritually blinded. The truth was present among them; "the way, the truth and the life," but many did not see it.

Yet, despite their rejection, and misunderstandings concerning his profound teachings of the Kingdom of God, Jesus moved on with great deliberation toward his destiny. His teaching, "My kingdom is not of this world," has stood the test of time and still stands today.

So, Jesus moved with great deliberation toward his destiny. From the selecting of his twelve disciples, to gaining a following of thousands, we find Matthew and Mark reporting that as Jesus was leaving Jericho, there was already, "a great multitude" following him.

Then, in the final stretch of his journey, sitting along the path, we hear the blind beggar, Bartimaeus, calling out incessantly, "Son of David, have mercy on me." He pleads, "Master, let me receive my sight." Jesus replies, "Go your way: your faith has made you well." (Mark 10:47). Bartimaeus, sight restored, now joins the others on the journey.

And happily, Mark records, "He followed Jesus on the way." From being blind both physically and spiritually, he is now a fellow pilgrim travelling to Jerusalem. What a wonderful, miraculous event this was! It illustrates Jesus restoring physical sight and restoring spiritual sight as well. So, we find that Bartimaeus has joined the others travelling to Jerusalem.

As they travelled, they came to Bethphage, where unnamed villagers provided a donkey for Jesus to ride on, and on to Bethany (also near Jerusalem) where more pilgrims began to follow Jesus in a grand entourage. Onward they went finally to the Mount of Olives where:

Jesus Enters Jerusalem - With such large following, surely, he would enter with great fanfare on a magnificent steed, a war horse, demonstrating an image of might and power, as was typical of the emperors and generals of the day. But, no, Jesus enters quietly on a borrowed donkey, "upon which no one had ever sat." In doing this, he fulfilled the prophecy of Zechariah. 9:9. You ask, but why did he do this? Why did he not show the power and authority of which he certainly was capable? Scripture teaches and the old gospel song proclaims, "He could have called ten thousand angels." The answer?

Jesus did not need to enter on a war horse He didn't need to ride on a horse to show his earthly power. His kingdom is not of this world. It is far above this temporal existence, confined by time. Even his message of peace passes beyond all understanding. Jesus' message teaches love, humility and peace, not war and disrespect of other human beings.

Jesus rides amidst rejoicing and praise from his disciples and believing followers. Some began to see the spiritual light of it all; that Jesus was their hope and so they chanted and sang "Hosanna," which means save us now. Even with their spiritual eyes only partly open, they began to glimpse Jesus as their Savior. And:

Jesus chooses to enter Jerusalem In spite of criticism from those Pharisees, who were determined to maintain their religious strangle hold on the people. In spite of the possible retributions from the Roman government. In spite of Jesus' many followers whom he knew would later forsake him and flee, Jesus enters Jerusalem. He enters from the Mount of Olives, the very place where the Old Testament prophets declared the Messiah was expected to enter.

Now picture this amazing scene; Jesus had just healed Bartimaeus who was blind and is now happily following him with the other pilgrims. But this happy scene changes when, from the Mount of Olives, overlooking the city, Jesus began to weep, not ordinary tears, but deep sobbing from within. He experiences deep rejection. Why is he weeping?

Jesus Weeps Over Jerusalem because he sees that this is Jerusalem's last chance for spiritual restoration and for peace before the impending disaster that now was certain to come to them. Here are Jesus' words as recorded in Matthew 23:37-39,

"O Jerusalem. Jerusalem, you who kill the prophets and stone those sent to you, how often I have longed to gather your children together, as a hen gathers her chicks under her wings, but you were not willing. Look, your house is left desolate. For I tell you, you will not see me again until you say. 'Blessed is he who comes in the name of the Lord.'

Yes, Jesus weeps He weeps because he cares so much.

Jesus weeps over their spiritual blindness - even after he had just healed a blind man restoring his sight.

He weeps because he knows their opportunity to accept him has passed. They are spiritually blinded by political, religious and cultural prejudices.

He weeps because he knows their fate - that they brought it on themselves.

Jesus Prophesies Concerning Jerusalem's Fall He foresees the destruction of the temple, the sacking of the entire city of Jerusalem and the utter chaos that would occur there. The city did fall in A.D. 70 along with the temple built by Herod the Great!

Sadly, over two thousand years have passed and there is still no real peace in Jerusalem. The piles of stones from the walls are still there as a silent reminder of Jesus' prophecy.

But there is hope today! Someday Jesus will return, will restore all things and there will be a new creation! Now, as we return to the scene where Jesus prophesied concerning Jerusalem, he declared,

"Your enemies will surround you." - Like he was saying, "You only think you are in control. God is really in control." Then Jesus continues:

"Your enemies will destroy you and this city." - Again, it was like Jesus was saying,

"The power and control you cling to so tightly will be gone." Finally, Jesus said,

"This will happen because you did not recognize the day when God visited you." But this did not include the followers of Jesus; they could express his presence in their lives, like the old gospel song, "It is joy unspeakable and full of glory."

Yes, as Jesus entered Jerusalem, the crowds of people shouted, "Hosanna to the King of Kings." - believers lovingly laid palm branches on the ground before him.

History was made that day when, with supreme bravery, deliberation and a Divine sense of purpose, Jesus' rode into Jerusalem. Though crowds cheered, some criticized and some of the authorities even tried to stop the cheering, but Jesus' rode on triumphantly, and peacefully through the streets of Jerusalem, undaunted.

Jesus knew who he was. He knew he was God incarnate, God in human flesh come to be with us here on the earth. And the greatest miracle of all, our salvation, through the cross and his resurrection, was soon to take place.

Religious prejudice strongly held customs, spiritual blindness and fighting for power caused many religious leaders and others to fail to see Jesus as he really was. Peter, James and John had a special privilege concerning this on the Mount of Transfiguration.

What a shame for those who didn't know Jesus, who refused to believe! Yet, those who saw Jesus as their Messiah, were overjoyed.

Today, we celebrate this great historic event, Palm Sunday, as believers who have great cause to rejoice.

Jesus is indeed our Messiah, our King of Kings and our Lord of Lords who came to save the world. And that means you and me. There is no greater love than this!

Joy in the Morning

Scripture lesson: John 20:1-18 Text: John 20: 18a

It seemed like an ordinary day. Yet sadness was in the air. It was:

"On the first day of the week, very early in the morning, the women took the spices they had prepared and went to the tomb. They found the stone rolled away from the tomb, but when they entered, they did not find the body of the Lord Jesus. While they were wondering about this, suddenly two men in clothes that gleamed like lightening stood beside them. In their fright the women bowed down with their faces to the ground, but the men said to them "Why do you look for the Living among the dead? He is not here; he has risen!"

It was Mary Magdalene, Joanna, Mary the mother of James, and the others with them who told this to the apostles. But they did not believe the women, because their words seemed to them like nonsense. Peter, however, got up and ran to the tomb.

Bending over, he saw the strips of linen lying by themselves, and he went away, wondering to himself what had happened."

What a wonderful day is today, Easter Sunday, a day to celebrate Jesus' resurrection and his victory over evil and saving everyone who believes in him. Think about it! Jesus has sealed our salvation forever! This is why we, as Christians, have such inner peace and great joy.

In today's account, after Jesus' trial, his crucifixion as the final sacrifice for sin, buried in the tomb of Joseph of Arimathea, he then, on the third day, arose from the grave, demonstrating his Deity and proving his teaching, "The Father and I are One, "

Without a doubt, this is the greatest miracle in the history of the world. But some folks still have secret doubts. Why? There is the desire for visible evidence. In court cases, circumstantial evidence can be compelling and physical evidence can also be convincing. With Christians it is a matter of faith.

All over the world, Christianity declares the resurrection event to be true, but some still do not believe. So, let's take a step-by-step journey into this amazing event. Assuming the biblical records tell the story with sincerity, we may ask, what about witnesses? Recorded in scripture, are many who witnessed Jesus' death and, over fe hundred who witnessed his resurrection! Then, after the Day of Pentecost, empowered by the Holy Spirit, the disciples began to carry the gospel to the world.

Mark's gospel tells us that even the centurion Roman soldier, who stood by Jesus as he died, attested to his death and affirmed Jesus' real identity when he exclaimed, "Surely this man was the Son of God." It was almost as if he impulsively blurted it out! Think of the implications! He said this after participating in Jesus' actual crucifixion! He stood there witnessing Jesus die in front of him on the cross, the cross he had helped erect! Yes, he was a trained Roman soldier, but he was nevertheless, human. I believe the situation finally got to him impelling to exclaim, "Surely. this man was the Son of God!"

After the Roman soldiers, who did the actual act of crucifixion, took Jesus down from the cross, placing him in a sepulcher, or tomb, following orders, they rolled a large, heavy, disk shaped, stone covering its opening. Following standard Roman procedure, the stone was then sealed at its edges by rope and wax, making entry unlawful and subject to severe punishment. (On our trip to Israel, my wife and I stood at the empty tomb entrance, saw the heavy stone and the grooved track that guided the stone to seal the tomb.)

Pilate, in command, instructed the Roman soldiers to guard the tomb. knowing if they failed in their duty, they would be subject to execution, literally guarding the tomb with their lives. Roman military training was strict and Roman law was severe.

Pilate's situation was also tenuous. The Jews, wanting Jesus crucified, put pressure on him saying, "If you let this man go. you are no friend of Caesar." What was this political statement about? Pilate, appointed by Sejanus, was plotting to overthrow Caesar!

Learning of this, Caesar had Sejanus and his appointees executed. Now, the circumstances were obvious. Pilate was in no position to get into trouble with Rome and the Jews, who through their lying, had led Pilate into the dilemma. He mistakenly thought, that if he released Jesus instead of Barabbas and word got to Rome that, Jerusalem was in rebellion, led by Jesus, he would be the first to go. So, to save his own skin, Pilate turned Jesus over to be executed. Thus, the accuracy of gospel account was confirmed! And explains the Jews threatening remark, "If you let this man go, you are no friend of Caesar." Pilate was out to save his own life. If Sejanus could be executed, so could he!

So, Jesus was crucified. And as time passed on to the first day of the week, this is when, early in the morning, Mary and others came to the tomb needing someone to roll the stone back so she could enter with her spices to prepare the body. To her amazement she saw:

The Open Tomb - The heavy stone with the seal around it, was rolled away. The Roman soldiers were not able to keep the tomb sealed. Powerful forces were at work!

Mary looked in amazement. There was the tomb, empty. But where was the body of her Lord? Jesus was definitely not there.

Quickly she ran to tell Peter and John. And as with all Jesus' followers, they too, were afraid. To them, all hope was gone, and they were left mourning the loss of their Master. However, an astonishing turn of events was about to unfold. Mary arrived and told them the wonderful, good news. The tomb was empty! What was their response?

Immediately, Peter and John left her and ran to the tomb. Why did they do this? Mary's testimony not convincing? The situation was incredible. Peter and John just had to see for themselves. They wanted proof. But then, could it be that what Jesus had predicted really did happen? Probably out of breath, Peter and John arrived at the tomb; then, the reality of Mary's story loomed large. There, right in front of them, was the scene just as she had told them. They saw:

The Empty Tomb - with the heavy stone rolled away from the entrance. Their Lord, having been placed there lovingly by Joseph of Arimathea, was not there. What, then, did they see as they gazed inside?

They saw the empty grave clothes nested neatly, in place, the graveclothes were lying there, "still in their folds." World authority, Dr. Wm. Barclay, explains that the Greek text, "still in their folds," means it was as if someone had literally vaporized out of them. And the latest three-dimensional photographs of the Shroud of Turin show the same thing, as if someone had vaporized out of the grave clothes. This finding gives us pause to reflect. And:

John saw the empty tomb, the grave clothes and believed! Yet, there were many unanswered questions. The disciples were astonished and confused. The reality of it had not sunk in yet, that Jesus was risen from the dead, as he told them.

We wonder why they didn't understand. After all, Jesus' resurrection was prophesied in the Old Testament, as in David's Psalm 16, verses 9 and 10, "therefore, my heart is glad and my tongue rejoices: my body also will rest secure, because you will not abandon me to the grave, nor will you let your Holy One see decay." The apostle Peter preached from this very passage in Acts 2:25-28,

"I saw the Lord always before me. Because he is at my right hand, I will not be shaken. Therefore, my heart is glad, and my tongue rejoices: my body will live in hope, because you will not abandon me to the grave. nor will you let your Holy One see decay. You have made known to me the paths of life: you will fill me with joy in your presence."

This prophetic, Messianic interpretation is also found in another relevant passage, Chapter 53 of Isaiah. It begins with "Who has believed our message and to whom has the arm of the Lord been revealed?" Later, more detail unfolds in verse 9:

"He was assigned a grave with the wicked, and with the rich in his death, though he had done no violence, nor was any deceit in his mouth. Yet it was the Lord's will to crush him and cause him to suffer, and though the Lord makes his life a guilt offering, he will see his offspring and prolong his days. Therefore, I will ge him a portion among the great, and he will divide the spoils with the strong. because he poured out his life with the transgressors. For he bore the sin of many. and made intercession for the transgressors."

And earlier in Isaiah, Chapter 52:7, we read these wonderful words:

"How beautiful on the mountains are the feet of those who bring good news. who proclaims peace. who bring good tidings. who proclaims salvation. who say to Zion, 'Your God reigns.' "

It is puzzling that with all the Old Testament passages pointing to Jesus, the disciples still didn't understand why he died and God's plan of salvation for the world. However, one thing was certain. The tomb was empty. Jesus was not there.

Peter and John went back to their lodgings with great wonderment and with many questions. But they were soon to have their eyes opened further.

And at this point, Mary still thought that Jesus was dead and did not know where his body was. She wanted to do the proper thing and care for his body with spices. Little did she realize that she was about to meet:

The Risen Lord! - As John's gospel has it:

Peter and John had left. Mary, now alone, stood weeping outside the tomb. Looking into the tomb she saw two angels who spoke to her. Then, She hears a voice ask, "Woman, why are you crying?" "Who are you looking for?" Mary answers, "They have taken the Lord out of the tomb, and I don't know where they have put him." At this, she turned around and saw Jesus standing there, but, likely in the early dawn light, thought he was the gardener, she said, "Sir, if you have carried him away, tell me where you have put him, and I will get him." Jesus said to her, 'Mary.' She turned toward him and cried out in Aramaic, "Rabboni" (My Master).

After Mary's glorious encounter with Jesus at the tomb, she went directly to tell the disciples of her remarkable experience. Mary was now an eyewitness! She could proclaim with great authority, "I have seen the Lord." Many others, too, witnessed the resurrected Lord. In fact, over 500 people saw the resurrected Christ.

The world is always looking for true witnesses, prime sources. Here they are in the biblical record, along with countless millions of Christians, who down through the ages, testify how Jesus the Christ has transformed their lives.

May we include ourselves among them as we say, "He is risen!"

The Lifestyle of Discipleship

Scripture lesson: Luke 6:20-38 Text: Luke 6: 23

We know that being a disciple of Jesus Christ is much more than making a statement of our belief. It is who we are! And that involves our lifestyle, what we do with our lives and what we avoid dong, which is what we call discipleship. Indeed, this is why we are known as the people of "The Way." When did this tag get started? Well, Christians were first called people of "The Way" during the first century by outsiders.

They saw Christians showing love for one another, who, in fact, are a loving people, that they live by a different lifestyle and by different values. This is what makes us different! Our lifestyle is based on our loving relationship with Jesus Christ, his teachings and the inspired New Testament writings.

The writer F. R. Maltby described the Christian life this way, he said, "Jesus promised his disciples three things - that they would be completely fearless, absurdly happy and constantly in trouble." He may have taken things a bit to the extreme, but with today's challenges to our faith, it often seems that way.

The famous British scholar, G. K. Chesterton, whose high principles often got him into trouble when dealing with people Living by lesser values, once remarked, "I like getting into hot water. It keeps you clean." Our Christian lifestyle can be discomforting to those who live by worldly values.

A lifestyle of discipleship begins with the spiritual aspect of our lives, being saved, born again, but this quickly progresses into a new set of values and a changed lifestyle. Difficult for the world to understand, but for Christians it is a win, win all around.

In today's scripture, Jesus addresses his disciples, looking them straight in the eye, and seeing all their hurts, calls them blessed! As disciples of Jesus, this also means you and me. In spite of our faults and hurts, and he knows them all, Jesus calls us blessed. It is true.

Blessed Are the Disciples of Jesus! - No matter if we are poor, hungry, hated, or excluded, our very name rejected because of following Jesus, we are blessed!

A Jesus says his disciples are to rejoice, leap for joy, because great will be their reward in heaven Why? Because the very ill treatment that Christians sustain for the gospel, is evidence that we are numbered with the prophets! How may we better understand Jesus saying his followers are blessed?

First, we will explore the real meaning of the words Jesus is using while addressing his disciples, and also include blessings from chapter 5 in Matthew. In Luke, Jesus is addressing his disciples, not the general crowd. And his pronouncements of blessing are, for them, important words of encouragement. They didn't know it yet, but they would be carrying the gospel to the world at large. So, Jesus begins addressing them saying:

1. "Blessed are you who are poor." - Poor here means abject poverty. Not merely the inconvenience of altering a person's lifestyle because of some minor limitation. Poor here really means poor, poverty where the only hope for the person, is to put their whole trust in God.

2. "Blessed are you who hunger now, for you will be satisfied." -Think of the 23rd Psalm, "The Lord is my Shepherd, I shall not want." Jesus' words, in Luke and Matthew chapters 5-7, have both physical and spiritual meaning.

3. "Blessed are you who mourn." - This person is truly sorry for their own sins and unrighteousness, and realize they need to change, when they experience the presence of a high and holy God. Again, to Matthew chapters 5-7, Jesus says,

4. "Blessed are the Meek." - In ancient Greek, meek means self- controlled, not like modern English that suggests it means weak. The Greek philosopher, Aristotle, said meek means to be angry at the right time and not angry at the wrong time. Meek during Jesus', time means to be entirely self-controlled.

5. "Blessed are those who hunger and thirst for Righteousness." - Righteousness here does not mean merely abstaining from sin, like the hermit or social isolationist. Righteousness is also proactive, doing acts of kindness motivated by love. To thirst after righteousness is also to do good things.

6. "Blessed are the Merciful." - These people care, they see the need and act on it. The Greek word here, for merciful is *eleemon*, the ability to feel and perceive like the other person for whom mercy is ge. Like the Nate American quote, "Walking in the other person's moccasins."

7. "Blessed are the Pure in Heart." - This person's motes are entirely unmixed, free of hidden purpose. No hidden schemes here. No hidden agendas. "Blessed are the pure in heart," are persons whose motes are pure.

8. "Blessed are the Peacemakers." - They are problem solvers, not troublemakers to just get their own way. They put peace above personalities and never put the other person down just to come out on top. Peacemakers focus on the issue, not the person. It reminds me of the Peanuts cartoon where Lucy says, "The trouble with Snoopy is he's your dog Charley Brown." It is humorous because you cannot address her remark logically as a problem to be solved because it requires dissolving a relationship. Definitely not an answer.

Then, Jesus pronounces woes on those who are not called blessed:

"Woe to You, the Selfish, Wealthy. Power Class!" - Strong language! Who is Jesus addressing here? Mainly the self-satisfied, wealthy Sadducees and the Pharisees both who had a sense of entitlement because of their social rank or position. The Sadducees belonged to the wealthy, political social class and the Pharisees had powerful religious influence. So, Jesus scolds them:

You are comfortable, well fed, but:

Woe to you for your lifestyle It identifies who you truly are, selfish, and self-satisfied in your wealth. You are in the same classification as the false prophets! How can Jesus say this? He knows his audience! And further, Jesus says, in effect, it is because the public image you present is not who you really are. To correct their problem, Jesus, then, gives them instruction, also good advice for us today:

Our Heavenly Father Has Shown Us - by proper example. How?

Do good deeds Often easier said than done. Easy when things are going right, but how do we do good to others who dislike us, and may misunderstand our motes? First, we can pray for them, and having love precede the action, we can let our acts of kindness shine. The love of Jesus Christ flowing through us makes the impossible, possible and can become world changing. Then, Jesus said:

Love our enemies Why? Because we believe, in the end, love will win the day. Loving can actually become a pattern in our nervous system and replace hate responses. This is good for mental health. Further, Jesus says:

Don't judge or condemn doesn't mean we are not to evaluate a situation. It means. Don't play God. God is the judge, the final judge. I had a Baptist friend say to me concerning this, "We are not to judge, but we can be fruit inspectors." I found this interesting as another way of saying that we shouldn't judge, but we can evaluate. Not a bad approach when used within proper limits.

Forge and ge of ourselves This, is, in some ways, an ideal and only possible when we allow God to enable us.

The Lifestyle of Discipleship is the lifestyle of those who truly follow Jesus. And although impossible to be absolutely perfect in every act or deed in this life, we can grow and move upward toward the mark, as the apostle Paul says, "the mark of the high calling in Christ Jesus." However, it is true that we can become more and more perfect in love. This is one very visible testimony to the world of the Christ who lives within us.

The world will know we are Christians by our love. And we must never forget that the world will never understand what we are about without experiencing Jesus Christ for themselves.

So, let us, no matter the obstacles, "press forward toward that mark of the high calling in Christ Jesus." For he is ever faithful.

As Christians, we are called blessed as we continue to love others with a love that is truly unconditional.

So, may we continue to press forward toward the mark of the high calling in Christ Jesus, for he is ever faithful. And what a happy thought that God calls us blessed when we truly love and care for others. It sounds impossible. But we can do it with the love of Jesus, enabled by his Holy spirit.

And how comforting it is to know, that Jesus, who loves us just the way we are, desires that we grow spiritually, so that we can experience his very best for us.

How would we define the lifestyle of discipleship? It is following Jesus and being a channel through whom God works. This, my dear Christian friends, is the highest plane of Living in the entire world.

So, may we go forth with renewed vigor, sharing the good news of salvation, and sharing the joy of our life with Jesus Christ!

Sweet Revenge

Scripture lesson: Genesis 45:3-18

There are lots of social dramas on television. Some of them are funny like "Everybody Loves Raymond" and some of the older Brit corns, like "Are You Being Served" and "Keeping Up 'appearances." Others are dramatic like "Downton Abby," full of social intrigue, or one of my old favorite detectives, the unassuming, Lieutenant Columbo, the reruns are still being aired. Everyone likes a story of intrigue, whether it be social intrigue, adventure intrigue or the intrigue of a mystery story.

Well, today's story of Joseph in the Old Testament begins like a soap opera, with family problems, jealousy and foul play. The narration continues full of intrigue and surprises. It is truly, drama 'par excellence.' However, different from fiction, this story is like a documentary; this story really happened.

It begins with the chief character, Joseph, eleventh son of Jacob, and the first-born of Rachel, Jacob's favorite wife. Jacob, born three generations after Abraham, is part of a long line of important personalities in the history of the Israelite nation. The number of Jacob's twelve sons takes on more meaning as the narrative progresses. And to ge us a time frame, archaeological evidence puts the generation of Abraham in the Middle Bronze age, when the combination of copper and tin was discovered to produce a much harder metal, bronze.)

During this time, the early patriarchs were mostly seminomadic, being in constant need of water and pasture lands. However, we know that Joseph's lifestyle growing up was not strictly nomadic because Jacob built a house in Succoth, in the area of Canaan. His tents were only used for his livestock.

So much for background; our story begins in Genesis 37:3 where Joseph was favored by his father Jacob because he was the son of his old age. Perhaps celebrating this is why Jacob made him a special garment - a long robe with sleeves and apparently of bright colors. The result? Jealousy, followed by hatred! (Notice. The biblical writer doesn't defend this action or try to get us to understand it at this point; he lets the facts emerge as the story unfolds.) It begins with a work situation; Jacob sends Joseph to the city of Shechem to look after his brothers, to see if they and their flocks are O.K. Traveling alone, and not finding them at Shechem, he goes on the Dothan where he did find his brothers, but alas, it was not a happy meeting. They hated him and saw their chance to get rid of him, to murder him. Discussion ensued, but Reuben persuaded the other brothers to sell him as a slave instead to protect his life. So, they threw Joseph into a dry water cistern, so he couldn't escape and waited for travelers a nasty business.

Soon, Midianite merchants came by, and his brothers sold him to the Ishmaelites from Midian as a slave. Wow! Where was the fairness in that? After all, he came to look after his brothers. Evil has no bounds. So, Joseph, favored son in the family, was lowered to the status of a slave. A bad situation? Yes! And, of course, slavery itself, is wrong.

But to properly understand slavery in this ancient culture, it is helpful to know that a slave was often treated more like a conscripted hired hand. It was like buying an indentured worker with the owner responsible for his care. Certainly, this was not right, but that was the way it was during those ancient times. And even harder to understand. Sometimes slaves became so devoted to their masters that they opted to serve as their slaves for their entire lives, even when freedom after three years would be granted.

Also, important is that slaves sometimes had skills and abilities, and even intelligence beyond that of their wealthy masters. So, within this strange, commonly practiced system, a slave could rise to a very high rank within a household.

For example, if there was need for a trustworthy person with administrative ability who could handle such responsibility, they could rise to that coveted position, even managing an entire household. This is exactly what happened to Joseph, a man, with such valuable talents that they did not go unnoticed.

So, Joseph, after being betrayed by his brothers, was sold to an Egyptian named Potiphar. Soon his skills and talents brought him the high promotion of managing the entire household! What a twist in this story of intrigue!

Joseph was the very model of an administrator, hard- working, honest, wise, and devoted. So, what happened next? The master of the household noticed that the Lord caused all of Joseph's efforts to prosper in his hands.

At last, it seemed that Joseph's fortunes were turning around. But were they?

In Genesis 39: 6b we read this dicey, provocative statement,

"Now Joseph was well-built and handsome, and after "a while his master's wife took notice of Joseph and said, "Come to bed with me!" What would he do?

He refused, reminding her of the trust put to him by his master, "And though she spoke to Joseph, day after day, beckoning him, he refused to go to bed with her or even be in her presence. But one day when he went into the house to attend to his duties, and none of the household servants was inside, she caught him by the cloak and said, "Come to bed with me!" But he left his cloak in her hand and ran out of the house. . . Then, like a woman scorned, she called her household servants and lied to them. 'Look.' she said to them 'this Hebrew has been brought to us to play sports of us! He came in here to sleep with me. but I screamed. When he heard me scream for help, he left his cloak beside me and ran out of the house.'

Here the drama gets very nasty. When the master came home, she repeated the lie and the master believed her; burning with anger, he threw Joseph into prison where the king's prisoners were confined.

Now what's going to happen to Joseph? Have you ever been in a situation where you felt trapped? Fortunately, we read that the Lord was with Joseph and perhaps the Prison Warden realized that Joseph was falsely accused. At any rate, the Warden trusted him, recognized his leadership abilities, and he put Joseph in charge of all the prisoners.

Time passed and sometime later, both the chief cup bearer and chief backer of Pharaoh offended their master and were thrown into prison where Joseph was. Later they came to him because they had dreams that puzzled them. And they had been told that he interpreted dreams correctly. But when they approached Joseph, he said to them, "Do not interpretations belong to God?" After going God, the credit for his insights, Joseph told them the meaning of their dreams, that the chief cup bearer would be reinstated, but the chief baker would lose his life. And it happened.

Two years passed - -And the Pharaoh, himself, had two dreams that were alike. None of the king's wise men or magicians could interpret them. But, at his cup bearer's advice, he sent for Joseph who said. "I cannot do it. but God will ge Pharaoh the answer he desires." Again, after giving God the credit, Joseph interpreted Pharaoh's dreams that predicted seven years of plenty and seven years of famine. He advised Pharaoh to store up grain during the plentiful years in preparation for the seven- year famine to follow. At this, Pharaoh put him in charge and Joseph administered the storage of huge amounts of grain in all the cities over the plentiful seven-year period.

Then came the predicted famine. And we find the family of Jacob, forced to go to the land of Egypt in search of grain. How strange is this with events that so turn a situation around! Joseph goes from being a slave, to being a prisoner, and now to a power position over his entire family! Talk about - "from rags to riches!"

Now, Joseph's entire family is literally at his mercy. What will he do? What is he to make of this situation? After all, years have passed. His family would likely not even recognize him, nor would he recognize them. But as it turned out, even though they didn't recognize him, he does recognize them.

Was he gleeful at this? Here is his opportunity for revenge! If so, what kind of revenge? What will he do? How does he see the situation? Keep in mind, as you hear the rest of the story, Joseph's administrative ability and that he is a very clever strategist!

As soon as his brothers are in search of grain, he asked, "Where do you come from?" They replied, "From the land of Canaan to buy food." Then, in a clever, strategic move, Joseph says, "You are spies; you have come to see the nakedness of the land.".

But says he will test them, keeping one brother and allowing the others to go with sacks loaded with grain to their starving households. Further, he tells them they must bring their youngest brother back with them. Then, Joseph gives the steward orders to fill their bags with grain, to secretly put each man's silver back in his sack, and ge them provisions for their journey. Off they went.

When they stopped for the night, one of them opened his sack to feed his donkey and found his silver in the mouth of the sack. The others found silver in their sacks, too. Not knowing that Joseph had the silver secretly placed in their sacks, they trembled and blamed God. They said, "What is this that God has done to us?"

When they returned to Canaan with the grain, and were ready to go back to Egypt, Joseph's brother, Judah, said to his father,

"Send the boy (meaning Benjamin) with me and we will go at once, so that we and you and our children may live and not die. I myself guarantee his safety."

Jacob instructed them to ge the man, he didn't yet know was Joseph, a gift, a little balm and a little honey, some spices and myrrh, some pistachio nuts and almonds and double the amount of silver, to pay for the grain and pay back the silver they found in their sacks. Jacob said, regarding the silver placed in their sacks, "Perhaps it was a mistake."

So, they took their brother Benjamin with them, so as to bring their other brother back with them to Canaan and left for Egypt. When they arrived and presented themselves to Joseph, he saw Benjamin with them and instructed his steward,

"Take these men to my house, slaughter an animal and prepare dinner: there to eat with me at noon."

Frightened, the brothers thought they were brought there because of the silver that was put back into their sacks the first time. They thought, "He wants to attack us and overpower us and seize us as slaves and take our donkeys." (Joseph, without saying it, was teaching them an important life on in trust, when in the past they, themselves, couldn't be trusted.) Understandably, the brothers were fearful of becoming slaves, just as they had sold their brother Joseph to the Ishmaelites of Midian. So, when they went up to Joseph's house, they nervously explained once again that they didn't know who put the silver in their sacks. "It's all right," he said, "Don't be afraid.

Your God and the God of your father has gen you treasure in your sacks: I received your silver." Then he brought Simeon back to them as was promised.

When Joseph came home, they gave him the gifts they had brought from Canaan.

He, asked how they were and then asked,

"How is your aged father you told me about?" "Is he still ling?" They answered,

"Your servant. our father is still ale and well."

When Joseph saw his brother Benjamin, his own mother's son he asked, "Is this your youngest brother. the one you told me about?" And he said, "God be gracious to you, my son." Deeply moved at the sight of his brother. Joseph went into his prate room and wept there. After washing his face. he came out and. controlling himself. said: "Serve the food." After the meal when they were preparing for the journey back, Joseph said to the steward, "fill the men's sacks, put silver in each sack. Then put my cup, the silver one, in the mouth of the youngest one's sack. along with the silver for his grain." (More sweet mischief afoot? More sweet revenge? We continue.)

As morning dawned, the men left, and had not gone far when Joseph instructed his steward to go after the men and find the silver cup in the sack of the youngest brother, Benjamin's, sack. When all the brothers came back, Joseph requested they get their father and bring him back to Egypt with them. These carefully contrived strategies resulted in bringing the entire family back to Egypt. Joseph, no longer able to control his secret identity, said to his brothers, "Come close to me." Then, he said,

"I am your brother Joseph, the one you sold into Egypt: And now, do not be distressed or angry with yourselves for selling me here, because God sent me ahead of you to preserve for you a remnant on earth and save lives by a great deliverance."

... "Now hurry back to my father and say to him, "This is what your son Joseph says: God has made me Lord of all Egypt. Come down to me: don't delay. You shall live in the region of Goshen near me - your children and grandchildren, your flocks and herds and all you have. I will provide it for you there ...

Then Joseph kissed all his brothers and wept over them.... And with an insightful, parting remark, he said, "Don't quarrel on the way." So, ends this amazing story. Even better when you read it right from the Bible.

To help us glean some valuable spiritual lives on: First, we note that:

Joseph Sees the Hand of God on His Life Many years passed for this to be made clear, but Joseph's faith remained firm. Seeing the hand of God behind it all, he tells his brothers:

"Do not be distressed or angry with yourselves for selling me." - It was like a veiled way of saying, "I forge you." Further, Joseph tells them:

"Behind all this was God's hand at work." -Joseph's spirituality shone through. He says,

"God sent me to save lives to preserve the remnant." - He knows that the building of the Israelite nation as God had promised Abraham, with all twelve brothers, none to be lost, was in his hands. They were the beginning of the twelve tribes of Israel! Now it is easier to see that God's hand in Joseph's life was ultimately for the greater good, the building of a nation! God's great purpose is shown in all of these events:

God Made Joseph Lord of all. (in the area of administration) - Here God shows how he can make the powerless powerful for his will to be made known.

Joseph, after testing his brothers' veracity, and after shedding many tears, reveals himself to them and then gives them the good news. This is the best kind of sweet revenge. He returns good for evil. He tells them, "You shall live in the land of Goshen - near me."

"I will provide for you there."- Though they had abandoned him when he was a youth, he chooses the love principle and takes care of them.

"And he kissed all his brothers." When they left and returned with their father, Jacob, now named Israel, carried with them Joseph's love for them. They came to Egypt, hungry and fearful and finally left with food in their sacks and love in their hearts. The sweetest revenge is to return love for hate.

God Took Them All Through the Famine God's will was to lead them, guide them and save their lives, thus preserving the remnant, the 12 sons, which were to become the Israelite nation the 12 tribes of Israel!

Joseph was led by God's wisdom - to store grain to get them through the famine.

Other nations were also helped - they too, could buy grain.

The remnant of Israel was preserved - thus, allowing the formation of the nation of Israel.

On our own faith journey, we may not always understand our circumstances, but let's be clear about this important truth, God has his hand on each one of us, on all of our lives.

The scripture is wise, so true and validating, Psalm 37:23,

"The steps of a righteous person are ordered of the Lord."

If we seek to do God's will, he will enable us and it will be done, even though in this life we may never understand When we feel down, may we remember the life of Joseph!

God is ever faithful!

Ezekiel Is Called to Be a Watchman

Scripture lesson: Ezekiel 33: 1-9 Text: Ezekiel 33:7a

It was 1946, shortly after the close of the second World War which ended in May 1945; my father took a new pastorate, so we moved from Nanticoke Pennsylvania to Moosic Pennsylvania, where we had been Living for three and a half years in Nanticoke, Pennsylvania. The experience of hiding under the school desks during the frequent air raid drills was still fresh in my memory. Loud sirens would go off during school, and we rushed to take shelter under the desks. The town officials were constantly on the alert and if the sirens went off in the evening, we would have a complete blackout with the windows of our house covered to keep out any light. The local police and neighborhood watch patrol combed the streets to make sure all citizens were inside and complying with the requirements of the blackout. With everything pitch dark and the daily evening radio news broadcasts with Walter Winchell we were kept on edge. Only a few years before this, on De7, 1941, the Japanese had attacked the U. S. Naval Base at Pearl Harbor. And adding to our anxiety, submarines were seen along our coastline, spotted by the concrete observation towers. And they are still standing along the Delaware and Maryland coastlines today. (You can see them on the left while going south toward Ocean City Maryland.)

Those were scary times. They are still etched clearly in our memory; but from this experience we learned something very important. The importance of being constantly on the alert. We were, in fact, all watchmen. We were warned to be careful even of ordinary conversations because of information that might help the enemy. On the radio were constant warnings, "The walls have ears." Those were difficult years.

But after the war was over, we moved from Nanticoke, Pennsylvania to Moosic, Pennsylvania, believing we were going to have a better life in this coal mining railroad town, named after the Mohican Indians. Upon arrival, we walked around to see what was there. As a railroad town, Moosic was similar in that respect to Dayton, Evansville, and Spring City.

Something curiously interesting, right in town near the drug store, pool hall and grocery store, caught my eye. There was a little shed close to the railroad tracks. I was told that there was a man in that mysterious shed whose job was to handle the gate and rail switches as the trains came through town. He was the gate keeper and the switchman. Well, as time went on and not seeing him, we took him for granted.

Then, one afternoon it happened; a bad wreck occurred. The gate keeper had fallen asleep and failed to put the crossing gate down when a train was coming. We students were on the high school band bus, and we saw the car, stopped on the tracks, get hit. Fortunately, the lady driving the car got out in time, but her vehicle, driven relentlessly down the track, was totaled. The scriptural lives on here are obvious. We are all watchmen.

As Watchmen, We Should Realize and Face Up to Our Responsibility.

When I was band director in Jackson Louisiana there was a bright, but mischievous ninth grade boy in the band. Upon returning after summer vacation, I noticed a big change in Cedric. He was sober and quite serious. I asked him why he was now so serious, and he told me that he had worked that summer for his uncle. I said, "That's fine.

What work did your uncle do?" With a serious look in his eye, he said, "My uncle is a funeral director." I then asked him what he had learned from his experience, and he said, "I learned to face up to my responsibility." It certainly was growing up time for Cedric and through his work experience he had matured into recognizing his need to take responsibility for his actions. This is akin to the experience of the prophet Ezekiel, who as a watchman, was led to proclaim God's message with serious resolve. We learn that:

The watchman is responsible to proclaim the Word of the Lord as authoritative, and to avoid listening to ill-informed, sometimes popular, persons who make misleading pronouncements. Ezekiel proclaimed the Word of the Lord as a watchman for Israel.

The watchman is to be alert to the danger of spiritual decline. Ezekiel was.

The watchman is responsible to warn the people of impending danger Ezekiel did this, sounding the trumpet of warning loud and clear. He spoke to his countrymen to warn them. Sometimes silence is golden, but his time it was not. And spiritually similar to Ezekiel's time, we are Living in times when Christians need to take a stand.

As Watchman We Should Execute Our Spiritual Responsibility The tragedy of some people's lives is that, avoiding their responsibility, they just walk away. By doing this they are really walking away from life. This is unfortunate and sad because, in spite of the possible stress, they are missing out on some of life's most fulfilling moments. History is replete with examples of folks who "woulda, coulda shoulda", but didn't.

There is a story of a, so called, holy hermit who in his daily prayer, after contemplating on the suffering in the world, questioned God. He asked, God, "why didn't you do something about it?" God answered, "I did do something about it. I made you."

Our lives as watchmen should be so led that we can hear God's voice. Among the many conflicting voices in the world, we must prayerfully, discern God's voice.

As watchmen, we should dedicate ourselves to the tasks God has given us. We should bloom where we are planted.

As watchman, we are leaders. So, it is vital for us to get on the right road and travel only on that road because there will be others behind us following our lead.

As Watchmen, we should Accept the Limits of Our Task We should not try to do God's part of the task. This is a common mistake for those of us who really care. We do well to remind ourselves of the apostle Paul's teaching, "one sows, another waters and God gives the increase."

There is an interesting account gen when someone questioned Mother Teresa's ministry. She replied with one of the sharpest, but wisest answers I ever heard, "God didn't call me to be successful. He called me to be faithful."

This frames God's call to us as well. God doesn't call us to be successful. He calls us to be faithful. We are to leave the success part up to him. Of course, this is difficult. We all want to be successful, So, how do we do this?

We live and ge the message. This is our responsibility. And we must never shirk opportunities that God gives to us, while remembering that God gives the increase.

After we share the message, it is the responsibility of the hearer to act on it. And seeing the receptive heart, God will ge the increase.

After recognizing our personal limits in sharing the gospel, we do well to leave the increase up to God. It is very important to let the results rest in God's hands.

I remember the time when, Josephine, answering our children's question as to how her flowers grew, said, "I planted the seeds, gave them water, put them in the sunlight and God just made them grow." She taught the children an important lesson on.

She did her part and God did the rest. The children understood. It just made good sense.

As members of the household of faith, we are all called to be watchmen. (And this, of course, includes the ladies.) For the Church of Jesus Christ to be as effective as it should be, we must, face our own spiritual responsibility. And, as we are enabled, execute that responsibility faithfully, leaving the rest up to God.

After all, the destiny of the Church is with those of us who have embraced the Gospel, to be faithful watch persons for God's kingdom. This is the great task of the Church.

May God help us to heed the call, as Ezekiel did, and be faithful to our task as we live and ge the message.

And may we do this in the name of the Father, the Son and the Holy Spirit. Amen!

To Whom Shall We Go?

Scripture lives on John 6:44-69 Text John 6:68-69

The Englishman, Thomas Edward Lawrence (1888-1935) - the famous Sir Lawrence of Arabia, was a close personal friend of the poet Thomas Hardy. And while still in the Royal Air Force Sir Lawrence often visited Thomas Hardy while in his air force uniform. Well, it so happened that on one occasion his visit coincided with that of the Mayoress of Dorchester. Sir Lawrence and the Mayoress had not met before. The Mayoress was affronted by the presence of the uniformed service man. And thinking that he certainly wouldn't understand French, she told Mrs. Hardy that never in all her born days had she had to sit down to tea with a prate soldier. There was total silence. Then, Lawrence, who did understand French, said to the Mayoress in perfect English, "I beg your pardon madam, but can I be of any use as an interpreter? You see, Mrs. Hardy knows no French." The Mayoress was properly embarrassed. This is a classic example of someone seeing a person superficially. Unlike the snooty Mayoress, Jesus, is no respecter of persons. We are all equal in his sight. "To whom shall we go?" We can all go to Jesus Christ on an equal footing.

A few months ago, I heard an interesting and amusing story. You see, as a fly fisherman, I know it's hard to beat a well-made bamboo fly rod, especially for dry fly fishing. And it so happens that there is a master rod maker friend of ours, who lives in Sweetwater. So, my son Bill, Jr. and I went to try out his rods. He is so revered as a rod maker, and his prices are so modest, you have to wait about a year before delivery. Well, after putting down a payment to get our orders logged in, he gave us a number. Then, with a grin, he told us about a CEO from a large company in the northeast who wanted to place an order. He told him he would put him in line with the others as number 17 and it would be about a year before he could receive his rod. The CEO wanted his fly rod right away and, feeling powerful, shouted over the phone, "Do you know who I am.?" "Yes, I do, "came the reply, "Your number 17." We all laughed but saw an excellent example of fairness by someone who, at the cost of losing a sale, refused to be a respecter of people. By the way this gentleman also happens to be a United Methodist. The lives on here are that we are all equal in God's sight. So far as God is concerned, humanity is a level playing field.

Many times, Jesus spoke in parables and mysteries. The crowd often missed the great lives of his teachings because, being blinded by tradition or misinformation, they saw things superficially. Here, in John's gospel we have at central focus Christ's humanity and his Deity as the supreme teacher and supreme sacrifice for all humankind but understood only by the person of faith. And with all our efforts in evangelism to lead persons to Christ, we must realize that:

God Alone Draws All Persons to Himself - Even in our seeking God, God is drawing us to himself.

In his own time - We are temporal, but God is Divine and eternal. We think in terms of time. God knows eternity.

In his own way- We have his Spirit to lead us, but in the end, his ways are really beyond our ability to them figure out. "To whom shall we go?" To Jesus. He is the link that has forged our way to God. Jesus is the priestly mediator between us and God. And God through his Holy Spirit is the great motivator. By doing his will we help to set the stage for him to work his Divine will and purpose for us. He wants us to be partners with him in this.

God Has Sent His Son to Draw Us to Himself -

Jesus is the bread of life "To whom shall we go?" To Jesus the bread of life.

Jesus is the very substance of our spiritual lives. And he wants a relationship so close that he literally dwells within us. And at that very instant we begin to truly experience the power of God and that special, spiritual sense of knowing.

Faith Brings God's Presence and Then We know- We have the knowledge that passes human understanding. We know as revealed to Saint Peter that:

Jesus Christ has the words of eternal life therefore, the mind of God.

We believe and something wonderful happens Spiritual insight begins to open up to us. The scriptures are no longer foolishness as they were to our former carnal mind. They are now light to us because we are spiritually enlightened.

After all, to properly understand the scriptures they must spiritually discerned. We believe and now see the world and ourselves differently because we are changed inside. We now have a Christian's view of the world. Though we see a world with much greed and hate, we experience God's love and hope in his salvation.

We experience a sense of knowing because God's Holy Spirit comes to abide within us. God's Holy Spirit affirms that indeed, Jesus Christ is the holy one of God. He is the one to go to. He, and only he, is our Savior. "To whom shall we go?" To Jesus the one who loves us, who has the words of eternal life and who has redeemed us.

The great theologian, Dr. William Barklay, tells of an artist who was painting the Last Supper. He looked for a model he could use for depicting the face of Christ. He needed a young man with a face of transcendent loveliness and purity. As a result of his search, he finally found such a young man and used him as the model for his painting. The painting took him many years to complete.

Later, it so happened that he was looking for a model to depict Judas. He went out and searched in the lowest haunts of the city and in the dens of vice. At last, he found a man with a face so depraved and vicious that it matched his requirement. When the portrait sittings came to an end, the man said to the artist, "You painted me before." "Surely not," said the artist. "O yes," said the man. "I sat for your Christ." So sad. And he was portrayed permanently on canvass as physical evidence of his own depraved life. This is not the life of a true Christian. The lines that may etch our faces as we grow older, may they be lines of determination as well as lines of many smiles.

Now, the crowds could accept Jesus as a teacher. Some could even accept him as a prophet, but when he began to teach the real purpose of his coming to the world, the crowds no longer followed.

And yet, there was one disciple, named Peter, who had on so many occasions spoken out impulsively and improperly, but this time he nailed it! He spoke with divinely inspired insight and faith. This time he posed the decisively important question. This time when all the crowds turned away to forsake Jesus, Peter's voice rang true. He asked the vital question. Then, he gave the only correct answer. By doing this he proclaimed himself as a true witness of Jesus Christ. Peter's voice still asks that vital question today. "Lord, to whom shall we go?" and he gives the only correct answer, "You have the words of eternal life: - Then he proclaims; and we have believed - What a powerful, declarative, positive statement! It is here that the transforming power of God works in us - where we also affirm with Peter "and have come to know - As we also declare our inner, spiritual sense of knowing And finally, Peter proclaims so decisively, "that you are the Holy One of God."

Today, may we, also, answer Jesus' question, "Will you also go away? "Echoing the words of Peter:

"Lord, to whom shall we go? You have the words of eternal life: and we have believed and have come to know that you are the Holy One of God."

Invitation!

God Calls Isaiah

Scripture lesson: Isaiah 6: 1-9

It is so interesting how God calls us all in a different way; yet there are common threads that seem to be in every story about doing God's will.

While it is certainly true that Christian leaders are to be good examples, it is equally true that all Christians are to be good examples of what Christ has done for them. In this although the playing field is level, those in leadership often reach more people and have more influence, therefore they have more responsibility. But we should remember that we all have equal responsibility within our own spheres of influence, that of leading others to Christ and caring for one another. And in spite of our failings, God calls us all in one way or another, and we may even say to ourselves, why me?

I have had this very experience and I said to myself, "I'm just another person on the face of the earth. Why me?" But deep down, we have that inner sense that somehow, we are moving in the right direction. As we prayerfully follow God's leading, we begin to have a clearer sense of purpose and rightness as to where we are headed and that where we are going is the right path right there before us, beckoning us on. This is a very personal experience and a sense of direction leading us to realize that, for us, this is God's will. It is part of our spiritual journey, with Christ as our guide, in spite of our imperfections.

Isaiah is an excellent example of this, where God reaches beyond Isaiah's imperfection, calling him to lead and to write some of the most important, inspiring, messianic writings in the Old Testament. Isaiah is, to me, an excellent example of venturing out, as thoughtfully described in Robert Frost's "The Road Not Taken."

Two roads diverged in a yellow wood,
And sorry I could not travel both,
And be one traveler, long I stood,
And looked down one as far as I could
To where it bent in the undergrowth.

Then took the other, as just as fair,
and having perhaps the better claim,
Because it was grassy and wanted wear;
Though as for them, the passing there
Had worn them really about the same.

And both that morning equally lay
In leaves no step had trodden black.
Oh, I kept the first for another day!
Yet knowing how way leads on to way.
I doubted if I should ever come back.

I shall be telling this with a sigh
Somewhere ages and ages hence:
Two roads diverged in a wood and I
I took the one lives traveled by.
And that made all the difference.

We may not know where our path in life will lead us, but this we do know! Jesus Christ, through his Holy spirit, will be with us and will lead us all the way.

Our spiritual journey actually begins when we accept, Jesus Christ as our Lord and Savior for ourselves. Not some vague, general idea that we go to church because it is the socially acceptable thing to do, like the nominal Christian who hasn't really accepted Christ into their lives. Our decision is not like those whom Jesus described when he said, "You call me Lord, Lord, but don't do the things I say." But when we make the commitment to truly accept Jesus Christ as our Lord and Savior, and say with the deepest meaning, "Lord, I believe; I truly believe" we will then begin to sense God's Holy Spirit leading us.

This is what today's scripture passage is about. Isaiah has a Divine encounter, a vision:

Isaiah Sees the Lord! - This certainly is, for Isaiah, a Divine encounter!

He sees the Lord seated on a throne. This is Divine power.

He sees the Lord high and exalted He recognizes the deity.

The Lord is Holy God is ultimate purity, love and grace. Although God is totally set apart from his creation, he is totally connected to it, totally infused into it. That is why Jesus could say, "I am in the Father and the Father is in me. I am in you, and you are in me." So, as a result of Isaiah's vision:

Isaiah Sees Himself! - He has a self-encounter. He faces himself for who he really is; all social masks are removed. What the scripture means when it says, "Know thyself." We all need the self-encounter experience; when we look into the mirror of our souls and face ourselves for who we really are, sinners in need of a Savior. Of course, this will be difficult, but it will have a positive, cleansing effect on our lives.

When God revealed himself to Isaiah, in all his majesty and holiness, he burst forth with, "Woe is me. I am a man of unclean lips." His fallen nature was exposed, and yet God chose him to be the spiritual leader of his people! Why? God saw his potential, willingness to do his bidding.

His experience with the holiness of God, also led him to recognize the sinful state of his fellow Israelites, and exclaim, "I live among a people of unclean lips." Think of it; Isaiah says this about God's chosen ones, called to lead the world to Jehovah, the one true God, and they haven't done it. Instead, they have moved away from their spiritual source, God, their heavenly Father. How did this affect Isaiah?

Isaiah experiences a personal spiritual cleansing atonement without any sacrificial rite. He experiences God's grace, in an amazing event. The angel takes coal from the altar and places it on Isaiah's lips, an example of pure atonement, the cleansing of the soul without any human action, the work of pure grace symbolized by fire. And so, Isaiah is cleansed, now ready to receive God's call. But will he answer the call? Yes, of course he will.

Isaiah Answers God's Call and as he does this, he realizes there is something missing in his life, spiritual fulfillment. This too, is where we realize we need spiritual fulfillment, the missing ingredient. It is a spiritual purpose that gives special meaning to our journey. Isaiah was now ready to do God's work because:

Isaiah is purified for Divine purpose It is not what he did. It is what God did for him! Isaiah is now a life Divinely pure through atonement. I emphasize. It is not what Isaiah did. It is what God did for Isaiah. God atoned for his sins, ready to lead him and Isaiah is now ready to act on his Divine call. So, what happens next?

God reveals his plan to him He needs someone to carry his message. And notice the wording, "Who will go for us?" This plural statement "us" seems to hint at the Trinity. At any rate, Jehovah God needs a messenger and Isaiah is designated as his messenger, to carry the message.

Isaiah is now a vital part in God's plan when he makes his commitment and says, "Here am I. Send me."

(As a personal note, I can't begin to describe the feeling I got when I answered the call to ministry and said, "Here am I Lord. Send me.") Doing God's will! There is nothing like it in this world!

After Isaiah's commitment, God, commands Isaiah, "Go and tell this people." Notice, God doesn't say "my people." This is significant because of the spiritual disarray of the Israelites at this time in history. God's call to Isaiah is to get him to pave the way to restore their lost relationship with their God.

In a similar way Jesus calls us to share the gospel with the world to restore that, much needed, spiritual relationship, that souls may be saved.

God calls us even when we do not seek him enough. He calls us even when we fail him. He calls us in our imperfection just as he called Isaiah, to do his will. And, like the experience of Isaiah, when we do God's will, we are also changed while, growing spiritually.

By doing God's will, we reach toward the mark of the high calling in Christ Jesus and he, in turn, reaches toward us, and there, simply, and beautifully is fellowship. Yes, there is friendship, like it was with Abraham who was known as a friend of God.

I pray, that as we sense God's leading in our lives, no matter what it may be, we will say as Isaiah, that great prophet of old, "He am I. Send me." He will!

Life Led in Contradiction

Scripture lesson: Jeremiah 17:5-10

There is an old saying, "To thine own self be true" and we know it is important to be true to ourselves by our actions as well as in our speech. This desire for self-understanding is probably as old as the human race, itself.

For example, "Know thyself" and "Nothing in excess" are ancient Greek phrases that were inscribed in the courtyard of the ancient Temple of Apollo in Delphi. This is where the Seven Sages, or we would say today, where the wise philosophers, met.

Most popular inscribed saying was, "Know thyself," quoted many times by Socrates and though often ascribed to him, he didn't invent it. However, here is a correct quote by Socrates, "An unexamined life is not worth ling."

Self-examination is good for all of us and one way to start is to ask, "Am I my job or am I simply a person who does a certain job?" Some people so identify themselves with their employment that they see themselves that way. It's common usage in our language to say, "He is a salesman, a doctor, a teacher, a lawyer, a laborer, a banker." We just accept this as a correct description; and that's all right for what it is, just a description, because we know that people are really much more than that. We are much more than the many lives we take in our lives. We are greater than the sum of our parts because we are eternal. You probably remember from high school or college the Shakespeare quote,

"All the world's a stage and all the men and women merely players. They have their entrances and their exits and one man in his time plays many parts."

So, we may ask, "Who am I?" Self-search is beneficial for everyone. The psalmist King David did it. Here is what he wrote in Psalm 77: 6,

"I call to remembrance my songs in the night; I commune with my own heart: and my spirit made diligent search."

This is the David, as Psalmist, describing how he searches within himself to know himself better and as the rest of the psalm shows, his search to find the heart of God.

Why is this inner search so important? By learning to know ourselves, we can form positive patterns of thought and behavior that, through God's help, enable us to become the best of who we are, and not try to be somebody else. This is what God wants for all of us, to be true to ourselves, as psychologists would say, to be our best self.

What do we find as we search deeply within ourselves? First, we will ask ourselves honest questions about what is important to us. For example, what are our values, our attitudes, our likes and dislikes, our skills? What do we deem our successes or our failures?

When we do this we not only lay bare our adequacies, but our inadequacies and we finally come to realize that, down deep, our need is spiritual. So important to deal with this as it takes us on a path to avoid Living our lives in contradiction.

The religious philosopher, mathematician and physicist Blaise Pascal, knew about these things and knew what the prophet Jeremiah meant in today's scripture reading. As a result of his searching into the fallen state of the human race, Pascal concluded,

"We are only falsehood, duplicity, contradiction; we both conceal and disguise ourselves from ourselves." He states further that the fault lies in the heart's commitments. He says,

"The heart naturally loves the Universal being, and also itself naturally. But, when the choice is for self as against God, the self becomes hatable. What emerges is life led in contradiction."

Here is a broad statement of the human condition, put into religious, philosophical terms according to Pascal's understanding of the fallen nature of man, which is based on biblical principles. Pretty lofty thinking! Can we understand what he is really saying here in plainer language? Yes.

Pascal believes that human beings have a natural love for God and love for themselves at the same time. This is a setup for conflict. When persons choose to live the selfish life, a journey that goes against God, Pascal says, they wind up hating themselves. Why?

Because this kind of life focuses on the self and the self is never satisfied. And, worse still, when they choose the selfish life, they are not only out of relationship with God, but they are also out of proper alignment with reality. Why? They have rejected the faith principle. What is the lifetime result of all this? They wind up unhappy, hating themselves.

The life led in denial of the relationship God desires for us, is a life led in contradiction with itself. The illusion, stemming from the Renaissance period of history, that human beings can somehow reach a point of total self-reliance is an empty illusion. Such fallacious thinking is a dead end. Considering the good things that came out of the Renaissance period, with its emphasis on the importance of the individual, the idea of total self-reliance is not one of them. Why, you ask? Is self-reliance bad? No. Of course not, but ultimately, we are really totally dependent upon God who gives and sustains life.

So, Pascal, with his deep religious understanding, gives us some insights as to why Jeremiah prophesies the way he does. True, Jeremiah's language is strong, even extreme, but necessary to persuade a wayward nation. For example, when he says:

Cursed Is the One Who Trust in Man Why such strong language? In cultures that put their trust in military might, Jeremiah is describing a person who denies the power of almighty God to intervene in the affairs of human beings.

Cursed is the one who depends on man for strength believing they can somehow live a really fulfilled life unaided by Divine help or intervention.

Cursed is the one whose heart turns away from God - who really lives in rebellion against God, the source of all guidance and strength, saying they can do it by themselves. They are really turning their backs on a loving God.

Their lives will not be fulfilled as life should be life should involve natural and spiritual maturing, led with a profound sense of meaning and fulfillment, with an unshakable sense of personal worth, cradled in a settled faith embedded deeply within one's inner being and with the knowledge of humanity's greatest hope - eternal life with God through Jesus Christ. So, Jeremiah goes on to say:

Blessed Is the Person Who Trusts in the Lord

Whose confidence is in the Lord not in man's might, but in the power of God, the Divine energy, within each of us, which is our strength. Blessed is the person who realizes the true source of their strength.

They will be nourished - Gen spiritual strength to live a full life with meaning.

They will bear fruit - Putting action into their lives through biblical values and being led by the Holy Spirit.

The Lord Knows the Heart of Humankind those deeply embedded thoughts and values within the human heart that can so easily go astray. It is the plight of fallen humanity:

The heart without Christ is deceitful above all things and beyond cure. Who can understand it? Who can understand a life led in contradiction? Yet, we know this does not have to be. When we accept Christ, we are enabled to live our lives in God's will, without contradiction.

The Lord searches the heart and mind - to reward a person as to how their life is led. There is a day of reckoning for all of us. But a life in Christ is safe and secure.

The answer to life's meaning and purpose is found in the teachings and life of our Lord and goes beyond human reason. As Jeremiah writes in verse 12,

"O glorious throne. exalted from the beginning, is the place of our sanctuary."

- and in verse 14, Jeremiah turns to the real source of his strength when he prays,

"Heal me O Lord, and I will be healed: save me and I will be saved, for you are the one I praise."

May we, as Jeremiah did, turn to the real source of our strength because redemption and healing are ours through Jesus Christ, his Son. It is Jesus who paid the supreme sacrificial price for our healing and salvation. It is Jesus who enables us to fulfill life and avoid Living our lives in contradiction.

Therefore, our trust is in God because therein lies our hope. It is in Jesus Christ, God's Son that is our redemption. And it is a joyful thought to realize that since redemption and healing are ours, we need never live our lives in contradiction, but in a loving relationship with God through Jesus Christ, by the indwelling presence of his Holy Spirit. Amen!

The Parable of the Loving Father

Scripture lesson: Luke 15:32 Text: Luke 15:32

Do you remember the day you left home? Granted, everyone's circumstances are different, but we can all relate to today's story because, at one time or another, except for unusual circumstances, we all leave home. I recall vividly, right after Josephine and I got married, my father, who did the marriage ceremony, said to me, "Well, son, now you're on your own." Of course, I knew I was on my own, but to hear him say it when he did, came as a surprise. But what really startled me was the sense of finality in his voice. It was like I had reached some kind of rite of passage and things would never be the same. They never were.

A few weeks after we got married, Josephine and I traveled to Springfield, Missouri where Josephine got a job as an execute secretary at the Gospel Publishing House and I got a job selling shoes, attended classes and so began the school year. Later, I also worked at the Gospel Publishing House in the printing department. We were very happy and very busy; time flew by and nearly a year and a half later we drove back home to Pennsylvania. It was good to get back, but life moves on and though our family and friend relationships were good, they were not quite the same. We were now a married couple with a child, planning our future, struggling financially, working hard and ecstatically happy; and though our relationships with our families were not quite the same, they were good. This, unfortunately, is not always the case, which brings us to today's story about The Loving Father, his Younger Son and complaining Elder Brother.

It begins with the younger son who didn't realize how good he had it until he left home. And, even worse, he was unprepared to face life and deal with hard times. There are three important parts to this story, beginning with a younger brother, who took for granted the good home where he was raised.

It reminds me of an interesting comment by Frank Tiger, editorial cartoonist, and columnist that shows some of his insight into human nature. He said, "Many people have known happiness, but didn't know it when they had it." An insightful statement. And, of course, we know that happiness is a state of mind, not something you get, even though some persons or organizations try to quantify happiness this way. Like the statement, "I want it all and I want it now," implying that, with their product, you really can have it all and have it now. Ridiculous? Yes, but unfortunately ideas like this can have a strong influence because they play on people's greed.

And some people, never satisfied, let their dissatisfactions get such a grip on them it spills over into other people's lives. Their constant complaining bewilders friends and even family, who choose to keep their distance. Of course, we know that nobody is completely satisfied all the time, and expecting some kind of utopian existence simply does not exist on this earth.

I once heard a silly story that speaks to the problem of dissatisfaction.

There was a man who became marooned on a desert island. Being alone and a Christian, he built a small church. Later, he built another church. Years passed. And finally, a rescue boat pulled up on the shore of the island. Climbing out of the boat, one of the sailors saw that the marooned man had built two churches. Puzzled, he asked, "Why did you do this?" He replied, "I didn't like going to the first one; so, I built another one and, frankly, I didn't like going to that one either, so now I just stay at home."

This silly story is of interest because the man, in spite of his attitude, was still stuck on the island, the one thing he couldn't get away from. Dissatisfaction sometimes creates its own kind of dilemma.

Well, the Prodigal Son in today's story didn't know when he had it good. Like the TV commercial, he wanted more, and he wanted it now. Not wanting to wait until his father died, he wanted all the inheritance that was legally his and he wanted it now! So,

The Younger Son Demanded His Share of the Inheritance. How was this possible?

In Jewish culture the eldest son was entitled to 2/3 of the estate.

The younger son was entitled to 1/3 of the estate.

Estates were sometimes divided while the father was still living, so the demands of the younger son, in this case, though they were selfish, were not entirely unusual. However, what he did with his inheritance is a very different story. As was expected,

The Younger Son Left Home He apparently, wanted to travel and see the world; so, he left the home place and even his native land - a young man on the move, with a careless attitude, and with no plans or sense of direction in his life. He just wanted to be free of his responsibilities at home. He may have thought that, since his older brother was still at home, he could do the work. Or perhaps, he thought that any place was better than home with its responsibilities, and his newly acquired money would set him free from the constraints and responsibilities of home life.

Whatever his thoughts were, he began to live recklessly and spend, spend, spend. But his new reality now was that he was a traveling man without a home, without a country, with no job and little common sense. He was a disaster waiting to happen and it was. His life was now the result of a series of bad decisions. Does this sound strangely familiar? It is. The prodigal's situation is not unique, even in today's world. Many people paint themselves into a corner through a lack of proper planning and the foolish use of money. Then, they wonder how life seems to have become so difficult for them. They are like the Prodigal Son in today's narrator who, unless he made some changes, had no decent future.

The Prodigal Son had rejected his heritage, made thoughtless, immature decisions, was selfish, overconfident and careless with his money; and all the time his life was bottoming out. The result?

He had wasted his entire inheritance like the old saying, "A fool and his money are soon parted." So, the Prodigal Son, (prodigal means wasteful), not only wasted his money, but he degraded the cultural and spiritual aspects of his life. Then,

Hard times came his way - How did this happen? Of course, we know the answer. The Prodigal had made a whole series of bad decisions that left his life in a downward spiral. And when confronted with hard times, he reached rock bottom! Talk about having to learn the hard way! This was it! Life had given him a large dose of reality and through his own bad choices, he landed in a pig pen eating corn husks. Being a Jew, this was the ultimate disgrace, living in a pig pen with animals that Jewish law forbade them to use for food. Now what would he do?

With nowhere to go and no apparent hope in his present condition, the Prodigal was driven to come to his senses, and he began to reflect on his past. He thought about the good life he had left behind, the good food, a clean bed to sleep in, a job, the security of home and the love of family. He faced the stark realization that even the families' workers had it better than him. Just what was he thinking, to leave home the way he did. He known happiness but didn't realize it when he had it. Taking it all for granted, he was now, sitting in a pig pen. The memories of what he had left loomed in front of him. What had he done to himself? Now, what? There was only one thing to do, go home, hoping he could find a place to begin again, perhaps with the status of a servant. So, nervous and insecure, he headed for home. And when he arrived, he found the one thing that hadn't changed during his absence, his father's love. As he was returning home, his father, seeing him in the distance, actually ran to him. He was not rejected as he had feared. He was greeted by a loving father who didn't even reprimand him. Instead, he prepared a feast to celebrate his return.

But another problem emerges in the story:

The Elder Brother Was Not Happy with His Father Celebrating His Brother's

Return Why? Why would he be unhappy about this, otherwise happy celebration? What was his problem? It was his personal situation while his brother was gone. He was at home working, maybe also doing his younger brother's work, while his brother, a prodigal, was out having his fling. The elder brother complained that the celebration for his younger brother wasn't fair. Why was there a celebration, anyway? Shouldn't his younger brother's indiscretions be taken into account? Shouldn't he be punished, or even rejected, for what he did? Surely, he should. But his father didn't think of punishment or rejection. He thought of celebration! After all, his son had repented. He came back home, and he humbly offered to work as one his father's hired hands. The father saw that his son repented and was trying to do what was right. So, he had a feast prepared and rejoiced that his son, once lost, was now found! Love wins out in the end!

There are many social dynamics woven into this narrative. And among the intricate threads we see in the tapestry, we might ask, "Is there one great lives on Jesus is teaching in this remarkable parable?" And if there is? What is it? Is it about the son's return? Not entirely. Is it about the unhappy elder brother? That too, is only a partial answer.

And the entire household was witness to what was happening. They saw the father worrying about his younger son, the son's return, the joy, the celebration! So, is it about the household? Not really. They are an important silent part of the story, but only a partial answer. So, what is the great lives on Jesus is teaching? It is about forgiveness.

It is about forgiveness that has no bounds with God! It is about love that is so wonderfully timeless, it demonstrates that forgiveness truly has no bounds with God.

Is there rejoicing in heaven for even one soul that is saved? Yes, there is! Is there limitless forgiveness? Yes, there is! Is there boundless love? Yes, praise God there is!

The parable doesn't spell it out literally, other scriptures do. But the implication is very strong. When you and I fail, we should never forget this great, comforting truth.

Forgiveness has no bounds with God. But:

It appears that the elder brother wasn't forging. He was jealous and felt he was treated unfairly when, in fact, just like his younger brother, he had also taken his own heritage for granted. His father pointed out that what was provided for his younger brother was always available for him as part of the household, but he did not afford himself of it. All he had to do was ask. But he didn't. Instead of celebrating the wonderful news that his brother had returned and was restored, he focused on himself and complained of unfair treatment.

He recounted his own life and felt it went unrewarded. Like his younger brother, he had happiness, but didn't know it when he had it. What an inaccurate, selfish perception he had of his life. He was loved and Living in his father's house with all the benefits of food, clothing, and shelter. But most importantly,

The elder brother failed to recognize the importance of his younger brother, the Prodigal, being saved from a terrible, lost and hopeless condition and then being restored. He thought only of himself. So, his father reminded him of the benefits that were already his as he was part of the household. He only had to ask.

There are many lives on for us in this remarkable story. First, it is important to realize and fully recognize the benefits of our own salvation and our blessed relationship as part of the household of faith. We are enlightened and enabled to live the most superior life on the face of the earth.

Second, it is good to remind ourselves that our heavenly Father is forging, loving and is sharing his eternal kingdom with us. As part of the household of faith, we are truly part of God's Kingdom.

Third, every time a soul is saved, there is rejoicing in heaven. Every soul matters. When the lost son returned, there was feasting, music and dancing. The father felt impelled to do it. He said,

"We had to celebrate and be glad because this brother of yours (reminding him that, after all he was his brother) was dead and is now ale again: he was lost and is found."

And so, it is with every person who is saved. With every single person who is brought into the household of faith there is rejoicing in heaven.

Among the many practical and spiritual lessons, we may take away from this story, one stands out. God's love has no bounds. And may we never take our inclusion into the household of faith for granted. May we never allow anything to turn us away from our high calling in Jesus Christ.

May we continually reflect on God's grace and the spiritual benefits gen to us because we are saved; the blessings of being a Christian, the privilege of praying directly to God, the precious experience of God's Holy Spirit within us to guide and comfort us, and to experience that deep settled peace and unsurpassable joy within our souls.

So, let us celebrate our salvation, that wellspring of Living water ever flowing within us and be eternally grateful for our Christian heritage, belonging to the household of faith, and for eternal grace all because of our Loving Heavenly Father.

Let Christ Enter and Really Le

Scripture lesson: Acts 2:14a, 36-4 Text: Acts 2:17-18

After the resurrection Luke records in Acts, "He appeared to them over a period of forty days and spoke about the Kingdom of God. On one occasion, while he was eating with them, he gave them this command:

'Do not leave Jerusalem, but wait for the gift my Father promised, which you have heard me speak about. For John baptized with water, but in a few days, you will be baptized with the Holy Spirit.'

After this Jesus ascended to heaven and the disciples returned to Jerusalem. Several days passed and the Day of Pentecost (fiftieth day) came. The disciples were in the Upper Room.

"Suddenly a sound like the blowing of a violent wind came from heaven and filled the whole house where they were sitting. They saw what seemed to be tongues of fire that separated and came to rest on each of them. All of them were filled with the Holy Spirit and they began to speak in other tongues as the Spirit enabled them."

Since it was the day of the Jewish festal of Shavuoth (their Feast of Weeks), now known by Christians as the Day of Pentecost (Pentecost meaning 50 days), there were God-fearing Jews from all the nations staying in Jerusalem. When these people heard this sound, a bewildered crowd gathered because they heard the Galileans speak in the native tongues of these other nations. There were Parthians, Medes, Elamites, residents of Mesopotamia, Judea, Cappadocia, Pontus, Asia, Phrygia, Pamphylia, Egypt and parts of Libya near Cyrene, visitors from Rome, Cretans and Arabs. This was a miracle event, to say the least. Still, some of them, not understanding what was happening, made fun saying they had too much wine.

Then, Peter stood up with the eleven, raised his voice and explained to the crowd:

"These men are not drunk as you suppose. It's only nine in the morning. No, this is what was spoken by the prophet Joel:

'In the last days, God days, I will pour out my Spirit on all people. Your sons and daughters will prophesy, your young men will see visions, your old men will dream dreams. Even on my servants, both men and women, I will pour out my Spirit in those days, and they will prophesy.

"Then, Peter, after going another prophetical statement regarding wonders in the heaven above and signs on the earth beneath, predicting "the great and glorious day of the Lord," gives them hope out of apparent chaos, when he, by Divine inspiration, declares, "And everyone who calls on the name of the Lord will be saved."

Then, later in his sermon, and I can almost hear him shout,

"Therefore, let all Israel be assured of this: God has made this Jesus, whom you crucified, both Lord and Christ."

One thing about Peter, he could tell it straight. He knew straight talk and he got right to the point. He told the people what they needed to hear. How did they respond?

"When the people heard this, they were cut to the heart and said to Peter and the other apostles, 'Brothers, what shall we do?" Peter replied, 'Repent and be baptized, every one of you, in the name of Jesus Christ so that your sins may be forgiven. And you will receive the gift of the Holy Spirit. The promise is for you and your children and for all who are far off - for all whom the Lord our God will call."

After this, about three thousand souls came to Christ. They heard the message, believed and were saved. The path for people of The Way is now clear and when Peter preached on the Day of Pentecost, he taught the multitudes, quoting the Prophet Joel, revealing that they were now part of a new era - a new dispensation. So, he taught them the first step:

Repent - Repentance requires an attitude - a frame of mind that needs to admit our need of a Savior and determines to change by God's help, God's Holy Spirit working within us. It is the atoning power of Christ that makes change truly possible. What change?

A change of mind and heart - which leads to a new world view.

A change of our life's actions - which leads to perceiving ourselves differently.

A changed life from the inside out - We learn to view our own lives in the light of eternity. A typical question sometimes asked of young people looking toward their future, "How do you see yourself fe years from now, ten years from now." A difficult question for anyone to answer because it will involve such things as education, marriage, having and raising a family, the usual financial responsibilities like renting or purchasing a home, a car, vacation time. All these matters, because we are saved, take on different meanings and different values. The next step after accepting Christ is that we should:

Be Baptized - Why? Why should we be baptized? Don't the scriptures say, "Believe on the Lord Jesus Christ and you will be saved?" So, we may ask. What, then, is the importance of Baptism? What is baptism?

Baptism is an outward testimony of an inward change, a mysterious means of grace as we follow the directive in the scriptures; it is an outward, public testimony of declaring our death to sin and our rising to newness of life in Christ Jesus.

And it is important to recognize that baptism is not just the outward act itself, the outward act that we see. What is most important is what the Holy spirit does within us through the rite of baptism, what we don't see, but what we experience inside. It is God acting within us. (And, by the way, which is why being baptized twice is not necessary and is, in fact, failing to recognize that it is God's action within us, not the outward act itself). And it is, also, very important to realize that we are baptized into the body of believers - the body of Christ. Where does this lead us? It leads to:

A change of community - God's Church now becomes our special community, within the community at large, of loving, caring believers and that leads us to, A change in our values - As sincere followers of Christ, we want to grow spiritually, to be positively influenced by our newfound faith. And we find that this loving, scripture-based community will have a positive influence on us that will lead us to, A change of direction in our lives - because a spiritually maturing life will find how fulfillment, meaning and true happiness in serving Jesus, all work together. This is because God is working within us affecting change within us daily. This is Living life beautifully. We may not always be aware of it, but as we seek to live as Jesus Christ would have us to le, change is there and continuing. This is how we grow in Christ, into life that is beautiful, and this is why we are different, so different from the world with its jealousy, hatred and greed. How does this happen in our lives?

God's Grace in all the fullness of God's Holy Spirit!

A change within us leads to - spiritual experiences that are very real to us and very personal and always right as long as they are scriptural.

A change is evidenced externally as well as within - It is change that shows on the outside as well as on the inside, the power to live our lives on a spiritual level that actually can be seen and observed by others. In fact, your spirituality will give others pause as to how they are Living their own lives.

They may even become critical of you, trying to drag you down to their level, because your life, without you saying anything, may point out what they should be doing and where they should be on their journey spiritually.

This explains one reason why the apostle Paul tells us to rejoice in our sufferings for Christ because our sufferings for Christ are actually a stamp of approval.

And this change in us, as we grow spiritually, can lead to:

Change that positively influences others - to seek Christ's power to affect positive change in their lives. This is one of the most powerful Christian testimonies - for others to witness for themselves Jesus Christ manifested in us, seeing us fulfilling life and seeing us, in spite of life's difficulties, enjoying the journey. When we let Christ enter into our lives, and become the very fabric of our lives, then, we can really le!

On the day of Pentecost, in the power of the Holy Spirit, the apostle Peter rose to the occasion and preached the gospel to the multitudes. What an amazing change had come over him! Boldly, he preached the good news as he related their present experience, the outpouring of the Holy Spirit, with what was prophesied by the prophet Joel, in the Old Testament. (Remember, the New Testament wasn't written yet.)

Peter not only preached a full and complete salvation gospel, but one that looked forward to changes within the new Christians that would alter the course of their lives and ultimately alter the course of history. What a sermon! It was more than the words. The apostle Peter was now preaching as a Spirit-filled proclaimer, full of energy and excitement. It was obvious to everyone. He had experienced Christ and was endued with the power of the Holy Spirit! The crowd saw and experienced the new Apostle Peter. One who preached the whole gospel for the whole person and for the whole world. For Peter, indeed, the world was his parish!

His message began with the need for repentance, followed by the experience and public testimony of baptism. The air was ale with spiritual energy.

It was the gospel foretold by the prophets of old, the gospel of a New Age, not some trendy new age idea, the real new age, the Age of Grace, when God's Holy Spirit entered into a person crowning that person's life as a temple. (Paul taught this very truth to the Christians, "Your body is the temple of the Holy Spirit." And this presence remarkably changes our lives, giving us the power to really live with meaningful purpose and genuine testimony really live with inner joy and hope - really live because we live our lives as a Living sacrifice unto God!

Who Really Heard the Gospel

Scripture lesson: Acts 14:8-18 Text: Acts 14:15

Do you find the tall stories and claims by son1e people and some advertising agencies believable? Granted, it is sometimes difficult to separate truth from fiction. But often it just requires common sense. For example, I once heard a fellow say that he saw a ground hog so large it was the size of a bear. A baby bear, maybe. A full-grown bear, not hardly.

And what about the wild stories of Big Foot, the Loch Ness Monster, ghosts in the woods and in so-called haunted houses? When Josephine and I led in Louisiana, we visited many of the old plantation homes and heard their interesting stories; some of them included ghosts that supposedly appeared at night and made creaking sounds in the house; a lot of fun to hear and entertaining but, of course, ridiculous nonsense.

Here is another example. When I was in the Boy Scouts in Moosic, Pennsylvania, at a springtime Camporee, a story was circulated among the boys about a spooky, eerie glow in the woods at night. Imaginations went a bit wild! The boys even claimed that they saw the lights move. This went on for a few days until an older scout leader took us to the spot where the glow occurred. What a surprise! There was our answer on the tree trunks. The mysterious glow, was the bioluminescence of a certain kind of fungi commonly called "Fox Fire." We boys wanted to know the truth and there it was in front of us, the glow of fungi on the tree trunks. And the perceived movement was likely caused by the movement of the boy's own eyes while they stared at the fungi, a common illusion.

Concerning fact, during that summer of 1949, a medicine show came to the town of Moosic, Pennsylvania. They set up their portable stage in a field on the other side of the street where our church was located. A crowd in the evening and they gave short, noisy and rowdy, but harmless, plays. During a break, the barker came out to sell his amazing medical products. What a laugh! He claimed special cleansing properties of the amazing bar of soap he held in his hand. After a short sales pitch, he needed a volunteer, the dirtiest little boy he could find. He called him to the stage, and with the motions of a master magician, washed the boy's face and hands as clean as a whistle. The crowd applauded. They were amazed. He sold a lot of soap to the folks in that coal mining town, especially since the minors came home every evening covered with black soot!

Hold on. There is more! Following the bar soap act, the barker introduced what he described as a mysterious burn treatment. He said it was a Nate

American medicine called Black Indian Salve. And all the time, while he pitched his sales talk, he was heating a metal fireplace stoker with a blow torch. While watching the metal stoker turn bright red, the crowd, mesmerized, stood silent, waiting in anxious anticipation. What was going to happen? After an invitation to participate, a volunteer came forward.

Dramatically, the "Master of Ceremonies" placed a large glob of the salve on the volunteer's hand. Then, lightly and carefully stroking the red-hot poker over the salve, caused the black grease to sizzle, smoke rose, the crowd gasped, and the man ran up and down the aisle, selling his amazing cans of Black Indian Salve. What a clever trick!

Even as a boy I could see that it was a trick. However, the crowd believed his spin and they bought many cans of "Black Indian Salve" that evening.

Sometimes people will believe the strangest things. Think of what is happening today. We hear outright lies and brainwashing techniques that are influencing people in many parts of the world. And alas, it is happening in our own beloved United States of America. I find it bizarre that some people, actually find it easier to believe in flying saucers than to believe in God. Don't they realize that for a spacecraft to travel into deep space, it would have to travel faster than the speed of light, which is 186,000 miles a second, and planets are many light years away? And they should remember that God created all this. Truly, their conception of God is too small.

In ancient times there was a mythical story told in the city of Lystra, that one time Zeus and Hermas (two of their gods) came to earth in disguise. They were turned away from a thousand homes, gen no hospitality except for two old peasants Philemon and his wife Baucis. Angered, the gods, Zeus and Hermas, wiped out the whole population except for Philemon and Baucis, who they made guardians of their temple. When they died, they became trees. Yes, you heard it right. The mythical story that the people of Lystra believed, says they became trees.

You respond, what a fanciful mythical tale. Yes, it is, but it is important that we keep in mind that these people who believed this wild mythical story were the same people to whom the apostle Paul and Barnabas would preach. How could they possibly handle this preaching situation? Would the people be so blind to the truth that all the apostle's efforts would be in vain?

It is obvious that Paul and Barnabas, evangelist/missionaries, definitely had their work cut out for them. The initial plan was that Paul was the designated one to preach the gospel. How would he do this? Would he turn the gospel message into an argument with the philosophers and sophists? Certainly not! That would lower the great message of the gospel to the level of a human argument. Paul already had made that mistake when he visited the Acropolis and his listeners, the sophists, said that they would talk about it another time. Paul learned his lives on, to not turn the gospel into an argument. He would not repeat his mistake. So,

Paul preached the Gospel and nothing: but the Gospel and there was at least one n1an in the crowd who really heard the message, the message of hope, while his own situation seemed hopeless.

Though he was lame since birth, as he listened his faith increased.

Though he had never walked in his life, he heard a message of hope for him.

Though many in the crowd did not really listen, he listened. He really heard the message that Jesus Christ was his Savior, and Savior of the world, and in spite of all the obstacles in his life, in spite of his previous feeling of hopelessness, at last here was good news! Here was hope, not just in general terms, hope for him. Hope in Jesus. Here was healing for him through the power of Christ. So, as:

Paul Preached the Gospel. This one person, lame in body, but certainly not lame in spirit, believed!

There were, as is typical in crowds, some who didn't believe - No matter. The lame man, who, for all appearances had no hope, believed! He really believed it!

There were some who allowed their prejudices to interfere The lame man pushed beyond this and believed.

While others around him were hostile to the gospel, the lame man pushed beyond the hostility and believed.

Paul Preached the Gospel He didn't get off track, letting his message become mired down in the politics of the time. He didn't try to persuade through philosophical argument. He didn't make a case by telling them how wrong their culture was and how wrong they were. No! Paul stayed on the message. He preached the gospel. And at least one man, the man who was lame, really heard the message. Not only did he listen, but he also allowed the message to enter his life space and become a part of him. He went beyond merely listening to really hearing, to really believing, and receiving the gospel in all its truth.

While most of the crowd acted in fear - the lame man acted in faith.

While most of the crowd missed the message of the risen Christ and saw only the miracle, the lame man saw and embraced the truth. The Spirit of Christ entered into him, and his spirit was healed as well as his body. And so, the miracle.

While others, in their blindness, missed the message and thought Paul and Barnabas were gods, the lame man met the true and Living God and was healed.

As is typical today, so many in the crowd came to see Paul and Barnabas merely out of curiosity. As is typical, today, some folks even attend church as mere observers. We, as Christians, are not like this, but we still must guard against ever letting the values of the world weaken our faith.

May we fix our eyes on Jesus, "the author and finisher of our faith," and may we always be the persons who really hear the message. May our faith become so stimulated by the glorious truth we hear that we truly believe that God through Jesus Christ, can and will meet our every need, according to his will!

Not only did the lame man really listen, but he also really believed and, acting on his faith, received what God had for him. He was healed in spirit and body!

So, too, may we listen, really hear, and really believe that through the work of the Holy Spirit, we will receive what God desires for us. God is ever faithful!

The Prophets of Old Revealed Jesus

Scripture lesson: I Peter 1:3-15 Text: I Peter 1:12

The coming of Jesus to the earth was foretold many times in the Old Testament. For example, in Genesis 49:8-10,

"The scepter will not depart from Judah, nor the ruler's staff from between his feet, until he comes to whom it belongs." In Micah 5:2,

"But you Bethlehem Ephrathah, though you are small among the clans of Judah, out of you will come for me one who will be ruler over Israel." In Isaiah 9:6,

"For unto us a child is born, unto us a son is gen, and the government will be on his shoulders. He will be called Wonderful Counsellor, Mighty God, Everlasting Father, Prince of Peace." In Psalm 72:10-,

"The kings of Tarshish and of distant shores will bring tribute to him; the kings of Sheba and Seba will present him gifts." In Psalm 8: 22-23,

"The stone that the builders rejected has become the capstone; the Lord had done this, and it is marvelous in our eyes." In Zechariah 9:9,

"See your king comes to you, righteous and having salvation, gentle and riding on a donkey, on a colt, the foal of a donkey." Then, in Jeremiah 31:31-34,

I will make a new covenant with the house of Israel and with the house of Judah. It will not be like the covenant made with their forefathers. I will write my law in their minds and write it on their hearts... "

These are just a few of the prophetic threads connecting the Old Testament, Old Covenant with the New Testament, the New Covenant. These threads all lead us to Jesus, who is the fulfillment of these prophesies and many others.

In today's scripture we are brought up to date, so to speak, in that Jesus beginning his ministry, is calling his disciples. The narrate begins with Jesus calling Simon Peter and Andrew. This interesting account gives us some insight into understanding the culture better and who the apostle Peter was.

We read in Matthew in chapter 4: 19-21:

As Jesus was walking beside the Sea of Galilee, he saw two brothers, Simon called Peter and his brother Andrew. They were casting a net into lake, for they were fishermen. 'Come, follow me,' Jesus said, 'and I will make you fishers of men.' At once they left their nets and followed him.

Going on from there, he saw two other brothers, James, son, of Zebedee and his brother John. They were in a boat with their father Zebedee, preparing their nets. Jesus called them, and immediately they left the boat and their father and followed him."

Remember, as we have said before, Jesus was a rabbi, and it was a great honor to be selected to be taught by a rabbi. It was every Jewish boy's dream to have such an honor. And here were working men who likely had gen up the dream for years. No matter. When Jesus saw the two brothers, Simon and Andrew, working as fishermen, casting their net into the lake, he called to them "Come, follow me and I will make you fishers of men."

Yes, it was an honor to be so called by a rabbi, but how strange is this calling! Fishers of men? What was he talking about? We can only imagine that they may have said something like, "Why has this rabbi selected us? We fish for fish. What does it mean to be a fisher of men? And why has he called us?" They had to be puzzled and they certainly knew what it was like to catch fish, but the idea of fishers of men? What does it mean? This was quite foreign to these men who led a very practical life in a world almost devoid of abstractions.

However, because it was such an honor to be so specially selected to be taught by a rabbi, they immediately left their nets and began walking with Jesus along the shore. As they walked, Jesus saw two other brothers, James and John, also working, but in a boat with their father, sewing up the tears in their nets, that occurred from fishing the day before and getting the nets ready for the following day's work. Jesus also called to them and them, too, immediately followed him, walking with him along the shore.

As we think about this situation. We might ask; just what was it like to be a fisherman, especially on the Sea of Galilee? To be sure it was a strenuous life requiring a strong physique to be able to deal with uncertain weather conditions, like storms. And, along with this, there was the need to constantly maintain their boats and equipment. And it didn't just involve catching fish. The fish had to be sold; so, this was also a sales operation requiring the fishermen to deal with people from many different cultural and ethnic backgrounds. These fishermen would likely have to be fairly fluent in at least Greek, Hebrew and Aramaic because merchants came from many different geographic areas. So, the fishermen had to be more than just basically proficient in business math. They would have to know the market value of each type of the more than 35 different kinds of fish caught there. Not a simple task, but historical records reveal that it was profitable. How do we know this?

The income of a successful fisherman, who owned the boat and the net, would be 40% and the rest would go to the crew. The researcher Murphy-0-Conner tells us that Simon Peter and Andrew's fishing operation worked in partnership with James and John, the sons of Zebedee, who had employees. That these were men of substance is confirmed, in part, by the quality and size of the house at Capernaum, known as Peter's house, which is larger than most of the other houses that have been excavated in Capernaum. The guides for the Holy Land will take you to see the house, which is part of the tour.

So, when Jesus said, "Follow me and I will make you fishers of men," he knew exactly what he was doing. He chose the right persons for the great task that would lay before them, and as hard-working men, with many different abilities, Jesus knew they could become world changers, and they have!

Could they do this right away? No. This would be possible much later after three years of education with Jesus, the master teacher. Now, after Jesus' ascension, we hear Peter, who now has become a strong apostolic leader, addressing a hurting, persecuted, and scattered Church. He speaks encouraging words. He tells them," You are "God's elect." Oh, how they needed to hear that!

And Peter reminds them that although they chose to follow Jesus, he first chose them!

They were chosen through the sanctifying (purifying), work of the Holy Spirit for obedience to Jesus Christ and the sprinkling of his blood. Then, Peter continues:

Jesus Christ Has Gen You Knew Birth Why does he remind them of this?

Because during this time of their difficulty, they may not feel born again, and even worse, they are scattered distances through persecution and are hurting so much they need encouragement. His words are like healing balm to them.

Knowing this, the apostle Peter reminds them of the meaning of their new birth, saying: It is a Living hope - There was a time you had no hope. It is through the resurrection of their Lord - who died and rose to save you.

It is beyond this present life, an inheritance that is incorruptible It is kept in heaven for us, we who are redeemed of the Lord, shielded (protected) by God's power! - until the day when Christ returns. Peter gives no promise of a life without suffering. He is very straight and clear about this:

Trials May Come: Grief May Cause Us to Suffer - but Peter reminds them, and us, that being a persecuted Church is not without purpose.

Trials are to test our faith to prove the genuineness of our faith. Do we really believe. Trials are to refine our faith, to refine our faith like the way gold is purified.

In an ancient time, perhaps around a campfire enclosed with stones, someone discovered that heat applied to certain rocks containing powders, we now know as oxides, would change the powders into a hard substance that could be worked and shaped. It was amazing! It was like magic to them. Heat changed the powder, iron oxide, into iron and thus the iron age was born. The heat drove out the oxygen leaving a pure hard metal, iron.

Metal refinement is an amazing process. When I worked at the Gospel Publishing House in Springfield Missouri, as a young man working my way through school, one of my jobs was to work the lead furnace. Lead was used to make pipe shaped molds, about the size of baseball bats, called pigs, which were put into linotype machines. The machine would re-melt the lead and the typist would type words on the top edge of domino shaped slugs, which were then arranged into columns, and finally made into pages for printing.

In order to do this, heat was applied to the reusable scrap lead and new pigs were made by pouring the lead into long, narrow molds. An interesting process. The heat melted the lead and that caused the dry ink and other impurities, to rise to the top to be skimmed off, leaving pure lead that was then poured into the molds to go back to the linotype operator.

This is similar to the way gold is refined. Heat causes the impurities to rise to be skimmed off leaving the pure gold. The apostle Peter uses this excellent example as to how our faith is refined. (How interesting. Peter, the fisherman, knew about metal refinement.) Then Peter proceeds to teach that the purpose of suffering for Christ is:

To bring praise and glory to the God of our salvation Today, as we live out our lives, we call our faith journey, we have not seen Jesus, yet we love him and believe in him. Partly because, in a very real spiritual sense, we experience his presence. This is the marvelous relationship we have with the Lord; and Peter, relating his own experience, as a fellow Christian, exclaims:

We Are Filled with Inexpressible Joy! - How does he are at this conclusion, in spite of all the persecution he has experienced? It is spiritual insight when he says,

"For you are receiving the goal of your faith." - This is making Christians aware of spiritual process working in them, the work of the Holy Spirit. All of this -

"For the salvation of your souls." - Peter reminds them of the most important thing, their salvation, not to be neglected or forgotten. Then, he reminds them of the words of the prophets saying,

The prophets spoke of this salvation and the grace that was to come to us. Down through the ages, sometimes separated by hundreds of years, the prophets spoke of the coming of the Messiah. And he has come; praise be to his name!

This is what is meant when we experience the joy of our salvation and feel that sense of eternity! Although, this inexpressible joy is beyond mere words, at least in part, worshipful music can help to lead us in worship. The joy of our salvation may also explain the spiritual feelings that well up inside us as we experience the marvels of God's presence and his truth working in our lives!

And it is true that, as we grow spiritually, we are changed toward the likeness of Jesus Christ. Jesus has given us new birth, a Living hope and an inexpressible joy in spite of all our sufferings and grief. What is this inexpressible joy? I repeat. It is the joy of our salvation and the hope of eternal life within us. God's Holy Spirit confirms this within the deepest resources of our being; an eternal well-spring of Living water that guarantees we will never again experience that unquenchable thirst Jesus spoke of, that longing for spiritual reality seemingly out of our reach, which is the problem for so many. What is the problem?

It is all about faith. Faith on a level that is not merely a decision on our part to believe. It is faith on a level that is a deep inward response to that inner voice that, like a magnet, draws us into relationship with Jesus Christ and his transforming power.

This is how we are transformed. It is rebirth, the work of Christ within us.

Certainly, it is true; our bodies are getting older, but because of Christ within us, our spirits are forever young, that wellspring of Living water!

Praise be to our Lord and Savior Jesus Christ! We have experienced new birth, a Living hope! Trials may come our way to test us as Christians; but we now view them as a source of refining our lives like the refinement process that turns what is impure into pure gold. So! We are filled with inexpressible joy, this Living hope that is the joy of our salvation!

John's Great Vision of Heaven

Scripture lesson: Revelation 21-1-5,10-18,21-23, 27.

22:1-7,17 Text: Rev. 21:27

Several years ago, in a clever commercial, a little boy, bleary eyed, waking up from his visit to the dentist, asked, "Is this the real world?" We laughed. It was cute and funny, but this situation had interesting implications. Why? Because it is a common experience, at the moment of waking, for a person to experience the shift from a dream state to the state of consciousness, the conscious, real world. In fact, this common experience has so intrigued scientists and artists that much has been written about it; and there are works of art attempting to depict it. The challenge for the scientist? Why does it occur and how does it happen? The challenge for the artist is to communicate the experience through art. And all this relates to what psychologists call the "stream of consciousness," a kind of dream state.

This idea has also interested composers. For example, the great French composer, Claude Debussy, wrote an orchestral composition called, "Prelude to the Afternoon of a Fawn." He creates a musical portrait describing a fawn just waking up and not knowing whether it is still dreaming or whether it is awake, experiencing what is real.

In another of Debussy's masterpieces, "Le Mer" (The Sea), you can hear waves lapping on the seashore, sea birds calling to each other, the thunder of a storm; and feel the intensity of the sun's brilliant light reflecting on the waters at high noon. live Mer is a wonderful musical experience, but, of course, none of it is real. Obviously, live Mer is an artistic expression of reality, not reality itself, which, in this case, is the sea. And, it almost goes without saying, that paintings and sculptures are also expressions of reality.

However, the vision of Saint John, the Divine was not a mere artistic expression, it was real; an experience into a future reality, a new dimension if you please. And John was not required to understand it; all he was required to do was to experience it and write it down. And he did, for present and future generations.

John saw amazing things. He saw events happening right before his eyes, yet they were of things still to come; John witnessed the power of God in greater measure than anyone had experienced before him. How can we dare to say this? John saw, flashed before his eyes, the destiny of the human race! He witnessed wonderful hope for Christians because their robes were made white by the cleansing blood of the Lamb, the final sacrifice for sin!

What did all of this mean? It is impossible to understand it all; but here are a few obvious clues to pique our curiosity. The robes, symbolic of our eternal soul, cleansed by the blood of the Lamb, signify spiritual purity and eternal salvation.

So, the narrate begins with John, the missionary, spreading the good news. But Domitian, the emperor, didn't think it was good news. In fact, he so strongly disapproved of John's efforts that he banished him to a prison colony in the Aegean Sea, on the isle called Patmos. Here, on this tiny island, where John is sent as a criminal of the Roman empire, is where the amazing account begins.

Of all the unlikely places, we would think that God, gives someone a vision of such magnitude, would choose a temple, or a church, or a beautiful garden; but no, God's choice was the penal colony on Patmos where John's situation seemed hopeless. Once again, God has turned the impossible into the possible, giving John an eternity-reaching, vision- experience in the midst of a seemingly hopeless, situation.

To my thinking, this vision of God's power and glory gen to Saint John the Dine, is similar to Christ revealing himself, in all his glory, to Peter, James and John, on the Mount of Transfiguration.

On the Mount of Transfiguration, Moses appears, representing the law; Elijah appears, representing the prophets; and Jesus is transfigured before them, revealing himself, glorified and as Savior.

In Revelation, John's vision also includes the elements of the law, the Prophets and Jesus our Savior, yet is more informant because it connects the past with the present and links the present with the future.

Though this Revelation to John is enigmatic, (puzzling), prophetic, startling, and gives warning; yet it is full of promise. It reveals God's limitless power over all creation. It is totally cosmic in scope and impossible to fully understand.

As a first read, I recommend that you read it entirely at one sitting, which is what I did for my first reading. Reading it this way will impact you with a profound sense of God's power. Its revealing scenes, say to us, "Be assured God is in control." "There is hope." For example,

Chapter 7 says: "Then one of the elders asked me, 'These in white robes - who are they, and where did they come from?' I answered, 'Sir, you know.' And he said, 'These are they who have come out of the 2reat tribulation: they have washed their robes and made them white in the blood of the Lamb.'

Here, God is definitely-in-control! And it is good to remember that the Revelation gen to John, is both personal and universal, and was copied to be shared. We can conclude this because John experienced the unlimited, timeless, loving, power of God, manifested in the mystery of the Godhead, the Holy Trinity.

So, under Divine command, John writes his experience, as far as humanly possible, to communicate his vision to the world, this amazing, cosmic book, Revelation.

Now, it is true, over the centuries, many students and scholars have tried various lines of reasoning to unravel Revelation's mysteries. Some have even tried to relate symbolic language to politics. Some scholars, thinking that the Revelation was written in code, believe that it must contain symbolic meanings. This idea spawned more than one code theory; some political, others merely speculate and still others, just mysterious. However, none of the code approaches is convincing beyond a reasonable doubt. Perhaps these investigators just can't bring themselves to believe that John's vision is authentic.

And some scholars have even tried to explain John's experience psychologically, saying that being isolated and lonely, he hallucinated the whole thing. The problem with this analysis is that John's vision describes events never heard of or seen before, is of amazing continuity and is full of inspiring promise for the redeemed. Hallucinations, by comparison, are shorter, illogically fragmented, and almost always negative. Conversely, John's vision is full of hope and eternal joy.

Other critics have tried to relate John's vision to the politics of the time. This approach only spawned more speculation and theories, each one creating its own set of problems.

So, we conclude. John's vision is authentic. However, now he has the challenging task of writing down his vision which describes a future reality completely different from the reality of a material world, but a reality full of wonderful promises for we who are the redeemed of the Lord. Revelation gives us hope, hope beyond compare. Eternal life with God.

Also, through the enlightenment of Revelation, we come to realize with greater insight, that God truly is in charge of this world and all creation. So, we can look forward to the fact that, within God's timetable, everything will be made new. Yes!

God Will Make Everything new! - There will be: A new heaven and a new earth, one that is parallel with our eternal existence. The new heavens and the new earth, like us, will be eternal, existing in a new dimension.

Eternal life and eternal joy will be ours. How can this be? Through Christ, we will be clothed with newly created, eternal, spiritual bodies. The old physical order will pass away and will make way for:

The new order, including our newly transformed existence, will be beyond a material existence. And, while it is natural for us to desire a long and useful life, we look toward heaven when our work on earth is done. After all, as the redeemed of the Lord, we are not citizens of this world. We, are citizens of heaven and as Saint John tells us in Revelation:

Heaven is a Beautiful Place! - He tries to describe it, but it is really beyond any earthly description. Why? Because heavenly things are eternal; they are not bound by time and space. This is the new reality, as John writes in Revelation 10:6, "When time shall be no more."

You may ask. Wasn't there always time? Well, some people think that time began at the instant of the "Big Bang," when, the theory declares, everything came into existence. Again, you ask, "Then, how can we describe such an existence?" Well, think of it this way. When time is no more, everything is always in the present, as it is with God. How can this be?

An interesting quote concerning this is from Exodus 3:13-15. Moses is directed by God to inform the Israelites that he is led of God to approach Pharaoh telling him to free the people from their existence as slaves.

"Moses said to God, 'suppose I go to the Israelites and say to them, 'The God of your fathers has sent me to you,' and they ask me, 'What is his name?' Then what shall I tell them?" God said to Moses, "I am who I am. This is what you are to say to the Israelites, "I AM has sent me to you."

Here is scriptural proof of the eternal, timelessness of God, who describes himself to Moses as the "I AM." And since he is the One who created time and is not restricted by time, He is therefore, timeless. This means God is always in the present.

This timelessness describes eternity, which molds the past, present, and future into the forever present. For us, as Christians, this means our being forever in the presence of God! This is heaven! And John tells us that Heaven is beautiful, eternal, and too wonderful for us to fully understand. But we do know some things as described for us by John:

Heaven radiates the glory of God Of course, heaven cannot be adequately described by a mere mortal, but Saint John, obeying the angel's command, manages to describe heaven beautifully. Like an artistic, impressionistic painting, John compares the brightness and reflection of color to the color and radiance of earthly metals and rare, exquisite jewels as they reflect brilliant light. It is like everything is aglow, bathed in the lovely, Divine light of God.

This is heaven!

Heaven is perfect It is pure. And its purity is incomprehensible to us because nothing in the material world is eternal, and nothing in the moral or ethical spheres is totally perfect or totally pure. Heaven, though, is all of these. Heaven is the manifestation of Divine perfection! Praise be to God:

Heaven is for us Jesus said he was going to prepare a place for us and at his ascension, the angel revealed that he was going to return to earth in like manner as he left. We know that while on earth, Jesus taught of heavenly things and about the kingdom of heaven through parables to help everyone learn what heaven is like.

Jesus said, "Be not afraid." Why? Because hell was not created for the human - race. Hell was created for Satan and his angels. Be assured. God wants no human to go there; that is why he sent his Son to us. Anyone who winds up there, sent themselves there against the will of God. Yes, against the will of God!

Heaven is for us, and the Bible tells us that everything will be created new, and we will all be changed, "at the last trump in the twinkling of an eye."

We, As Christians, Will live There - In Heaven - In the Perfect Presence of God - Forever!!!

Heaven contains the tree of life. This speaks of eternal life in God's presence.

God's throne is within the city This speaks of perfect love and perfect order.

God's people will reign with Christ forever and ever the final demonstration and declaration of Divine victory over evil, of Christ's triumph over Satan and all satanic forces. And it is the culmination of all the promises gen to us by Jesus Christ, and eternal joy for all of God's children. These promises are for us.

We have the promise from Jesus, and from the angel at the time of Jesus' ascent into heaven, that He will return to the earth. The promise is clear. It is true. It is proclaimed in the gospels and in the epistles and also here, as spoken in the Revelation, "Behold, I am coming soon."

We do not know when that will be, for we know that with God, "A Day is as a thousand years and a thousand years as a day." But Jesus has promised that he will return, and He will return!

And when Jesus comes back to earth again there will be a cosmic change akin to the original creation, a new heaven and a new earth. And all things, including you and me, will be transformed, will be made new.

So, we must not falter in our faith. Jesus has promised us eternal life with him, and he will do what he has promised.

Revelation 22:17 says, "Come! Whoever is thirsty, let him come; and whoever wishes, let him take the free gift of the water of life."

Jesus Prophesies Concerning His life and Ministry.

Scripture John 16:1-32a Text: John 16:22

How strange is early morning fog. We often experience it on Dayton Mountain or on the Smokey Mountains. We love our mountains, but we well know how dangerous they can be under certain weather conditions, especially when we are in heavy rain, snow, or fog.

Since we can see only as far as conditions permit, we may be able to see only a short distance in front of us, especially if it is dark. And traveling forward, only being able to see the road a little at a time, what is ahead of us is almost daunting, but the way becomes gradually clearer as we travel forward.

Often this is the way our journey through life is. We plan or try to plan, yet we cannot see far enough ahead to anticipate all the possibilities. So, in spite of our careful efforts, a part of our lives, like the fog on the mountain, while seeming to stubbornly remain a mystery, gradually unfolds to greater clarity. I think we can all agree. This is life.

And so, it was with Jesus' disciples. In their daily walk with him and listening to his teaching for three years, the fog of spiritual understanding gradually lifted. Now they were ready to hear, with greater understanding, who Jesus really was. He was much more than a carpenter, a respected maker of yokes and a rabbi; he had a Divine mission on the earth as God incarnate, God in human flesh, among them. So, now was the time.

Jesus would reveal this Divine aspect of himself: So,

Jesus Prophesies Concerning His Death and Resurrection.

He says, "In a little while you will see me no more." - He was referring to his death on the cross and burial in the tomb for three days.

"Then, after a little while you will see me." -This is his time with them after the resurrection.

"You will experience grief, but it will turn to joy." - This probably refers to his ascension and their joyful experience on the Day of Pentecost. Then,

Jesus Prophesies Concerning, "the Day of the Lord." - This was the day spoken of in the Old Testament, fear of the wrath of God. Then, and now, there is no longer any need for fear of The Day of the Lord. Salvation through Jesus' saving work on the cross and his resurrection completes the initial work of redemption. Thus, Jesus says:

We will rejoice! - We have eternal life!

We will be able to pray in Jesus' name We no longer need a mediator. We can go directly to God, our heavenly Father.

We will have a spiritual completeness. This is not of ourselves. It is the work of the Holy Spirit and God's grace through Jesus.

Jesus Prophesies Concerning His Origin and His Ascension.

He came from the Father His origin is that he is Divine and came to the earth to live among us as fully human as well as being fully Dine; this he specially revealed to Peter, James, and John on the "Mount of Transfiguration."

He entered the world as a baby His birth was a divine entrance heralded by an Angelic Host, revealed to shepherds while they were watching their sheep in the field, and to "Wise men from the East," who saw a special star and traveled a great distance to see the Christ-child.

He tells them that he is going back to the Father Jesus' ascension was the final proof that Jesus really came from the heavenly realms to the earth where, as was promised, he someday will return!

Finally, as Jesus reveals himself in greater measure, the fog of spiritual insight is lifted. He unveils his mission which is to die and claim victory of the greatest magnitude - over Satan, sin and death.

Now, the disciples are convinced and truly believe who Jesus really is, but Jesus warns them that even with this new knowledge, they will forsake him and flee; but he gives them great hope and comfort as he tells them, and his message is for us today. "In this world you will have trouble but take heart! I have overcome the world!

The Power That Came at Pentecost

Scripture lesson: Genesis :1-9; Acts 2:1-2 Text: Acts 2: 21

We use many popular phrases and sayings in our everyday language that are syn1bolic and mean son1ething different from their literal 1neaning. For example, what does "Let's think outside the box," mean?" What box? There is no box. Of course, the box is symbolic and means to think beyond the ordinary.

Another phrase, used symbolically, comes from the Old Testament book of Daniel, chapter 5. While King Belshazzar was giving a party, a hand appeared, writing on a wall, "You have been weighed in the balances and found wanting." The king sees the handwriting and knows that it is predicting his punishment. However, today we use this phrase, "seeing the handwriting on the wall," simply to predict a future event.

Another common saying, "That's as clear as mud," means something is not clear.

Another symbolic saying "smashed into smithereens" means being smashed into very small pieces like shooting a pumpkin with a shot gun and don't ask me how I know this.

We say "The crack of dawn" describing the instant daylight appears? Another illusive phrase that found its way into the English language. Some phrases are even more difficult.

What does "being paddled within an inch of your life" mean? As a little kid I heard someone say that. It scared me, but even worse, I didn't know what "an inch of my life" meant. And I couldn't figure out how to measure it. It's humorous now, but it wasn't then.

My last example, from the farm, "Don't put all your eggs in one basket," could mean several things like, avoid using one solution to solve a problem or avoid putting all your savings in one place. How interesting is it that we can understand symbolic expressions.

And language development, especially in young children, is truly amazing. My fascination increased after I had courses in childhood development at Millersville University in Pennsylvania. And when our children were born, I couldn't wait for them to begin to talk. Josephine and I would hold them, play with them, and talk to them every day. What we soon learned was that they could understand much more than they could express. And they became more and more attentive as we talked to them. Knowing that children are wired for imitation, we would say Mama or Da-da over and over, trying to teach them and one day when we heard them say Da-da or Mama, what pride we felt! Our names - it was like, now they know who we are; of course, they already knew before they could say it; but now they could express it. What a marvel is the development of language in human beings!

And if a child is born into a culture where several different languages are spoken, that child will grow up speaking those languages. This is common in some countries, for example in Africa, or the Mid-East, for children to become bi-lingual or even tri-lingual. Language development is truly a wonder of the world.

Today's, scripture, Genesis chapter, deals with language, tribalism, and rebellion; it is the story of ancient Babylonians, a proud, arrogant people, who rebelled against God. They chose to live as though they were gods, having to answer to no one, but themselves.

Babylon was located along the Euphrates River, near what is now Iraq. This part of civilization was localized in what is called the Fertile Crescent; a fertile land surrounded by desert sand. This was their world, a limited environment surrounded by the harsh desert with its dangers and surreal limitations. Here were a people living with a broken relationship with the God who made them and was sustaining them. Here were the Babylonians, a people filled with pride and self-sufficiency, who decided to take total control of their destiny by building a tower toward the heavens. This action declared that they thought could conquer their environment without God's help. Very dangerous.

So, the Babylonians decided to build for themselves a city to contain their civilization and a tower to reach the heavens. An action of rebellion. Why so? Well, God told Noah in Genesis 9: lb, "Be fruitful and increase in number and fill the earth." The Babylonians did not want to be scattered over the earth as God had commanded. So, they rebelled, deciding to build a city and a tower.

Now, building Babylon, the city, was not wrong in and of itself; but their reason for building it was wrong. They built it in rebellion to keep from populating the earth as God commanded; and their reason for building the tower? To focus on the city and to keep the people contained in Babylon. Talk about control!

But their very reason to build the tower was foolish because the horizon line, for a six- foot person at sea level, is only about three miles away and for someone standing about a hundred feet above sea level, is only about twelve to fifteen miles from where Babylon was located. Anyone going beyond that distance couldn't even see the tower and could easily get lost. Truly, the tower idea was ridiculous.

These people were very misguided. So, God, seeing their rebellion and misguided plans, confused their language to put an end to their foolishness. God confused the people, with the only language they knew, to where they couldn't understand each other.

The point? It is about God punishing the Babylonians for their rebellion and disobedience. It is about an arrogant people, filled with pride and self-sufficiency, who ignoring God's command to populate the earth, attempted to take a God ordered destiny into their own hands. Even trying to reach heaven by building a tower, which historical records say was only about three or four stories high. Ignoring allegiance to God, trying to make a name for themselves in a self-contained city and not be scattered over the face of the whole earth.

It is important to note that this event occurred sometime after Noah and his family were saved from the flood. Civilization, known to the writer of the book of Genesis, was apparently limited to the area of the Fertile Crescent. Here was their world, living with a broken relationship with God, the One who made them and was sustaining them.

The Babylonian's venture was short-sighted, at best, and in a practical sense, ridiculous.

A Godless scheme doomed to failure.

Going now to the New Testament, an amazing story, also involving language, is recorded in the book of Acts, on the Day of Pentecost. There is an interesting connection where God confused the language of the Babylonians in Genesis and the coming of the Holy Spirit as recorded in Acts. The connection? The language confusion of the rebellious Babylonians is now replaced with the disciples proclaiming the gospel in several different languages. A kind of restoration of God's original purpose.

This New Testament account contrasts the confusion of language in Genesis with the restoring of lost communication through believers filled with the Holy Spirit on the Day of Pentecost. And it is also amazing that this great event was prophesied in the Old Testament by the prophet Joel and others.

Believers, speaking through the power of the Holy Spirit, proclaimed fearlessly the gospel message that resonated in the different languages of the people who heard it. It was truly amazing! The believers proclaimed the gospel in the languages of theses foreign countries and were understood. Such an event had never happened before. The coming of the Holy Spirit to believers was the beginning of a new era for the infant Church. The Holy Spirit had come exactly as Jesus had promised. What had happened?

The Holy Spirit Came to Dwell Within Every Believer. God's Holy Spirit was the amazing, manifested presence that would now reside within Christians in the Christian community, transforming every believer who was there. The witness was clear, unprecedented and a singular occurrence. Nothing like it had ever happened before. God sent his Holy Spirit to dwell within the life of every believer, and it empowered them all. A crowd gathered:

They heard the sound of Pneuma, the sound of a rushing mighty wind.

They saw what appeared to be tongues of fire - that sat on each believer.

The entire crowd witnessed the coming of the Holy Spirit The seeking Christians experienced the Holy Spirit, being endued with power from on high, they declared the gospel in different tongues, languages, they had never learned. And the Church of Jesus Christ was now empowered for service.

The Crowd Sought for Meaning in the Event They were on the outside looking in, not the believers who experienced the event. They were merely observers. So,

Some made superficial observations like someone thoughtlessly watching a ballet.

Some were amazed. These were the open-minded observers who realized something truly amazing had happened.

Some were troubled The event conflicted with their previous life experiences. And it was the time for them to hear the gospel to help their understanding. And now:

The Gospel Was Proclaimed! - Who rose first to proclaim it? It was Peter, the one who was so afraid of the Roman authorities that he denied that he knew Jesus, three times. Yes, it was Peter, the impulse one, who seemed to so often put his foot in his mouth by saying the wrong thing. Witness now the new Peter, the apostle, a man full of the Holy Spirit, declaring the gospel totally unafraid, standing boldly before the crowd and openly declares:

These are not influenced by the effects of alcohol. They are not drunk. After all, its morning. And neither are they insane.

You are witnessing prophecy being fulfilled as spoken by the prophet Joel - an outpouring from God that has never happened before. And we will add:

This was the beginning of a new age. God's Spirit come to dwell within all believers.

We know that after Jesus ascended into heaven; the Comforter, the Holy Spirit, came, as was promised. The gospel, now revealed through the Pentecost event, is for all the peoples of the world. This is Pentecost. And this spiritual power is available to every believer. The Pentecost event heralds a new era, a new dispensation for all the world!

Indeed, may we continue to rejoice in our salvation through Jesus Christ, and rejoice in the coming of the Holy Spirit into our lives. As Peter proclaimed and as the Prophet Joel prophesied:

"For everyone who calls upon the name of the Lord will be saved."

So, may we continue to cultivate the precious presence of God's Holy Spirit within us for our own inner peace, personal strength, and personal witness for God's kingdom.

After all, the power that came at Pentecost is for us today and for every day!

Jesus Prayed for Us

Scripture lesson: John 17:20-26

Without a doubt, prayer is our royal telephone line. The old gospel song by Frederick Lehman says it well:

"Central's never busy always on the line; you may hear from heaven almost any time; 'Tis a royal service, free for one and all; When you get in trouble, give this royal line a call. Chorus: Telephone to glory, of, what joy dine! I can feel the current moving on the line, Built by God the Father for his loved and own, we may talk to Jesus thro' this royal telephone."

Prayer is our connection to God. This has been shown throughout history. So, regarding today's scripture, we ask, why with the knowledge the disciples had of the Old Testament, with their religious training in synagogue school, did they feel impelled to ask Jesus to teach them how to pray. Certainly, this was a legitimate request; but before we answer the why, let's consider the disciples' religious background. To begin with, how did they understand the role of their religious leaders, and who were they? Mainly there were the Scribes, Pharisees and priests.

The Scribes copied the scriptures and kept the records of Jewish history; they were the text authorities, guardian-scholars of the written Old Testament.

The Pharisees, mostly middle class, were held in high regard, for their knowledge of the scriptures, often memorizing entire books of the Old Testament. Recognized legal interpreters of the law, but unfortunately, sometimes used their authority to impose legalistic requirements on the people that went far beyond Mosaic law.

The Sadducees were the outliers, the secular minded group, wealthy aristocrats, politically friendly with Rome, who didn't believe in an after-life, nor God's involvement in history.

Now, contrast this with the Rabbis. They were highly regarded teachers in the Jewish community, and it was a great honor to be selected as their student. This explains why, when Jesus called, "Come follow me," the busy fishermen immediately went to him; perhaps, even running to catch up with him as he walked along the shore of the Sea of Galilee. Just imagine the many thoughts that were racing through their heads. When Jesus, the revered Rabbi, called them to follow him, it was certainly an honor; but it also meant something else of the greatest importance. When they answered the call to follow a Rabbi, it meant that they were no longer following any other religious leader. Since Jesus was now their Rabbi, he was their only spiritual leader. So, they would now follow Jesus and no one else. An important lesson for us today.

And as a result of their decision to follow Jesus, we wonder, what was their spiritual status? Well, because of their former Jewish religious leaders, with their ceremonial exclusiveness, praying to God instead of them, they didn't know how to pray for or by themselves. Their religious leaders had, apparently, always done the praying.

So, it is obvious why personal prayer was a mystery to the disciples? They may even have felt inadequate regarding prayer, not even knowing the words to use. This is probably why they concluded that they needed help in learning how to pray?"

They felt they needed to be the ones praying. This was a legitimate request, keeping in mind that the priests and prophets were their former religious leaders. But now, they were following Jesus and sensing a profound change taking place within themselves through his life and teachings and not knowing how to pray, they wanted him to teach them how.

Answering their request, Jesus gave them the beautiful prayer, known as the Lord's Prayer, which could be titled "A Model Prayer for Disciples." With its beautiful, very meaningful words, we should always reflect on its profound meaning and expression.

"Our Father" recognizes God and as our Father, our relationship to him. "Who art in heaven" establishes his domain. "Hallowed be Thy name" expresses worship and the utmost respect for his name. "Thy kingdom come" recognizes God as supreme King over everything and petitions that His Kingdom come to the earth. "Thy will be done on earth as it is in heaven" implores that God's will be done on this imperfect earth as his will is done in heaven which is perfect. "Ge us this day our daily bread" requests and also recognizes God as the source of our sustenance. "And forge us our trespasses as we forgive those who trespass against us" recognizes that we are sinners, in need of forgiveness, but we must also forge. "And lead us not into temptation" petitions God that we be led away from situations that may tempt us. "And deliver us from evil" declares the power of God over Satan, the source of evil. "For thine is the kingdom, and the power and the glory forever. Amen," is a beautiful doxology that was added later.

Prayer is the most powerful spiritual resource we have, and we need to pray every day. Jesus knew more than anyone else, the importance and power of prayer.

In today's scripture we learn that Jesus knew his ministry was coming to a close. He knew that he soon would be left alone to stand trial and he knew he would be crucified. On one occasion, he shocked his listeners when he told them, "For this purpose I came into the world."

But Jesus knew much more. He also knew that he was the hope of the world. That through his teaching about the kingdom of God, through his death as the final sacrifice for sin and his victorious resurrection, he would lay the eternal foundation for his Church. He prophesied this when he said to Peter, "On this rock will I build my Church and the gates of hell will not prevail against it."

Now, at the precisely right moment, ready to redeem the world from the clutches of Satan, Jesus prays his beautiful "High Priestly Prayer." It reaches beyond the imperfections and spiritual chaos of this world, extending beyond finite uncertainty and points forward, with a hopeful, promising, prophetic arch toward the great future ministry of his Church. First,

Jesus Prays for the Ministry of Others.

He prays for his disciples those he mentored for three years, that they all would be one, as he and the Father are One.

He prays for those who believed through the disciple's message - that they, too, would be in unity and be one, as he and the Father are One.

He prays, "May they also be in us so that the world may believe that you have sent me." - This implies that our bodies are the temple of the Holy Spirit!

Then Jesus says, "I have gen them the glory that you gave me that they may be as one as we are one, I in them and you in Me. May they be brought to complete unity to let the world know that you sent me and have loved them even as you have loved me." - This is love in its purest form!

These beautiful words of Jesus leave us breathless with amazement. This high priestly prayer of our Lord is the deepest, most powerful message for believers in the entire New Testament.

Jesus explains why he came into the world, what salvation's goal is and what salvation's final destiny is for us as the redeemed of the Lord. Yes, Jesus prayed for us, all of us; its meaning, of our oneness with Jesus Christ and oneness with fellow believers, drawing us toward a more perfect relationship with God and God's people.

Jesus Prays for Unity in His Church - "That they may be brought into complete unity to let the world know that you have sent me and have loved them as you have loved me." - Complete unity means love in action and love fulfilled. We pray for unity in the Church of Jesus Christ, everywhere!

A "That all of them may be one, Father." - Jesus describes the spiritual goal of oneness in his Church, knowing the fragmented state of humanity over the world.

"Just as you are in me, and I am in you." - The Divinestate of spiritual oneness,

Christ in God and God in Christ. This is love in action, perfect love. Then, Jesus says,

"I have gen them the glory that you gave me, that they may be one as we are one, I in them and you in me." - This is how, as Jesus' disciples, we are given the glory, are bonded into oneness with him and are infused into oneness with his Father. Jesus wants us, his Church, to be infused as one as he and the Father are one.

Jesus Prays for Our Eternal Life with God It is why he came to save.

Jesus wants us to be with God - where God is, which is in heaven.

Jesus wants us to experience his glory - because it is the ultimate confirmation of Jesus' Deity- and confirming his oneness with his Father!!!

Jesus wants us to realize his eternalness - not just know about it, but to experience that Jesus is indeed God incarnate, eternal, timeless God come to dwell with finite man. This is one important reason why he prayed, "the glory you have gen me before the foundation of the world." This affirms Jesus' deity and his timelessness - existing before time began.

So, Jesus prayed, to his heavenly Father as our Savior, our Heavenly High Priest and as our teacher:

"I have made you have known to them and will continue to make you known in order that the love you have for me may be in them, and that I myself may be in them."

Here, Jesus teaches the manifest love of God that may also be demonstrated in us. The

Holy Spirit of Jesus, also manifested as God's Holy Spirit is part of the Holy Trinity.

The great spiritual insight, then, is knowing God as our heavenly Father, Jesus his Son and the Holy Spirit as a Divine Unity infused inseparably in love. This explains why God is love, not a mere attribute; it is who God really is. "God is Love."

So, God's Holy Spirit, the Divine Presence, sent by Jesus to dwell within us, is real!

The apostle Paul's affirmation, that we are the temple of the Holy Spirit, means that we are not alone. God's presence will go with us throughout our lives giving us a faith inspired eternal view.

Free from the bondage of a sinful life that degrades the human condition and destroys the human spirit, we are free from that gnawing sense of hopelessness, which results from Living a spiritually empty existence.

Through Christ, our lives now have spiritual meaning. Our life is in Christ because of Christ's love for us and his Spirit within us; we are free from that deep sense of despair that grips the life without Christ. Remember, Perfect love really does cast out all fear. And since we know that God wants us to be happy, may we pray earnestly, especially in times of stress, "God fill us with your love."

It is so profound and meaningful! Jesus prayed for us to be one with him, and one with each other as he and the Father are one. May we seek to grow in the faith to become more like Jesus, more at one with him and more at one with each other.

It is precious to know that the loving presence of the Holy Spirit can unify us, his Church to truly be one, as God and Jesus and the Holy Spirit are One.

So, let us rejoice, knowing that we are saved, and in his unifying, loving care forever!

Blessed be his holy name!

Justification Means the Slate Is Clean

Scripture lesson: Romans 5:1-1 Text: Romans 5:1

My father, Alfred Dawson Boyd, was born in Belfast, Ireland. He came to this country, on a freighter ship in 1929, worked as a gardener for Wurlitzer, and in the Botany 500 garment factory. Following that, he enrolled in, Beulah Heights Bible Institute, now Valley Forge Christian College, and then served as a pastor for over forty years.

As children, we grew up hearing about his life on the farm in Ireland, the milk maid, the house maid, the farm hands and thatched roofed cottages. How he thought old uncle Jacob, the owner, was a slave driver, but his brother Bill, when visiting us, said dad just didn't like farm work. But dad did like to ride horses bare back, play soccer with the neighborhood boys and tell us what tough players the Boyd brothers were. The Boyd's typically have longevity. Dad lived to be 98, his sister Evelyn, in New Zealand, lived to be 99.

My Irish heritage is my father's side; my mother's side is English. Historically, the reputation was that the Irish were uncivilized wild heavy drinkers, perhaps the reason for the name the Fighting Irish football team of Notre Dame University.

As pastor and father, dad was hard working, sometimes impatient and at times quick tempered, but we knew he loved us. I learned about Irish tempers early on.

Some folks think that a pastor and his home should be some kind of perfect example. This is not reality. We were just a family with the usual family problems and in need of the wisdom of the scriptures in our daily ling.

However, some families do not even try to live with Christian values, carrying grudges and unresolved grievances, sometimes for years. As a young man, I learned of the fierce feud, 1863-1891, between two Scotch/Irish families, the Hatfield's and McCoy's. With their long standing, bitter disputes and fights, it seemed violence was in their blood. In fact, their escapades captured the attention of Hollywood producers, and the feud was made into a movie and in 2012 into a TV mini-series. And it is currently being replayed in a restaurant in Pigeon Forge. Nobody needs this kind of negative notoriety. But hold on to your McHat!

Any family tree, if traced back far enough, will reveal its own set of problems. During my first appointment in 1986, the Darlington-Center Charge, the Hatfield/McCoy feud came into focus again. The lay leader at Darlington,

Fritz McCoy, a farmer and computer expert. An excellent lay leader, and all-around nice guy and his wife, Mary, a regional insurance executive, often invited us, during our six and a half years of pastoring there, to dinner after church.

As we got to know them, I asked Fritz about the Hatfield/McCoy feud. He said he knew little about it except that it was a long bitter fight that finally got resolved, was in the past and of little consequence to him. Understandable because Fritz and Mary, were devoted Christians and raised their boys with Christian values. In fact, both boys became presidential scholars. Of course, their home wasn't perfect. No home is. But their Christian lifestyle was strong in their lives and made all the difference.

The Hatfield and McCoy debacle is not unique. It mirrors the dark side of humanity that needs a dean slate. Life can be wonderfully fulfilling and joyful; the way God wants it to be. However, regretfully, in our country and over the world, there is much discord and violence.

But, you say, hold on a minute; my life is not like this. Our family doesn't live that way.

Excellent! Neither does ours. We just need to be thankful for our Christian lifestyle.

Of course, we know that even in a Christian home there can be unresolved problems and hurt feelings. Here is where we should prayerfully seek sensible solutions. We want the family slate to be clean.

At this point, perhaps frustrated, we ask, "Why can't people just learn to get along with each other? When people are frustrated and dissatisfied with themselves, their internal spiritual conflict spills over into society. What the world needs is salvation and the wisdom of Jesus, the Prince of Peace; and it is our mission to tell them about the transforming power of Jesus who is the answer to that gnawing, unsettled feeling inside of them. Christ's presence has transformed us, changing the way we view the world and our approach to life's problems. We should use and share our spiritual insights!

Sometimes, conflicts in the home or workplace are often quietly pushed aside and remain unresolved. This is to be avoided. Time doesn't heal wounds. Unresolved problems never go away; they fester in our subconscious and only get worse. Human relations need to be handled prayerfully, with love and understanding, to make the social slate clean. How?

One way is if we are wronged, forget or if we are in the wrong, ask for forgiveness.

Difficult? Yes, it is, but remembering that at the base of every problem in human relations is a spiritual problem, accepting that there is a problem is the first step. Then, as we pray and deal with it, the problem will be more easily solvable. Difficult to do? Yes, but recognizing the problem while considering its spiritual dimensions will move us toward a clean slate. If the problem is us, we need forgiveness; if it is someone else, we need to solve and forge. The human relations slate needs to be clean. A deep spiritual search is helpful.

The life that struggles without Jesus will always continue to struggle for meaning.

Our lives are meant to have purposeful spiritual meaning. How futile are the attempts to answer life's questions without considering the spiritual! And futile are the so-called answers to life's meaning without a deep positive spiritual sense of purpose!

And without a sense of the Divine within us, the presence of the Holy Spirit, none of life's experiences will have the kind of meaning they should have. Why? We need the deep sense of personal worth Jesus gives us because he died for us and rose victorious! Praise the Lord! We need not travel alone. Have you invited Jesus into your life? Are you tired of traveling alone? Traveling with the Lord brings us to realize that life goes far beyond the immediate to what is eternal, and that the good life is found in the Living of it, a life led unto God!

Jesus answered the question of meaning at Calvary. His saving, purifying work gives spiritual meaning to our lives. Being born again, we are justified before God. Knowing this we can shout, "O Happy Day!" - the slate is clean! We can now move forward unfettered and with real purpose knowing that:

Justification Is Salvation's Beginning Now that the slate is clean:

We sense great peace. Our lives are cleansed, enabling us to 1nove through life unfettered by the bondage of sin. Praise the Lord! At last, we are truly free!

A. We sense a spiritual bonding with Christ. He is in us, and we are in him.

We realize we truly are loved! And now we have total access to God's grace, firmly positioned spiritually and able to share in the glory of God.

Suffering For Christ Can be Part of Our Spiritual Growth. The apostle Paul says we can rejoice in our suffering because:

Suffering allows perseverance which can make us stronger. The result?

Perseverance molds character because perseverance pushes beyond pain.

Character (through faith) leads us to hope in our salvation through Jesus, who left heaven to enter our finite world to save us.

Our Hope Is in Jesus, Our Precious Lord and Savior. The wonderful truth is, though we were undeserving of God's grace, Jesus died for us that:

While we were yet sinners, Christ died for us!!! - Perhaps, even ignorant of our hopeless condition, we were loved. And through Jesus, God forges us and reconciles us to him. This means we are justified (made pure) by his blood poured out for us on Calvary. This means our slate is clean!

We are reconciled to God through Christ's death and his resurrection. (Jesus was the final sacrifice for sin.) The result?

We are saved, born again! - This means that our slate is clean in the eyes of God, justified. We stand pure as if we had never sinned. Scripture says that our sins are cast into the sea of God's forgetfulness never to be ren1embered against us anymore. This is justification! So, how dare we allow our past sins to eat at us? God has forgiven us of every sin we have ever committed! Self-deprecating thoughts are not who we now are. Being born again, our lives, are washed, made whiter than snow. Praise the Lord! Our slate is clean!

To only know about salvation is not enough. But to realize that by confessing our sins we are completely forgiven. This is our point of purification, our justification, when our lives are cleansed, cleansed by the blood of the Lamb.

Salvation is not through something we have done; it is what Christ has done; we are saved through Jesus Christ. Now, our slate is clean, really clean, now firmly positioned with our new life in Christ. Even our suffering takes on spiritual meaning.

The Holy Spirit enables us to persist through suffering and as our character is molded, we become stronger and stronger. Growing in the faith leads us to realize that all life should be centered in Jesus Christ, not ourselves. And His grace is sufficient for us and being reconciled before God, we come to really know and love Jesus because we are truly cleansed. Our slate is clean! Praise the Lord!

A Soldier's Faith Amazes Jesus

Scripture lesson: Luke 7;1-10 Text: Luke 7:9b

Today's scripture is of special interest because the qualifications and responsibilities of a Roman Centurion identified him as a soldier of colnmand being responsible for 100 men. Along with this, he represented military law and could chastise a soldier with whips. And following the upward chain of command, the general, a rank above the Centurion, could sentence a soldier to death for dereliction of duty. And Roman soldiers, of every rank, executed their duties under the command and authority of the Roman government. Roman soldiers knew authority.

The Roman soldier was highly trained. This included strenuous physical demands like climbing mountains, swimming rivers and training to fight in battles. He was not to seek danger, when faced with it, he was to always hold his ground, even to die at his post.

The Centurion began his training as a regular soldier, similar to a Prate, in the United States Army. After completing his basic training, he could seek to climb through the military ranks, with each level giving him increased authority. Finally earning the rank of Centurion, he could command a hundred soldiers. One thing is certain; the Centurion knew power! Yet, had his own limitations and he knew it.

One limitation was that he could not help his highly valued servant who was near death. In this situation he was powerless. But, to his credit, he sought someone with the power to heal his servant. This person was Jesus.

He believed that Jesus could heal his servant. A remarkable decision, in spite of the Roman occupation. Nevertheless, the Centurion decided to seek the help of a Jewish Rabbi whose name was Jesus. How would he do this? He would follow the chain of command:

The Centurion Sent the Jewish Elders to Jesus for Help. The implications of his decision are complex. Why? First, the Jewish elders were forced to recognize Jesus. Second, being Jews, under Roman occupation, they knew that they had better comply with the Centurion's request. Third, the Centurion asked highly respected Jewish leaders to approach Jesus, to increase the chance that Jesus would heal his servant.

Also, extraordinary for a hardened Roman soldier, was his show of caring. He put himself aside to get help for his servant. We see desperation mixed with caring. He did care and had nowhere to turn, so, wisely, he turned to Jesus for help. Not only believing that Jesus could heal his servant, but he also believed that if Jesus only spoke the word his servant would be healed. Now, that is faith! Further,

The Centurion showed respect for Jesus. He sent Jewish elders to make the request.

The elders pleaded with Jesus on the Centurion's behalf. They thought they had to convince Jesus, a Jewish Rabbi, that this Roman Centurion, who represented Rome's control over the Jewish nation, was worthy of his help. So, what did they do to try to convince Jesus to heal the Centurion's son? Their answer was the Centurion's works.

The elders declared that the Centurion's good works made him worthy. They said,

"He loves our nation, and he built us a synagogue." Their pleading was not only important for the immediate situation, but it was also important as part of salvation history. As early as in Genesis we read, The Lord said to Abram,

"I will make you into a great nation and I will bless you. I will make your name great, and you will be a blessing. I will bless those who bless you and whoever curses you I will curse and all peoples on earth will be blessed through you."

Notice the important faith implication. The Jewish elders said, "This Centurion, by his faith, has blessed Israel and is therefore, placed under that particular part of the covenantal relationship and is worthy of God's blessing." - Not by his works but by his faith. So,

Jesus Goes to the Place of Need.

Jesus goes with the Jewish Elders to the Centurion While on their travels,

The Centurion sends another message saying, "I do not deserve to Have You Come Under My Roof." It is as if the Centurion, experiencing some kind of epiphany, recognizes Jesus' Dinity. It reminds us of the prophets of old when sensing God's presence, felt unworthy.

It is a curious thing that the Elders of the Jews didn't recognize Jesus as their Messiah, but this Roman soldier, surrounded by idolatry and Roman culture, senses the presence of God in Jesus, his greatness, his Dinity, and declares, "Just say the word and my servant will be healed." Then, the Centurion follows his statement of faith, further recognizing Jesus' Divine authority, by saying, "Just as my word has authority, so does yours." The Centurion knows power, and he believes in the power of Jesus' words. Like a flash of insight into the power of Create God, who spoke the worlds into existence, the Centurion really believes in Jesus. Upon hearing his words:

Jesus Proclaims the Centurion as a Man of Great Faith!

Jesus affirms the Centurion's faith Imagine the bewilderment of those who heard the Centurion. I can imagine what they might have thought. Could this gentile have faith? He didn't belong to any Jewish religious organization. And as a gentile, in their minds, he was a lost soul. They probably thought he was faithless, hard and uncaring. Well, if they did think that about him, they misjudged him. If they thought because he was a Roman and a Roman soldier, he was faithless, hard and uncaring, they got it all wrong. Very wrong.

Jesus actually compares this Centurion's faith with the nation of Israel. An astounding comparison! Why? Because the people of Israel, God's chosen people, were covenanted to be God's people of faith to lead the nations of the world to God! And certainly not someone like this Roman Centurion could a path of faith be forged as an example to them. But forge a path, he did! Not by his works, though honored by the people and commendable, but by his faith. So,

Jesus Healed the Servant according to the Centurion's faith not his works. Notice: Jesus did not say that the Centurion's fine works made him worthy or because of his good works his servant would be made whole. Jesus said it was his faith!

Understandably, the elders of the Jews saw goodness in the Centurion and, being people of the law, argued for his worthiness through his works. But Jesus did not say that because of his fine works he would heal his servant or that because of his works he was made worthy. Jesus knew the important ingredient was his faith.

On the surface this all seems so simple, but it is not. Why? First, though good works are important and a beautiful thing, no one is made worthy before God through their works. Second, what Jesus did say revealed the great theological truth that is key to all spiritual, covenantal relationships,

"I have not found so great faith. no not in Israel."

Third, Jesus' commended the Centurion, a Roman and a gentile, for his faith and Fourth, Jesus' statement was an insightful criticism of Israel's lack of faith, the very people Jesus came to save, who, at this time in history was not the nation of faith they were covenanted to be. They were to be spiritual leaders to lead the world to the one true and Living God.

Here in this Roman soldier, a Centurion, a man of considerable earthly authority, we find fine qualities that demonstrate God's prevenient grace, which is an open door to all who have faith. God's grace is for all who believe.

We find in this Centurion soldier, of unusual temperament, a noble caring about others. He even cared about his servant which was not typical of the

Romans, who usually treated their servants as Living machines.

But we find this Centurion caring about the Jewish people, and actually loving the nation of Israel, a people of a different religion. When they needed a synagogue, in spite of his own religious differences, he built it for them; here we find in this powerful man, trained fighter and military leader, humility. He sought for help, even declaring himself unworthy to have Jesus come under his roof since he was a Roman.

And more amazing, he said to Jesus, "Just speak the word and my servant will be cured."

It was faith that moved the Master. It was faith that led to his servant's healing. It is our faith, too, that will bring healing into our lives and into the lives of others. O Lord give us such faith!

Jesus Calls a Tax Collector to Follow Him

Scripture lesson: Luke 5: 27-35 Text: Luke 6:32

Social stratification is a reality! Circumstances, such as the family into which we were born, economic situations, government regulations or oppression, religious ideas and other factors, affect us. Positive or negative circumstances can affect our self- esteem and can even keep us from bettering ourselves. In America we have the, so called, "'American Dream," the belief that we can better ourselves through education, careful planning and hard work. And many people have done this, but the opportunities that exist in a free society don't always exist in other countries. For example:

In India there is a caste system that, at birth, places a person into a certain caste or excludes that person from any caste, being an outcast, at birth, and it is that person's status for life. The ancient custom dictates that the person is not to socialize or even talk to someone of a lower caste. And even worse, if born so low as to not even being in a caste, that person is known as an outcast and is an outcast for life. Some people have come to America to be free from this kind of fixed social stratification.

In American culture, this same term, outcast, is also common in our language and it means that the person so identified is generally cast out from society. Thankfully, in America citizens are not doomed to live within a certain caste or be forever considered an outcast. In our country, normally, a person, through education, an improved socially accepted level of living, or through accomplishment in the workplace, is able to enter into the mainstream of society. We know of some people in our own community who have done this.

However, various levels of social, economic, and intellectual status are found, in cultures all over the world. Even in a free society, such as ours, we find social stratification everywhere, based on wealth, political power, family status, social connections, academic achievement, or achievement in the workplace. Some people even carry a sense of status because of where they live and may view their status as giving them a kind of entitlement.

I remember, with amusement, an old western movie where a young girl saddled up to a stranger and threatened him in no uncertain terms, "'My daddy is mayor in this here town and you had better do what he says." The young girl felt powerful through the position of her mayor daddy and so she felt entitled. However, as amusing as this is, on a serious note, we ask ourselves. What place does social stratification have in the Church of Jesus Christ? And the answer is that it has no place in the Church of Jesus Christ because we are all of equal value in the eyes of God. The highly educated, apostle Paul leveled the field when he wrote in Corinthians 3:9, "We are God's fellow workers; you are God's field, God's building." Today's scripture lives on gives us an excellent example of the renowned Rabbi, Jesus honoring a social outcast by selecting him to follow him. Unusual because of the social barriers in their society, yet:

Jesus Calls a Social Outcast, a Tax Collector, to Follow Him. A tax collector? Yes. Why would Jesus call a social outcast, someone hated by his fellow Jews, and not even allowed in the synagogues to worship with them, to follow him? Why would Jesus' call Levi from his workplace while he was collecting taxes from fellow Jews who hated him. Why would Jesus' honor this hated man by even speaking to him, as was forbidden by the Pharisees? And everyone knew it was an honor to be selected and called by a Rabbi. So, why would Jesus call this social outcast Jew, seen as a traitor because he worked for the Roman government, to follow him?

And would Levi, the tax collector actually follows Jesus? There was a lot for him to consider. Would he ge up his lucrative job, that of collecting taxes to follow Jesus? Would he ge up his allegiance and employment benefits of Rome to now ge allegiance to Jesus? Yes! In front of those standing there he made his decision. The call was simple. His decision was immediate and life transforming. Jesus simply said, "Follow me." And Levi got up immediately, left everything, and followed him.

Then, Levi did a beautiful thing; after receiving the honor of being called by Jesus, Levi, in turn, wants to honor Jesus. How would he do this? He chose to have a great banquet in his house, not an ordinary meal, a great banquet. Why would he do this? Levi understood the magnitude of his call and wanted to celebrate it at the level he saw it. He understood that Jesus calling him was an honor.

So, who were invited to this great banquet to celebrate with him? His friends, and among his friends were his fellow tax collectors. There was a large crowd of tax collectors and others sitting at the table with them and apparently the Pharisees and their scribes were also there. (An important clue here is that during this period of time, important figures took scribes with them to record important events, which explains, in part, how some scriptures were recorded.) Important to recognize that here,

The Pharisees and Scribes (teachers of the law) saw Levi's life change a change of allegiance away from Rome to that of allegiance to Jesus. Did they celebrate with him? No, of course not, their own religious authority was diminished since Levi was now following Jesus, his new religious authority. Not understanding what had happened, they complained, seeing the situation through narrow legalistic eyes, blinded by their own social customs, they didn't approve of Jesus eating with sinners. Perhaps, they tried to imply guilt by association. But whatever their reason, instead of rejoicing with Levi, honored to be called by a Rabbi, they shifted the celebration to criticism about Jesus. They asked,

"Why do you eat and drink with the tax collectors and sinners?" - We know the scribes and pharisees wouldn't break their social codes and do what Jesus did, eat and drink with tax collectors and sinners. So, instead of trying to understand, they criticized Jesus by questioning, what was to them, a liberal lifestyle. It was like they were asking:

Why have you crossed over the social line? - Why would you dare to cross the social taboo, probably inferring that, by doing this, Jesus was contaminating himself.

Why are you allowing yourself to be numbered with the outcasts of society? - We don't do this. It is forbidden. How does Jesus answer their critical questioning?

Jesus States His Purpose for Coming to the Earth Here, in the eyes of everyone, Jesus calls Levi, the tax collector, considered to be one of the lowest of the low in the eyes of the Scribes and Pharisees. And further, Jesus uses this situation to affirm his purpose for being there. He came to save the lost. To make this even clearer, Jesus called Levi, in their eyes, among the lowest of the low. Speaking plainly, Jesus tells them,

"'I have not come to call the righteous," - You Scribes and Pharisees, who see yourselves as not needing help. You who think you are already righteous, take note:

"I have come to call sinners to repentance." - Here, Jesus made them think about their own situation. How did they fit into the scheme of things? And then, concerning their criticism about fasting Jesus told them,

"But the days will come - and when the bridegroom is taken away from them in those days they will fast."

Jesus left the heavenly realms and came to the earth so save all who are willing to follow him. He calls us to salvation; he calls us to experience his love and his peace, and he calls us to service. We should celebrate his calling us to salvation, and to experience his love and peace, and also his calling us to service.

To be in the service of the Lord, in whatever ministry we find opportunity, is an honor. The secular world knows little of this. What they know is self-centeredness and greed. And those persons who wrap themselves in the rags of selfish values and the fleeting goal of worldly status, actually exclude themselves from the eternal joy of salvation and a life that knows the joy of following a spiritual calling and engaging in joyful service.

But those who embrace the Lord's provision for salvation saying, "yes, I will follow Jesus." will receive salvation and the promised hope of eternal life and know the joy of serving Jesus.

Jesus called Levi to follow him, as he calls us today and every day, and Levi deciding to follow Jesus, honoring Jesus with a great banquet.

Though despised as a tax collector, Jesus saw Levi's potential as a powerful force for spreading the gospel throughout the world. Jesus knew that Levi had great potential as a writer as well as a proclaimer.

We know Levi today by his Greek name, Matthew the writer of the gospel of Matthew.

What a beautiful legacy Matthew has gen to us in his divinely inspired writing!

Jesus simply says to us today, as he said to Matthew, the tax collector, "Follow me."

The Standards of Real Discipleship

Scripture: Luke 9:57-62. 10:1-2 Text: Luke 10:1-2

A disciple is someone who accepts the role of a student, is willing to follow a teacher and be taught by that teacher. Disciples, then, are people who are teachable. So far so good, but since discipleship concerns the human experience, discipleship is not simple. Why? Discipleship involves the complexity of human behavior with its multiplicity of life experiences. However, these life experiences can become better understood when broadened and clarified through interaction between the teacher and the student.

Yes, discipleship is a school, a school of lifetime learning. But what about the student's readiness to learn? It will be helpful to consider the student's readiness to learn. Readiness is a necessary, but little known, understanding to the general public. But it is an essential part of every professional educator's training. Often, simply called readiness, it means that a student is ready to learn a particular subject. When done properly, the order of courses in school is carefully structured, according to the student's readiness to learn.

Jesus knew the importance of and requirements of discipleship. He had schooled the disciples for three years. He knew that his time was short on the earth. So, after all his teaching, including the parables, and prophesies, what was the last commandment Jesus gave to his disciples? And it is good for us to observe that he did not lay down a list of laws or rules for his disciples to memorize. Nor did he threaten them with consequences if they failed to meet a list of legal expectations. No! Jesus summed up his three years of teaching his disciples with one commandment: John 13: 14-15 "A new commandment I ge you: Love one another. As I have loved you, so you must love one another. By this everyone will know that you are my disciples, if you love one another."

Now, since we know, by Jesus reminding his disciples, "As I have loved you," that love is active, and the correct meaning of love is love is caring. And that Jesus set love as the gold standard for his disciples "Love one another as I have loved you," this tells us a most important concept. Love is more than a noun. Most importantly, love is a verb. And this tells us that love is active; love means positive action.

Love is not a fall, even though we may use the phrase "fall in love." But, thinking about it, we know this is not correct. Love is not falling. Love is a positive dynamic. In fact, love is the most positive dynamic in the world because it involves the most positive action. To support his we think of that wonderful scripture,

"For God so loved the World that he gave his only begotten Son that whosoever believes in him will not perish but have everlasting life."

The full meaning of love tells us it is best understood as a verb; how so? Love is dynamic. Love is action. By verbal definition, to go from potential energy to dynamic energy, love means positive action.

Jesus knew this and it is why he said to his disciples, "A new commandment I ge you. Love one another as I have loved you." Since, Jesus referred to his statement as a commandment, we can easily conclude that love is, indeed, a matter of the will. And, by inference, this explains why Jesus called his statement to his disciples a commandment.

This leads us to ask, "What is real discipleship?" And further:

What Are the Indicators That Are Marks of Real Discipleship?

The first indicator is time. It takes time to be a disciple. These days we are all busy; so often we must take time to put love into action as we minister together as the disciples of Jesus.

Second is Self- denying. We may plan for things we want to do, but to follow where the Holy Spirit is leading us, we sometimes have to put our own plans aside. And remember, even a cup of cold-water gen in the name of the Lord is ministry. This is real discipleship and shows devotion to our Lord.

Third is proper priorities - adopting biblical values means avoiding materialism, especially in the false sense that getting material things means happiness. Certainly, enjoying and having things is fine, as long as we see material things only for what they are. (To remind you of what is temporary, look at a junk yard.)

Fourth is Being Futuristic, facing forward - It is important to avoid getting bogged down by constantly looking back. This is especially true when we have experienced painful experiences. So, it is important to remind ourselves that the past cannot be changed; and while we are Living in the present, it is important to plan for and look to the future. As real disciples, guided by the Holy Spirit, we are enabled to press forward, able to look beyond our limited, personal circumstances and see the big picture, the grand adventure, of which we are a part.

And, considering the unexpected, it is important to identify important, even crucial moments and not lose opportunities to make a positive difference. Sometimes chances come only once, which means we should avoid letting the emotion of the moment become a substitute for positive action. It is easy to fall into the trap that the longer we put something off, the bigger the task seems to become, and the more likely it will not be accomplished.

What Are the Indicators That Show Jesus' Plan for Discipleship?

- He taught his disciples for three years. Then, he appointed 70 men.

- He sent them out before he came to the town, they were his ambassadors.

- He made clear what he wanted them to do. They were on a mission.

What is the Visionary Challenge of Discipleship?

To realize that the harvest is great. Considering the immense spiritual need, many workers are needed because the need is great. There are many lost, misguided souls in this world that need Jesus as their Savior.

To consider that the workers are few. Many more workers are needed because the need is greater than it has ever been. Increasing population, weather conditions, climate change, criminal activity and the ravages of war have multiplied the spiritual need over the entire earth.

To Pray for those who work in the harvest fields. No one can do it all, but we can do what we are able and pray for those who are able and active, making contributions to the various sectors of life. This includes law enforcement, first responders, medical personnel, businesspersons and educators, and the important vast labor force, the backbone of our nation, and Christian ministers, to name a few. And remember as Real Disciples, Jesus says to all of us today, "I am sending you."

Finally, it is important to realize that we are all in various stages of physical, emotional, and spiritual development. And that the Lord knows our abilities as well as our limitations. So, as we pray for each other and ourselves, may we pray that our own lives be spiritually strengthened to better meet the standards of real discipleship, looking forward instead of backward, avoiding the trap of being locked in past pain with humanly unsolvable problems and unsolved conflicts of the past. May we leave these matters in God's hands, moving forward to do his will, not allowing emotions to become a substitute for the solution to a problem.

May the Lord equip us to put love into action, as his disciples, to help us meet the challenge of the harvest of souls in our generation. For that is our responsibility as real disciples of Jesus Christ.

Jesus Gives Life Amidst Despair

Scripture lesson: Luke 7:17

It was a hot summer day in the peach orchards of Scotland, near Chambersburg, Pennsylvania. Several of us boys, proudly wearing our straw hats and feeling our manly stamina, were picking peaches, spraying the trees and doing other farm work.

Suddenly, one of the fellas, trying to fix a piece of equipment, hit his hand with a hammer. Ouch! A loud cry of pain startled us and then, complete silence. All the work stopped.

Silently, we stood transfixed gazing at the young man, his face white with pain. He stood there silently, holding his hand ever so tightly. We were frozen at that moment. Then, one of them looked at me, the new guy in the group, and explained his silent response, with admiration, "He's being Stoic." Being Stoic? What does that mean? While I was looking puzzled, he explained that being Stoic is dealing with painful situations bravely and silently. They saw bravery and discipline in their friend's silent face blanched white with pain; and he didn't even cuss.

This, to them, was being Stoic. He demonstrated bravery and strength silently. His silence was golden. And I had experienced a grass roots interpretation of Stoicism, actually not very far removed from its ancient philosophical roots.

Stoicism was founded in Athens, Greece by Zeno around 308 B. C. Later it was taught by the eccentric philosopher Diogenes whose ideas led him to become a cynic, thus, his dubious title as the founder of Cynicism.

The brilliant Diogenes was a strange character. Publicly, he did vulgar things, rebelling against common decency and rebelling against socially accepted norms; yet some of his ideas still have influence today. For example, one afternoon, while sunning himself in a tub, Alexander the Great came to see him. Looking down at Diogenes, he asked, "'Are you afraid of me?" Unruffled, Diogenes quipped, "Are you a good thing or a bad thing?" Alexander, surprised at Diogenes throwing a question back at him, quickly replied "'I am a good thing." Diogenes quipped back 'Then, why should I be afraid of something good! "Alexander, thrilled at Diogenes' answer, asked if there was anything he could do for him. Diogenes, simply requested, "Please move over. You are blocking the sun."

This gives us a small glimpse into the mind of the eccentric, philosopher Diogenes, whose thinking influenced the ancient Greek world and whose own ideas morphed into a deadly, downward spiral that finally led him from Stoicism to Cynicism.

Nevertheless, in ancient Greece, Stoicism became, the noble philosophy of many intellectuals.

Granted, some of its principles, self - control and strength to overcome destructive emotions, are of value to strive for. To be a clear, unbiased thinker who understands universal reason is also a noble ideal, as is the importance of improving one's ethical and moral well-being. Stoicism's idealism requires its followers to be free from anger, envy, and jealousy and to accept all people as equals because all people are products of nature. At face value, this sounds good, but it doesn't recognize that the fallen nature of mankind needs redemption. So, here are the problems. Distorted understandings of human nature and unattainable ideals. In spite of all the idealistic, philosophical rhetoric, no one could actually follow its demands. This left the Stoics and others frustrated, still searching and unfulfilled. They needed salvation.

In this respect, the Stoics were like the Jews who, because of man's fallen nature, could not keep the law perfectly either. So, they too, were left frustrated, unfulfilled and in spiritual despair.

Happily, at the right time, Jesus Christ and His Church came bringing the good news. And by the third century, Stoicism, as a philosophy to replace religion, faded. Jesus had pointed the way, 'You must be born again."

However, during Jesus's ministry, Stoicism was still influential, continuing into the apostolic era until it faded in about 300 A.D. So, it is very likely there were Stoics in the crowd when Jesus performed the miracle in today's scripture. (And knowing about the influence of Stoicism and Hellenistic Philosophy during the time of Jesus and the apostolic era, helps explain some otherwise obscure writings in the New Testament.) The Stoics felt alone, subjected to the forces of nature, while still trying to follow Stoic propositions. Not good. Impossible to achieve. If unchecked Stoicism leads to cynicism and finally to Nihilism. You say, who would ever think that life could be understood this way? Well, read Solomon's book of Ecclesiastes. It opens with,

"The words of the Teacher, son of David, king of Jerusalem: "Meaningless! Meaningless," says the Teacher. "'Utterly meaningless! Everything is meaningless."

Are these words really in the Bible? Yes, they are. And by king Solomon? And yes, and it seems that Solomon has gone ranting; but don't stop reading yet. Read Ecclesiastes to its dramatic end and Solomon writes:

"Now all has been heard; here is the conclusion of the matter: Fear God and keep his commandments, for this is the whole duty of man. For God will bring every deed into judgment, including every hidden thing, whether it is good or evil."

In the beginning of Ecclesiastes, the teacher, Solomon, addresses life's meaning from a purely secular point of view. Its cynical tone continues until toward the end of the book. So, where is wisdom in this writing? It is this. Without God everything is meaningless. A similar conclusion was reached by the Stoics, but their fatalistic thinking gave no hope.

Thankfully, Solomon, goes further than the Stoics, that life does have meaning because he instructs his pupils to fear God. And since fearing God has meaning, keeping God's commandments also has meaning. Therefore, our life has meaning because God feels it important enough to keep account of it, even every hidden thing.

So, Solomon finally concludes, 'For this is the whole duty of man." This is Solomon's understanding of life and God's commandments summed up in one word, 'duty." And we should remember, Solomon reached his conclusions, under law, long before Jesus Christ came into the world and the coming of the Age of Grace. Solomon didn't know grace. He knew law.

So, under law, Solomon's line of reasoning makes sense in that it points readers toward God.

Stoicism does not do this, and while some of its prescriptive ideas are noble, they can't enable someone to follow their ideals. And still worse, its followers are left abandoned to frustration and despair, trying to deal with life by totally controlling or eliminating emotion.

This Stoic attempt at control led to the mind/body dualism of the Greek philosophers. We know today this is impossible. Emotions are part of being human. Scientific tests have shown that we can't even think without emotion. The Achilles heel in Greek Hellenism and Stoicism, is the person' inability to realize its ideals in actual practice. This led to frustration, cynicism and fatalism which has led some, even today, to Nihilism, doing away with life. Still, you may be asking, "Are Hellenism and Stoicism still important in today's world?" Yes, be assured, these ancient ideas, often clothed in different terms, are still influencing many people today.

What the world needs is Jesus. He can ge peace in a war weary world, hope instead of despair, love in place of fear. The problem is that people need to realize their spiritual need; then they will be ready to accept Christ. As Christians, that is what we did.

So, the Stoics, going through life seeking secular answers to meaning and wisdom through strict discipline and faith in nature, are left frustrated with a sense of despair because they can't measure up to their own ideals.

Attempting to be indifferent to pain or pleasure, gritting their teeth in painful silence, amidst the perplexing uncertainties of life, the Stoics are left comfortless without hope. Why? Because human logic, bereft of Divine revelation, leads the mind and soul to a sense of hopelessness. This is why Solomon, in his book Ecclesiastics, assuming the role of the Teacher, declares in unvarnished language, "All is vanity and vexation of spirit."

Shocking? Yes, it is. But no need to panic since the coming of Jesus, we are now privileged to live in a new Dispensation, the Age of Grace. Easily available to us are many writings in the New Testament containing spiritual wisdom and hope. For example, in I Peter 2:9 we read:

"But you are a chosen people, a royal priesthood, a holy nation, a people belonging: to God, that you may declare the praises of him who called you out of darkness into his wonderful light."

Be assured, some of the secular philosophy courses in universities, including Stoicism do not answer or properly address the question as to why we are here, let alone approach the catechetical question, "What is the chief end of man?" - Joyfully, we have the beautiful, wise answer, "The chief end of man is to glorify God and enjoy him forever."

Stoicism, in its attempts to be a successful moral/ethical system, fails miserably when it tries to replace religion because meaning is all about a personal, spiritual relationship. Where Jesus said, "I and the Father are one," and "I am in you and you are in me," is an insight into the spiritual realm and about a beautiful, Dine, relationship. This relationship is unknown to the secular mind because it is spiritually discerned.

So, Stoicism, and other strains of human wisdom that seek understanding purely through ideas and systems of thought fail. Why? Because these ideas and teachings are devoid of a Divine relationship, with the One who makes a Divine relationship possible, our heavenly Father.

The writer of the book of Hebrews said it well. In describing the hope of eternal life through Jesus Christ, our heavenly high priest, he wrote, "The new is better than the old." Indeed, it is!

Today's scripture teaches us about Divinely inspired hope and about a loving, caring God who, indeed, does experience emotions as part of his loving nature. After all, "God is love," not merely an attribute of God. It is who God is and as our heavenly Father, wants the best for us. God's love is shown in today's miracle lives on where Jesus, in great love takes care of a humanly impossible situation. As we enter the scene:

Jesus Sees the Need - and is deeply moved because he sees the humanly impossible situation.

The young man is dead, But Jesus knows that though the end of life in this world is everyone's experience, he is, ""the resurrection and the life." What is the situation here?

His mother is a widow. So, it is likely that her son was her only means of support since during this period of time widows often went begging and some entered prostitution to survive. At any rate, Jesus knew their circumstances. He had the opportunity to save their desperate situation and affirm his power over death and life.

The young man's mother was grieving and in great despair - and the community, also grieving, was unable to change her situation and bring the man back from the dead. Now, during this time of grief and desperation, Jesus arrives on the scene and:

Jesus Performs a Miracle. He Raises Her Son from the Dead Instantly their circumstances were changed! Jesus met the needs of both of them, performing his first miracle of restoring someone to life.

Jesus took command of the situation Everyone else was helpless to do anything.

A miracle resulted - demonstrating Jesus' power over death and life.

Jesus gave the young man back to his mother - and it was a touching moment. Thinking her son was gone, never to return, there he stood restored to life.

The Crowd Saw the Miracle And remember, there were actually two crowds, the large crowd that followed Jesus and the great crowd of townspeople with the widow. This means there were many, many witnesses to this miracle, the first raising from the dead that Jesus did. There was certainly no doubting what happened. Talk about a crowd of witnesses! Multitudes of people knew what they saw, and their reaction was how we would certainly respond.

The crowd was filled with awe. A kind of fear seized them because they knew this wasn't a trick. The young man, who had died, was being carried to his grave on a stretcher. Then, wonderful to behold, Jesus, God incarnate, Creator God, restored life right before their eyes. They saw the power of death broken and the restoring power of life overcoming it.

Did the crowd praise Jesus for the miracle? No, they did not. Why not? After all, they saw Jesus perform a miracle with their own eyes. However, they still perceived Jesus as a prophet, merely a vessel of God. But the large crowd from town and the large crowd that followed Jesus all saw the miracle and, of course, it was astounding! There was no doubting the event so:

The crowd praised God for the miracle They saw Jesus as the channel through which God restored the man back to life. And we should take note that Jesus did say, on other occasions, that everything he said and did came from his Father in heaven. So,

The crowd exclaimed, "A great prophet has risen among us." and "God has come to help his people:' So, could there be another reason for this miracle? Yes, for every miracle that Jesus did, there were broader, more far-reaching implications than the miracle itself.

Remember, that during this same time John the Baptist was in prison. He was isolated, inside prison walls, wondering what was happening to Jesus and the events surrounding him. Scripture does tell us.

"John's disciples had told him about all these things; so, John sent two of his disciples to the Lord asking, "'Are you he who is to come, or are we to look for another?'"

It appears that, under the strain of prison with its uncertainty, John had doubts. He needed some affirmation. Was Jesus really the Messiah as he had previously declared at Jesus' baptism? What would Jesus say? Would he, with reasoning, try to defend who he was? No. Instead, he recounted his many miracles and ended his remarks by showing keen insight into the minds of the people he was trying to reach. He told John:

"The poor have the Good News told to them; and blessed is he who does not find a stumbling -block in me." - It appears Jesus is confirming his Messiahship to John.

Today's scripture began with a deceased young man, his desperate mother and a large crowd in mourning, but it ended with a miracle and an amazed crowd. There were, without a doubt, mixed in the crowd, unbelieving Stoics, Greek Hellenists and other nonbelievers, who viewed life fatalistically and without hope of eternal life. Here, they witnessed a miracle and it totally upset their fatalistic thinking. They were forced to rethink their feeling of hopelessness.

Here, right in front of them, was hope. Jesus had the power over death and life.

And with great power, as is this miracle, Jesus sent his Holy Spirit to live within us, to be among us and to transform us daily. Be assured, spiritual growth is, itself, a great miracle. It changes us to become more like Christ!

God loves us. He cares about us which is why he gives life amidst despair. We know this because he sent his Son to the cross for our sins, to literally love us into the kingdom; he taught us the power of prayer, and to experience him in our own lives.

We experience answers to prayer, miracles in our own lives and in the lives of others. And we experience the wonder of personal transformation as we grow in faith, praying, living in the Spirit and rejoicing as we go from glory unto glory! Isn't salvation grand!

The Challenge of Truth

Scripture lesson: Jeremiah 29: 1-17 g John 8: 31-36

Text: Jeremiah 29: 9

Today's scripture reminds us of the problem of false news. Because of this problem we tend to doubt any news item we hear or read and frustrating to legitimate broadcasters and journalists who really try to be accurate and truthful. And it seems to be a problem worldwide.

Some time ago on televised news, someone made one of the most outrageous, deceptively false statements I have ever heard. Information was given out that was obviously false and this person, facetiously trying to defend it, calmly described the falsehood as an alternate truth. An alternate truth! I couldn't believe my ears. Talk about deception, blatant misinformation! There is no such thing as an alternate truth! An alternate interpretation? Yes, Certainly, there are different ways of looking at any subject or problem. So, what is the problem? How to regard the base line. The information is either accurate or it is not; it is truthful, or it is false, real or an illusion. But to categorize any information as an alternate truth is sheer nonsense! Why? The very definition of truth means that it stands alone as an absolute. Someone may ask, "What about interpretations?" A legitimate question, but interpretation is entirely different. An interpretation is a person's understanding of something; and there may be many different understandings or interpretations. Truth itself is different. Truth stands alone because it is an absolute. Truth is truth. So, we easily conclude that truth is God breathed and scripture is Divinely inspired.

Away with any system that tries to dilute logic into shades of gray. Why? Because such an approach implies that you can't really know anything. It is thought that Socrates started this idea and Plato continued it. Their problem? As I see it, they didn't know Divine inspiration, have spiritual understandings and, apparently, rejected the reality gen by their senses. So, borrowing a British term, I say, balderdash! English translation, nonsense! Scripture teaches us, "You shall know the truth and the truth will set you free." That you and I can know the truth, ultimate truth, not an opinion, not mere perception, the absolute truth. Truth exists without qualification. It stands alone. As an absolute, it does not allow for an alternate. Why? The alternate would have to be inaccurate and would lower the pristine quality of truth to mere opinion or interpretation. An alternate truth is impossible because truth is an absolute!

Certainly, there is more than one way of looking at something, whether it is a situation or problem, but in the end, something is either true or it is false. In these, often confusing times, we must constantly remind ourselves, there is no such a thing as alternate truth. Some ideas and proclamations are false, and sometimes just propaganda or various perceptions of an event or an idea, but truth itself, has no alternate.

To try to fool the public with such an obviously false remark is outrageous and an insult to the public's intelligence; but alas, this kind of distortion is not new. It has been used by unscrupulous leaders down through the centuries. It has been and is still considered an allowable practice by some high-ranking officials in governments of the- world. It can be found in their manuals and is widely distributed in the world's universities. It teaches that, at their discretion, it is all right for government leaders to lie and decree the public if they feel it is necessary.

And there is one treatise that has had more influence than all the rest, the document called, "The Prince." It has influenced leaders all over the world and is found in universities and public libraries virtually everywhere. Who wrote it? Here is your answer.

In 1532 Di Niccolo Machiavelli published a political treatise that he called "The Prince." The general themes of his treatise are that the aims of princes are glory and survival, and these are important enough to justify the use of immoral means to achieve those ends.

Flat out, Machiavelli is really saying, "'the end, "'glory and survival," justifies any means to achieve them." He then describes his idea of the way a virtuous Roman can hold on to a newly acquired province or land even if taken by force. Machiavelli uses the Roman republic as his example and from it he teaches how new princes can act to assure and maintain their position of power. Here is his advice to the new prince:

1. Install colonies of one's people there. This means of the same tribe or same country, and smacks of racism or a kind of tribalism. Next, he advises the prince,

2. Indulge the lesser powers without increasing their power - being friendly with lower government officials to gain their confidence and better control them. Further, he advises:

3. Put down powerful people, - never being defense and always attacking anyone who criticizes or disagrees with you. Attack relentlessly critical leaders, putting them down so to undermine the public's confidence in them.

This was an important tactic of the former Soviet Union and is still being used.

While there loomed the real threat of war, the Soviets really wanted rival nations to lose faith in their established institutions. That way they could win without firing a shot. Of course, they haven't succeeded in the U. S., but their calculated threat still remains. Then, the fourth piece of advice Machiavelli gave in his book, "The Prince" was:

4. Do not allow a foreign power to gain reputation to keep a foreign nation at bay and from becoming a threat. Later, after adding some background reasoning to his arguments, Machiavelli wrote,

"'Therefore, a prince must have the means to force his supporters to keep supporting him even when they start having second thoughts, otherwise he will lose power." Later, he writes, "'A prince is praised for keeping his word," but he advises, "'A prince should only keep his word when it suits his purposes, but do his utmost to maintain the illusion that he does keep his word and that he is reliable in that regard." - Then in chapter 15 he writes, "'The prince must appear to be virtuous, and should be ·virtuous, but he should be able to be otherwise when the time calls for it; that includes being able to lie, though however much he lies he should always keep the appearance of being truthful."

These chilling words of advice are read and practiced by some world leaders. Shocking! Yes.

Machiavelli's ideas are totally against the teachings in the Bible, and against the writings of Aristotle and other great thinkers, including the framers of our constitution who, wisely, were for representative government, democracy and a republic that uses representative government. Far from perfect, though it is, thank God we are a democratic republic that practices democracy, the balance of powers, and still seeking to form a more perfect Union. May we never lose this vital deterrent to tyranny even though truth will always have its challenges.

Down through history to the present, some have tried to hide behind the notion that truth is ever evasive, that we cannot know the truth. The Bible says that we can know the truth and the truth will set us free. Truth connects us to the real world.

For example, when during Jesus' trial, he said, "•Everyone on the side of truth listens to me." Pilate, trying to dodge Jesus' statement, responded with, ·'What is truth'?" Then, in a dramatic gesture, going to a basin, he ceremonially washed his hands in front of the angry crowd and declared, "am innocent of this man's blood. It is your responsibility." Not true. It was Pilate's responsibility and he dodged it. He allowed his decision to be made by an angry mob.

Just think how amazing this scene is, while Pilate, was reiterating the age-old question, "What is truth?" the very embodiment of truth was standing right there in front of him.

We know there are professionals who specialize in building and preserving the images of public figures, telling them what to say, when to say and how to say it. We ask. Is image building bad? No. Done honestly for the right reasons, it is good. We all want a good image, but to some people image is everything, even if it is fake. For Christians, this is a problem. We want, not only to know the truth. We want to live truthful lives, our lives exemplifying authenticity, the truth. So, we ask, "How can put my best foot forward without being deceitful?"

The business and political world place enormous emphasis on personal and corporate image. A good, truthful image is a fine goal. Our image should speak the truth about us and not make us feel that we are hiding our real selves. And we do have a right to privacy.

While interacting with someone on a personal level, we may wonder, "What is that person really like? Who is the real person behind the social mask'!" We may even ask ourselves, "Can we ever get to know the real person or are we always left with an image of who they want us to think they are?"

This thinking can sometimes be amusing.

I was surprised to see a clever sign in a tourist shop that read, "Oh God, help me to be the person my dog thinks I am."

As for the truth in social and in other situations, it is sometimes really difficult to discern the truth when something is told to us and sometimes it is stressful to tell the truth when we know it is unpopular to say it.

The prophet Jeremiah found himself in such a situation. He had the difficult task of proclaiming the truth to an unresponsive and unsympathetic Public is similar to difficulties we find ourselves in today while holding and proclaiming Christian standards in front of an unsympathetic public standards can we use? First, prayerfully ask, what does scripture say'? Second, where does reason lead us? Third, how does past tradition inform us? Fourth, how do we balance careful reasoning in light of scriptural truth and with our own life experiences?

Well, Jeremiah knew the truth because God had revealed it to him, and it was up to him to deliver it. But there was another voice, a more popular one, but it was not the voice of truth. It was:

Hananiah's Prophecy- He told the people what they wanted to hear, not what they sorely needed to hear. His message was a self-serving political event, proclaiming what Judah wanted to believe as truth, his version of an alternate truth. He lied to them. Of course,

Hananiah claimed Divine authority. That was what prophets did. He claimed to be the voice of God, also, what the prophets claimed. Hananiah was called to proclaim the truth to the people, but his message was not the truth. He lied.

Hananiah prophesied peace for Judah and the quick destruction of Babylon. He said all this, in the midst of Israel's waywardness, their backslidden condition, their practicing idolatry and their immoral ling.

Hananiah ignored the real problem that the people had They had forsaken the true and Living God and spiritually regressed, going back to their former primitive practices of idolatry and immorality. Hananiah told the people what they wanted to hear instead of the truth. He tried to convince them of an alternate truth and there is no such thing. He lied.

Jeremiah's Prophecy- Jeremiah told the people the truth. Their sinful Living must stop.

Jeremiah, too, claimed Divine authority to be the voice of God, but Jeremiah doesn't overlook their sinful lifestyle. He bravely preaches that their sinful Living must stop. He tells the truth. If they embrace it, they would be set free.

Jeremiah prophesies that because of their sin the tribe of Judah will experience defeat and punishment. King Nebuchadnezzar, a pagan king, will be used as God's instrument in Judah's punishment. Why is this so important? The answer is found in prophecy concerning Jesus. Several hundred years later Jesus would come from the tribe of Judah, and he is called the Lion of the Tribe of Judah.

Judah, as a nation, veered further and further away from God's desired plan for them. Backslidden, out of God's will, Judah lost its spiritual direction and was spiraling spiritually downward. Judah was spiritually desolate. Judah needed to repent.

Denying the truth of the gospel is a downward slippery slope, ending in a bottomless pit of meaninglessness and despair. This is not God's desire for the human race. He wants us to live as people of the way, as true Christians because he is "The Way, The Truth and The Life."

In the Old Testament we read in Proverbs 3:6, "In all your ways acknowledge him and he will make straight your paths."

As we live out our lives, may we prayerfully apply reason and wisdom in the light of scripture.

While living authentic lives, may we proclaim truth we know to a sinful world, to proclaim the Christian message.

It is certainly possible to know truth and possible to live the truth of the gospel. So, let us determine to proclaim and embody this wonderful truth that sets us free, in the name of the Father and of the Son and of the Holy Spirit. Amen!

The Giant King David Couldn't Slay

Scripture lesson: Samuel 21:15-17 Text Sam. 21:17

The nation of Israel began as a Theocracy, which means it was led by prophets and other spiritual leaders, who were, ideally, led by God and were the ultimate authority. But as the twelve tribes grew, they became like a federation of tribes, with each tribe becoming more a law unto themselves. This created fragmentation rather than unification, weakening them militarily.

Surrounding nations, notably the Philistines, posed an increasing threat to this tribal federation of Israelites. For national security, as well as for internal organization, Israel needed to be unified as one nation. This was done. And Saul became the first king of Israel. How does David enter the picture? Employment.

Saul learned to know David, first as his armor bearer and court harpist since David stayed at Saul's court for some time; later, when David returned to his home, he resumed his work in the fields as guardian of the sheep - a shepherd.

Well, it seemed that conflict between the Philistines and Israel's twelve tribes was bound to happen. The predator Philistines and the city of Gath, one of their fe city states, were not far from the encampment of the new nation of Israel. Gath was the home of King Ashish and the Philistine warrior Goliath. (Of recent interest to archaeologists is that the monumental gates of Gath and its surrounding fortifications were finally uncovered in Israel on August 4, 2015, proof that the large city of Gath did indeed exist).

Our narrator continues with mischief arising from the Philistines, a challenge daring anyone from the Israelite army to meet their giant warrior, Goliath, in a duel. No one in Israel dared to face this hulk of a man, until David stepped forward. He slew the giant with his sling and was now, in the eyes of his countrymen, a hero. The result of all this caused Saul to become jealous and fearful of losing his throne. Saul then sought after David and David had to flee for his life. He first went to the priestly city of Nob, then to Gath and with numerous supporters, he went on to hide in the cave of Adullam.

Where were David's parents while he was avoiding Saul's attempts on his life? It is to his credit, and showed moral fiber, that during this time he did not forget his aged parents. He took them to the friendly Moab nation, putting them under the protection of the Moabite King.

The chase of Saul for David continued. And one evening when Saul fell asleep in a cave, David cut a piece from the hem of Saul's garment to show that he could have killed him, but he didn't, even though Saul was after his life. Another time David and his cousin stole into Saul's camp in the hills below Hebron and they actually made off with the kings' own spear. Outwitted again, Saul was furious, frustrated and embarrassed. In Saul's relentless pursuit, David needed to find a place that was safe and he, very cleverly, took refuge, of all places, among the Philistines. Saul wouldn't think to look for him there. David actually became their vassal (a kind of subordinate person in servitude) for a while. Anything to escape Saul's vengeance and determination to kill him.

However, this part of the drama comes to an abrupt end when Saul went to battle in the northern plain of Jezreel and was slain. Remarkably, after all these spine-tingling events, David wrote a moving lament for his dead friend Jonathan and his King and father-in-law for whom he still had admiration and affection.

Go figure!

By the time David became king in 1,000 B.C., international affairs were relatively quiet. Since Egypt's might and prestige were crumbling it was no longer a threat to Israel.

David, genius of a man that he was, musician, writer of psalms, composer of music, statesman, great organizer and excellent businessman, was to establish a kingdom with Jebus (which later became Jerusalem) as the new capital city.

This city was strategic and was the main highway to the east and to this day is venerated by three religious groups. the Jews, the Moslems and the Christians.

Proceeding with his foreign policy, David entered into league with the Phoenicians, principally with Hiram, king of the fabulous city of Tyre. These significant events were of great importance, in part, because the Phoenicians developed the alphabet, derived from Egyptian hieroglyphs, which is similar to what we use today.

All seemed well, a time of progress and peace, but the Philistines marched into the valley of Rephaim, a few miles southwest of Jerusalem. However, they were driven out and when they attacked again, they were driven all the way back to their homeland.

Then, David brought the sacred ark of the covenant to Jerusalem. The Philistines made one more desperate attempt, but David took possession of their city, Gath. Remember Gath? - the home of the Philistine giant Goliath?

From then on, for a while, David had little trouble with them as a nation; but as Israel grew, other nations became nervous and the Ammonites together with the Syrians, attacked Israel. They were defeated and, in the meantime,

David discovered great wealth in the iron and copper mines of Edom. Its ores were useful for many things, not the least were for weapons.

So, over time, David's kingdom grew in spite of continuing skirmishes; but time was taking its toll. David was in his later years. Yet he went out, once again, with his men, to battle the Philistines who were taunting the Israel army with another giant warrior, named Ishbi-Benob, who said he would kill David.

What was to be done? Could David step forward one more time and save the day? Time had taken its toll. The famous shepherd boy, sweet singer of Israel, slayer of Goliath, who finally became King was growing old. And those pesky, Philistines never ceased stirring up trouble. This time, David was, simply, not able to face another giant warrior like Goliath. What was to be done? Would the Philistines finally be able to cause Israel international embarrassment?

Thankfully, no. "Abishai son of Zeruiah came to David's rescue; he struck the Philistine down and killed him." The crisis was over. But an important lesson was learned. David, much older now, was the one who needed to be protected. The lesson was well learned for we read:

Then, David's men swore to him saying, "Never again will you KO out with us to battle. so that the lamp of Israel will not be extinguished."

There comes a time for all of us when we realize we are not just sharing our knowledge, we are teaching the new generation to take our place. This adds a great deal of meaning and depth to what we do and share. Many things are caught by example rather than taught by precept.

So, the question arises. Are we bearing our responsibility so that, when we finally step down, the younger generation will be well equipped to seize the mantle of responsibility and caring? Will they share the gospel message and exemplary Christian Living to their generation as we did for them?

Our task, indeed, the task of the Church, the world over, involves both nature and nurture. Believing in Christ as our Savior and following him changes our nature. Teaching the Bible by example and by precept is nurture.

So, let's be clear, nurturing and caring are the main responsibilities of the Church. From birth to baptism to understanding and embracing the Christian faith, nothing is more important than nurturing, caring and sharing!

From being a young inexperienced warrior of the cross, to becoming an older, wiser one is crucial to the life of every believer and to the life of the Church.

Contrary to some misguided subcultures of today, the Church, and society at large, needs the old wise head! On a practical note, for example, the young may have an excellent understanding of technology. The older wise head can often ge them the wisdom to use it properly.

Broadly, the task of the church is caring for our generation in every way. This includes the new, fragile young children, the vibrant young adults, and the mature older adults whose energy is not what it once was in their youth.

The task in the Church's spiritual life is active love in the context of prevention - to train the young and guide them in the right way and to set them on a proper spiritual path. The task of the Church is as protector and overseer of the spiritual lives of all in their care. The task of the Church is caring and healing - to help each other when we fail and hold each other up in prayer and support because we all need help at one time or another. This is our task! May God help us to do it well! We all, at one time or another, need help with the challenge of a threatening situation in our lives that looms big like the giant enemy warriors of David's time. May we seek the Lord for help and strength, and may we be available to help one another when the task seems too great for us.

Jerusalem's Last Chance

Scripture lesson: Luke 19:28-43 Text Luke 19: 44b

Luke's scriptural account shows Jesus as an assassination target. How could this be? This wise teacher, this Rabbi who went around teaching love and caring, who taught his followers righteous ling, who healed the sick and bound up the broken hearted, who was so in touch with his feelings that at Lazarus' tomb he wept. And later, overlooking Jerusalem, he wept again. This Jesus, who taught his disciples how to pray, who had the power to forge sins, was now the target of a plot designed to kill him. We question why? Why would anyone even think to do such a thing to this wise, caring, kind, loving man?

Jesus' words of wisdom had such power that they moved thousands toward believing in him. The result? He came to be perceived as a threat to established religion. In short, the power structure of the religious community wanted him gone. You may ask. What about the Roman government? At this time, it couldn't care less. But this was not the case with some people in the religious community.

Along with this bias, Jesus knew that after all the healing miracles he had done and after all the things he had taught his disciples about the kingdom of God, one of his chosen twelve disciples was going to betray him. Yet, Jesus showed such supreme love that even at the last supper he invited Judas, the devious betrayer to participate in the meal.

In spite of his personal example of grace and love, and his very existence in jeopardy, Jesus continued to move toward his destiny with deliberate intent. How could he do this? Totally contrary to what a natural reaction would be, but he moved forward because he knew he was following his Father's will. And this knowledge did not make his mission any easier. However, Jesus continued to move forward with unwavering assurance.

At such a critical time it was necessary for Jesus to have a crystal-clear conception of who he was and an awareness of the magnitude of his mission. Just what was his mission? Jesus was to carry the sins of the entire human race, past, present and future on the cross.

And strangely, after this singular event, the sacrificial system of the Jewish nation was abolished after his death. And this happened after the emperor Titus conquered Jerusalem and sacked the temple in A.O. 70, just as Jesus had predicted. And it is worth noting that this temple has not been rebuilt after over 2,000 years, with the evidence of piles of stones at the temple's base still in a heap like trash. We saw the piles of stones on our trip to the Holy Land.

Further, Jesus' own identity could not be derived from anyone else's conception of who he was. He realized that many of his followers did not really know who he was, and some allowed their own religious prejudices to keep them spiritually blinded. The truth was present among them; "the way, the truth and the life," but many did not see it.

Yet, despite their rejection, and misunderstandings concerning his profound teachings of the Kingdom of God, Jesus moved on with great deliberation toward his destiny. His teaching, "My kingdom is not of this world,' has stood the test of time and still stands today.

So, Jesus moved with great deliberation toward his destiny. From the selecting of his twelve disciples, to gaining a following of thousands, we find Matthew and Mark reporting that as Jesus was leaving Jericho, there was already, "a great multitude" following him.

Then, in the final stretch of his journey, sitting along the path, we hear the blind beggar, Bartimaeus, calling out incessantly, "Son of David, have mercy on me." He pleads, "Master, let me receive my sight." Jesus replies, "Go your way: your faith has made you well." (Mark 10:47). Bartimaeus, sight restored, now joins the others on the journey.

And happily, Mark records, "He followed Jesus on the way." From being blind both physically and spiritually, he is now a fellow pilgrim travelling to Jerusalem. What a wonderful, miraculous event this was! It illustrates Jesus restoring physical sight and restoring spiritual sight as well. So, we find that Bartimaeus has joined the others travelling to Jerusalem.

As they travelled, they came to Bethphage, where unnamed villagers provided a donkey for Jesus to ride on, and on to Bethany (also near Jerusalem) where more pilgrims began to follow Jesus in a grand entourage. Onward they went finally to the Mount of Olives where:

Jesus Enters Jerusalem - With such large following, surely, he would enter with great fanfare on a magnificent steed, a war horse, demonstrating an image of might and power, as was typical of the emperors and generals of the day. But, no, Jesus enters quietly on a borrowed donkey, "upon which no one had ever sat." In doing this, he fulfilled the prophecy of Zechariah. 9:9. You ask, but why did he do this? Why did he not show the power and authority of which he certainly was capable? Scripture teaches and the old gospel song proclaims, "He could have called ten thousand angels." The answer?

Jesus did not need to enter on a war horse He didn't need to ride on a horse to show his earthly power. His kingdom is not of this world. It is far above this temporal existence, confined by time. Even his message of peace passes beyond all understanding. Jesus' message teaches love, humility and peace, not war and disrespect of other human beings.

Jesus rides amidst rejoicing and praise from his disciples and believing followers. Some began to see the spiritual light of it all; that Jesus was their hope and so they chanted and sang "Hosanna," which means save us now. Even with their spiritual eyes only partly open, they began to glimpse Jesus as their Savior. And:

Jesus chooses to enter Jerusalem In spite of criticism from those Pharisees, who were determined to maintain their religious strangle hold on the people. In spite of the possible retributions from the Roman government. In spite of Jesus' many followers whom he knew would later forsake him and flee, Jesus enters Jerusalem. He enters from the Mount of Olives, the very place where the Old Testament prophets declared the Messiah was expected to enter.

Now picture this amazing scene; Jesus had just healed Bartimaeus who was blind and is now happily following him with the other pilgrims. But this happy scene changes when, from the Mount of Olives, overlooking the city, Jesus began to weep, not ordinary tears, but deep sobbing from within. He experiences deep rejection. Why is he weeping?

Jesus Weeps Over Jerusalem because he sees that this is Jerusalem's last chance for spiritual restoration and for peace before the impending disaster that now was certain to come to them. Here are Jesus' words as recorded in Matthew 23:37-39,

"O Jerusalem, Jerusalem, you who kill the prophets and stone those sent to you, how often I have longed to gather your children together, as a hen gathers her chicks under her wings, but you were not willing. Look, your house is left desolate. For I tell you, you will not see me again until you say, 'Blessed is he who comes in the name of the Lord.'

Yes, Jesus weeps He weeps because he cares so much.

A Jesus weeps over their spiritual blindness - even after he had just healed a blind man restoring his sight.

He weeps because he knows their opportunity to accept him has passed. They are spiritually blinded by political, religious, and cultural prejudices.

He weeps because he knows their fate - that they brought it on themselves.

Jesus Prophesies Concerning Jerusalem's Fall He foresees the destruction of the temple, the sacking of the entire city of Jerusalem and the utter chaos that would occur there. The city did fall in A.D. 70 along with the temple built by Herod the Great!

Sadly, over two thousand years have passed and there is still no real peace in Jerusalem. The piles of stones from the walls are still there as a silent reminder of Jesus' prophecy.

But there is hope today! Someday Jesus will return, will restore all things and there will be a new creation! Now, as we return to the scene where Jesus prophesied concerning Jerusalem, he declared,

"Your enemies will surround you." - Like he was saying, "You only think you are in control. God is really in control." Then Jesus continues:

"Your enemies will destroy you and this city." - Again, it was like Jesus was saying,

"The power and control you cling to so tightly will be gone." Finally, Jesus said,

"This will happen because you did not recognize the day when God visited you." But this did not include the followers of Jesus; they could express his presence in their lives, like the old gospel song, "It is joy unspeakable and full of Glory."

Yes, as Jesus entered Jerusalem. the crowds of people shouted, "Hosanna to the King of Kings," - believers lovingly laid palm branches on the ground before him.

History was made that day when, with supreme bravery, deliberation and a Divine sense of purpose, Jesus rode into Jerusalem. Though crowds cheered, some criticized and some of the authorities even tried to stop the cheering, but Jesus rode on triumphantly, and peacefully through the streets of Jerusalem, undaunted. Jesus knew who he was. He knew he was God incarnate, God in human flesh come to be with us here on the earth. And the greatest miracle of all, our salvation, through the cross and his resurrection, was soon to take place.

Religious prejudice strongly held customs, spiritual blindness and fighting for power caused many religious leaders and others to fail to see Jesus as he really was. Peter, James and John had a special privilege concerning this on the Mount of Transfiguration.

What a shame for those who didn't know Jesus, who refused to believe! Yet, those who saw Jesus as their Messiah, were overjoyed.

Today, we celebrate this great historic event, Palm Sunday, as believers who have great cause to rejoice.

Jesus is indeed our Messiah, our King of Kings and our Lord of Lords who came to save the world. And that means you and me. There is no greater love than this!

Joy in the Morning

Scripture lesson: John 20:1-18 Text: John 20: 18a

It seemed like an ordinary day. Yet sadness was in the air. It was:

"On the first day of the week, very early in the morning, the women took the spices they had prepared and went to the tomb. They found the stone rolled away from the tomb, but when they entered, they did not find the body of the Lord Jesus. While they were wondering about this, suddenly two men in clothes that gleamed like lightening stood beside them. In their fright the women bowed down with their faces to the ground, but the men said to them "Why do you look for the Living among the dead? He is not here; he has risen!"

It was Mary Magdalene, Joanna, Mary the mother of James, and the others with them who told this to the apostles. But they did not believe the women, because their words seemed to them like nonsense. Peter, however, got up and ran to the tomb.

Bending over, he saw the strips of linen lying by themselves, and he went away, wondering to himself what had happened."

What a wonderful day is today, Easter Sunday, a day to celebrate Jesus' resurrection and his victory over evil and saving everyone who believes in him. Think about it! Jesus has sealed our salvation forever! This is why we, as Christians, have such inner peace and great joy.

In today's account, after Jesus' trial, his crucifixion as the final sacrifice for sin, buried in the tomb of Joseph of Arimathea, he then, on the third day, arose from the grave, demonstrating his Deity and proving his teaching, "The Father and I are One, "

Without a doubt, this is the greatest miracle in the history of the world. But some folks still have secret doubts. Why? There is the desire for visible evidence. In court cases, circumstantial evidence can be compelling and physical evidence can also be convincing. With Christians it is a matter of faith.

All over the world, Christianity declares the resurrection event to be true, but some still do not believe. So, let's take a step-by-step journey into this amazing event. Assuming the biblical records tell the story with sincerity, we may ask, what about witnesses? Recorded in scripture, are many who witnessed Jesus' death and, over fe hundred who witnessed his resurrection! Then, after the Day of Pentecost, empowered by the Holy Spirit, the disciples began to carry the gospel to the world.

Mark's gospel tells us that even the centurion Roman soldier, who stood by Jesus as he died, attested to his death and affirmed Jesus' real identity when he exclaimed, "Surely this man was the Son of God." It was almost as if he impulsively blurted it out! Think of the implications, He said this after participating in Jesus' actual crucifixion! He stood there witnessing Jesus die in front of him on the cross, the cross he had helped erect! Yes, he was a trained Roman soldier, but he was nevertheless, human. I believe the situation finally got to him impelling to exclaim, "Surely, this man was the Son of God!"

After the Roman soldiers, who did the actual act of crucifixion, took Jesus down from the cross, placing him in a sepulcher, or tomb, following orders, they rolled a large, heavy, disk shaped, stone covering its opening. Following standard Roman procedure, the stone was then sealed at its edges by rope and wax, making entry unlawful and subject to severe punishment. (On our trip to Israel, my wife and I stood at the empty tomb entrance, saw the heavy stone and the grooved track that guided the stone to seal the tomb.)

Pilate, in command, instructed the Roman soldiers to guard the tomb. knowing if they failed in their duty, they would be subject to execution, literally guarding the tomb with their lives. Roman military training was strict and Roman law was severe.

Pilate's situation was also tenuous. The Jews, wanting Jesus crucified, put pressure on him saying, "If you let this man go, you are no friend of Caesar." What was this political statement about? Pilate, appointed by Sejanus, was plotting to overthrow Caesar!

Learning of this, Caesar had Sejanus and his appointees executed. Now, the circumstances were obvious. Pilate was in no position to get into trouble with Rome and the Jews, who through their lying, had led Pilate into the dilemma. He mistakenly thought, that if he released Jesus instead of Barabbas and word got to Rome that, Jerusalem was in rebellion, led by Jesus, he would be the first to go. So, to save his own skin, Pilate turned Jesus over to be executed. Thus, the accuracy of gospel account was confirmed! And explains the Jews threatening remark, "If you let this man go, you are no friend of Caesar." Pilate was out to save his own life. If Sejanus could be executed, so could he!

So, Jesus was crucified. And as time passed on to the first day of the week, this is when, early in the morning, Mary and others came to the tomb needing someone to roll the stone back so she could enter with her spices to prepare the body. To her amazement she saw:

The Open Tomb - The heavy stone with the seal around it, was rolled away. The Roman soldiers were not able to keep the tomb sealed. Powerful forces were at work!

Mary looked in amazement. There was the tomb, empty. But where was the body of her Lord? Jesus was definitely not there.

Quickly she ran to tell Peter and John. And as with all Jesus' followers, they too, were afraid. To them, all hope was gone, and they were left mourning the loss of their Master. However, an astonishing turn of events was about to unfold. Mary arrived and told them the wonderful, good news. The tomb was empty! What was their response?

Immediately, Peter and John left her and ran to the tomb. Why did they do this? Mary's testimony not convincing? The situation was incredible. Peter and John just had to see for themselves. They wanted proof. But then, could it be that what Jesus had predicted really did happen? Probably out of breath, Peter and John arrived at the tomb; then, the reality of Mary's story loomed large. There, right in front of them, was the scene just as she had told them. They saw:

The Empty Tomb - with the heavy stone rolled away from the entrance. Their Lord, having been placed there lovingly by Joseph of Arimathea, was not there. What, then, did they see as they gazed inside?

They saw the empty grave clothes nested neatly, in place, the graveclothes were lying there, "still in their folds." World authority, Dr. Wm. Barclay, explains that the Greek text, "still in their folds," means it was as if someone had literally vaporized out of them. And the latest three-dimensional photographs of the Shroud of Turin show the same thing, as if someone had vaporized out of the grave clothes. This finding gives us pause to reflect. And:

John saw the empty tomb, the grave clothes and believed! Yet, there were many unanswered questions. The disciples were astonished and confused. The reality of it had not sunk in yet, that Jesus was risen from the dead, as he told them.

We wonder why they didn't understand. After all, Jesus' resurrection was prophesied in the Old Testament, as in David's Psalm 16, verses 9 and 10, "therefore, my heart is glad and my tongue rejoices: my body also will rest secure, because you will not abandon me to the grave, nor will you let your Holy One see decay." The apostle Peter preached from this very passage in Acts 2:25-28,

"I saw the Lord always before me. Because he is at my right hand, I will not be shaken. Therefore, my heart is glad, and my tongue rejoices: my body will live in hope, because you will not abandon me to the grave, nor will you let your Holy One see decay. You have made known to me the paths of life: you will fill me with joy in your presence."

This prophetic, Messianic interpretation is also found in another relevant passage, Chapter 53 of Isaiah. It begins with "Who has believed our message and to whom has the arm of the Lord been revealed?" Later, more detail unfolds in verse 9:

"He was assigned a grave with the wicked, and with the rich in his death, though he had done no violence, nor was any deceit in his mouth. Yet it was the Lord's will to crush him and cause him to suffer, and though the Lord makes his life a guilt offering, he will see his offspring and prolong his days. Therefore, I will ge him a portion among the great, and he will divide the spoils with the strong, because he poured out his life with the transgressors. For he bore the sin of many and made intercession for the transgressors."

And earlier in Isaiah, Chapter 52:7, we read these wonderful words:

"How beautiful on the mountains are the feet of those who bring good news, who proclaim peace, who bring good tidings, who proclaim salvation, who say to Zion, 'Your God reigns.' "

It is puzzling that with all the Old Testament passages pointing to Jesus, the disciples still didn't understand why he died and God's plan of salvation for the world. However, one thing was certain. The tomb was empty. Jesus was not there.

Peter and John went back to their lodgings with great wonderment and with many questions. But they were soon to have their eyes opened further.

And at this point, Mary still thought that Jesus was dead and did not know where his body was. She wanted to do the proper thing and care for his body with spices. Little did she realize that she was about to meet:

The Risen Lord! - As John's gospel has it:

Peter and John had left. Mary, now alone, stood weeping outside the tomb.

Looking into the tomb she saw two angels who spoke to her. Then,

She hears a voice ask, "Woman, why are you crying?" "Who are you looking for?" Mary answers, "They have taken the Lord out of the tomb, and I don't know where they have put him." At this, she turned around and saw Jesus standing there, but, likely in the early dawn light, thought he was the gardener, she said, "Sir, if you have carried him away, tell me where you have put him, and I will get him." Jesus said to her, 'Mary.' She turned toward him and cried out in Aramaic, "Rabboni" (My Master).

After Mary's glorious encounter with Jesus at the tomb, she went directly to tell the disciples of her remarkable experience. Mary was now an eyewitness!

She could proclaim with great authority, "I have seen the Lord." Many others, too, witnessed the resurrected Lord. In fact, over 500 people saw the resurrected Christ.

The world is always looking for true witnesses, prime sources. Here they are in the biblical record, along with countless millions of Christians, who down through the ages, testify how Jesus the Christ has transformed their lives.

May we include ourselves among them as we say, "He is risen!"

The Power of Resolve

Scripture: Joshua 24:13-15; Romans 8:35-38

Joshua, chapter 23, describes the current peaceful state of Israel and that Joshua, now advanced in years, wishes to leave them with some final words of wisdom: "After a long time had passed and the Lord had gen Israel rest from all their enemies around them, Joshua, by then old and well advanced in years, summoned all Israel - their elders, leaders, judges, and officials - and said to them: 'I am old and well advanced in years.'

Realistic about his age, Joshua recognizes that his time on earth is short and wants to ge his fellow Israelites some important parting words. He begins by reminding them that their victories are a result of God's help, so,

Joshua reminds them of the source of their victories He declares,

"It was the Lord who fought for you ... 'Be very strong, be careful to obey all that is written in the Book of the Law of Moses. So, be careful to love the Lord, your God ... Now I am about to go the way of all the earth. You know with all your heart and soul that not one of the good promises the Lord your God gave you has failed. Every promise has been fulfilled; not one has failed. But just as all the good things that the Lord your god promised have been fulfilled for you, so the Lord will bring upon you all the bad things, until he has destroyed you from this good land that the Lord your God has gen you. If you transgress the covenant of the Lord our God, which he enjoined on you, and go and serve other gods and bow down to them, then the anger of the Lord will be kindled against you, and you shall perish quickly from the good land he has gen o you."... "Then Joshua, assembling all the tribes of Israel at Shechem and reminding them again of God's works among them, declared, "Now fear the Lord and serve him with all faithfulness. Throw away the gods your forefathers worshipped beyond the river and in Egypt and serve the Lord....

Joshua requires them to make a vital, spiritual decision - It would involve the future spiritual direction of their nation, placing the responsibility on them. He continues,

"But if serving the Lord seems undesirable to you, then choose for yourselves this day whom you will serve, whether the gods your forefathers served beyond the river, or the gods of the Amorites, in whose land you are ling. But as for me and my household, we will serve the Lord." Then the people answered, "Far be it from us to forsake the Lord to serve other gods....

This was the answer Joshua wanted to hear so:

In an ancient time, perhaps around a campfire enclosed with stones, someone discovered that heat applied to certain rocks containing powders, we now know as oxides, would change the powders into a hard substance that could be worked and shaped. It was amazing! It was like magic to them. Heat changed the powder, iron oxide, into iron and thus the iron age was born. The heat drove out the oxygen leaving a pure hard metal, iron.

Metal refinement is an amazing process. When I worked at the Gospel Publishing House in Springfield Missouri, as a young man working my way through school, one of my jobs was to work the lead furnace. Lead was used to make pipe shaped molds, about the size of baseball bats, called pigs, which were put into linotype machines. The machine would re-melt the lead and the typist would type words on the top edge of domino shaped slugs, which were then arranged into columns, and finally made into pages for printing.

In order to do this, heat was applied to the reusable scrap lead and new pigs were made by pouring the lead into long, narrow molds. An interesting process. The heat melted the lead and that caused the dry ink and other impurities, to rise to the top to be skimmed off, leaving pure lead that was then poured into the molds to go back to the linotype operator.

This is similar to the way gold is refined. Heat causes the impurities to rise to be skimmed off leaving the pure gold. The apostle Peter uses this excellent example as to how our faith is refined. (How interesting. Peter, the fisherman, knew about metal refinement.) Then Peter proceeds to teach that the purpose of suffering for Christ is:

To bring praise and glory to the God of our salvation Today, as we live out our lives, we call our faith journey, we have not seen Jesus, yet we love him and believe in him. Partly because, in a very real spiritual sense, we experience his presence. This is the marvelous relationship we have with the Lord; and Peter, relating his own experience, as a fellow Christian, exclaims:

We Are Filled with Inexpressible Joy! - How does he arrive at this conclusion, in spite of all the persecution he has experienced? It is spiritual insight when he says,

"For you are receiving the goal of your faith." - This is making Christians aware of spiritual process working in them, the work of the Holy Spirit. All of this - "For the salvation of your souls." - Peter reminds them of the most important thing, their salvation, not to be neglected or forgotten. Then, he reminds them of the words of the prophets saying,

The prophets spoke of this salvation and the grace that was to come to us. Down through the ages, sometimes separated by hundreds of years, the prophets spoke of the coming of the Messiah. And he has come; praise be to his name!

The income of a successful fisherman, who owned the boat and the net, would be 40% and the rest would go to the crew. The researcher Murphy-0-Conner tells us that Simon Peter and Andrew's fishing operation worked in partnership with James and John, the sons of Zebedee, who had employees. That these were men of substance is confirmed, in part, by the quality and size of the house at Capernaum, known as Peter's house, which is larger than most of the other houses that have been excavated in Capernaum. The guides for the Holy Land will take you to see the house, which is part of the tour.

So, when Jesus said, "Follow me and I will make you fishers of men," he knew exactly what he was doing. He chose the right persons for the great task that would lay before them, and as hard-working men, with many different abilities, Jesus knew they could become world changers, and they have!

Could they do this right away? No. This would be possible much later after three years of education with Jesus, the master teacher. Now, after Jesus' ascension, we hear Peter, who now has become a strong apostolic leader, addressing a hurting, persecuted, and scattered Church. He speaks encouraging words. He tells them," You are "God's elect." Oh, how they needed to hear that!

And Peter reminds them that although they chose to follow Jesus, he first chose them!

They were chosen through the sanctifying (purifying), work of the Holy Spirit for obedience to Jesus Christ and the sprinkling of his blood. Then, Peter continues:

Jesus Christ Has Gen You Knew Birth Why does he remind them of this?

Because during this time of their difficulty, they may not feel born again, and even worse, they are scattered distances through persecution and are hurting so much they need encouragement. His words are like healing balm to them.

Knowing this, the apostle Peter reminds them of the meaning of their new birth, saying:

It is a Living hope - There was a time you had no hope.

It is through the resurrection of their Lord - who died and rose to save you.

It is beyond this present life, an inheritance that is incorruptible It is kept in heaven for us, we who are redeemed of the Lord, shielded (protected) by God's power! - until the day when Christ returns. Peter gives no promise of a life without suffering. He is very straight and clear about this:

Trials May Come: Grief May Cause Us to Suffer - but Peter reminds them, and us, that being a persecuted Church is not without purpose.

Trials are to test our faith to prove the genuineness of our faith. Do we really believe.

Trials are to refine our faith like the way gold is purified.

Twisted Religion

Scripture lesson: Mark 7:1-23 Text: Mark 7:15

As we mature, we begin to examine our personal lives, how we fit in with the scheme of things. This is a normal and valuable exercise. During this self-examination we learn about our gifts and graces, our strong points and our weak points. We may even catch ourselves taking a bad turn and avoid a bad direction our lives may be taking.

Through this self-examination we also learn that everyone has certain God-gen gifts and graces. We should celebrate our gifts, use them and celebrate the gifts of others. If you are happy with yourself, you can do this and not be jealous of others who may have gifts you do not have. And it is good to remember, God, our heavenly Father, only wants us to be the best we can be, not somebody else.

And there is the matter of traditions; as we learn what God expects, sometimes what society expects is not in line with what Jesus teaches us. In today's scripture lives on Jesus and his disciples were criticized for not practicing the Jewish ceremonial hand washing before eating. (The ceremony requires the person to first wash the left hand twice; then, wash the right hand twice; reversed if the person is left-handed.) Jesus answered their criticism by quoting the scriptures from Isaiah:

"Isaiah was right when he prophesied about you hypocrites, as it is written: "These people honor me with their lips, but their hearts are far from me. They worship me in vain; their teachings are but rules taught by men." Jesus continues:

"You have let go of the commands of God and are holding on to the traditions of men."

Jesus then, addresses a bad tradition involving a parent, child relationship; and he continues teaching, clarifying their misunderstandings about food. He states firmly, "Listen to me and understand this. Wow! "Nothing outside a man can make him unclean by going into him. It is what comes out of a man that makes him unclean." In saying this, Jesus declared all foods clean.

Jesus now goes into detail, "What comes out of a man is what makes him unclean. For from within, out of men's hearts, come evil thoughts, sexual immorality, theft, murder, adultery, greed, malice, deceit, lewdness, envy, slander, arrogance and folly. All these evils come from inside and make a man unclean."

In contrast to this, the apostle Paul describes the various gifts and graces listing:

Wisdom - using insight to make excellent decisions.

Knowledge - having a command of fact.

Faith - looks prayerfully beyond every situation to envision positive results. Healing - is its own miracle of God no matter how it happens, which through faith restores our body, soul mind, emotions and spirit.

Prophecy- the gift to proclaim the gospel as God's will and intuitively see into events that are shaping the future.

Distinguishing between the spirits - the ability to read people and discern whether a person's desires, actions and motes are upright.

The ability to speak a different language as inspired by the Holy Spirit - is a spiritual gift of worship and proclamation.

Gifts of administration - the ability to see the big picture, delegate authority while demonstrating servant leadership, and inspire folks to get involved for the cause of Christ.

The gift of helping others - to be able to help in practical matters or counsel and deal effectively with people in difficult situations. This gift inspires a person to affirm the goodness in others which, in turn affirms the goodness that is in us. It becomes a growing experience to better know ourselves. This self-understanding has a long, even ancient, history.

The philosopher Plato (c.a. 347 B.C.) declared that before he could enter the world of philosophical dialect. "I must first know myself." And self-knowledge has theological roots at its base. How can we say this? Well, arrogance is replaced by humility and humility is seen as a path leading to God's grace and to salvation through Jesus Christ. Many thoughtful people have long been aware of this. They see the concept of self-knowledge on both an intellectual and spiritual level. So, at this point, we might ask, "How can we come to better know ourselves and thereby avoid twisted thinking and twisted religion?" A few practical examples might be helpful:

Arnold Toynbaee (1889-1975), renowned historian and philosopher, in his landmark text, "A Study of History' wrote, "Unless we can bear self-mortification, we shall not be able to carry self-examination to the necessary painful lengths. Without humility there can be no illuminating self-knowledge." His statement certainly has a solid theological base that encourages us to know ourselves.

Listen to what Louis Johannot said. He was director with Helen Schaub, of the famous Institute live Rosey, a boarding school ages 7-18, that has for generations educated students from 56 countries and royalties from around the world. Knowing the school's international background, it is especially noteworthy to learn of Louis Johannot's interesting, somewhat amusing comment, concerning understanding a student's behavior. He writes: "The only reason I always try to meet and know the parents better is because it helps me to forge their children."

Just imagine. And from a famous teacher of the children of royalty. Oh, the challenge of understanding others and ourselves. Even royalty is no exception to this.

Then, there is Carl Jung, Swiss Psychiatrist, who wrote, "Everything that irritates us about others can lead us to an understanding of ourselves." How insightful is that?

Have you ever heard a family member say, "You sound just like your father" or "That is what your mother would say, or an uncle or an aunt?"

And isn't it interesting, those of us at midlife and beyond often find ourselves telling our children, grandchildren or great-grandchildren things our parents told us? This is good. It's a sign of our own maturity and in the process, we even come to know ourselves better.

Concerning self-knowledge, a lifelong pursuit, here is an amusing, insightful comment concerning this by the English writer and actor, Quinten Crisp.

"It's no good running a pig farm badly for thirty years while saying, "Really, I was meant to be a ballet dancer." By that time pigs will be your style." Although this is a lighthearted way of saying, "Know thyself," it really is important for us to take time to think and find out who we are. To make rational decisions based on this self-knowledge, and accepting who we are is mentally very healthy. And, of course, we should be constantly growing, no matter what our age. In short, run your own race! One person said this, "Be careful of taking other people's advice; you may wind up Living your life making other people's mistakes!

The famous American philosopher and poet, Ralph Waldo Emerson wisely advised, "Whatever games are played with us, we must play no games with ourselves." And in the process of knowing ourselves better, it is valuable to question and examine our own traditions and practices, as well as the traditions and practices of society at large. The caution here is that sometimes traditions start with good intentions but become so twisted that they no longer serve us personally or the common good of society. This is the tragedy of good traditions gone bad as it was with the Pharisees during the time of Jesus when washing one's hands before a meal became unnecessarily, an involved rigid religious ceremony. This leads us to consider:

The Demands of Traditions - Some are good and helpful; some are harmful, and some do not really matter much.

We have many fine traditions - such as table manners when eating, dressing appropriately and general cleanliness that show we care about ourselves to be presentable to others and to avoid disease. Then, traditionally, there are holiday observances and other special celebrations. All societies have their various traditions and questions may be raised about some of them that are doubtful as to their value. So, we might ask:

Are all of our traditions intended for the common good? Are they efficient for us personally and for society? And what about people trying to start traditions or practices not for the common good that may even be harmful? Should we just be passe and accept a bad tradition? I think not! Often people look to the government to tell them what is right or wrong. In this way the government becomes their Bible. Certainly, we are to respect government and governmental process, but the government is not our Bible!

Governmental branches have the authority to declare things illegal or legal, but that doesn't make their decisions legal morally or ethically right, if they are not up to biblical standards. And if they are not, we have every right to question their decisions, whether by legislation or by the high court. We, as Christians, must guard against twisted ideas, twisted philosophy and twisted religion at every level and in every form. And this includes any person's attempts at starting traditions or practices that are not biblical.

This causes problems for Bible-believing Christians because down through history:

Governments and Societies are notorious for punishing tradition breakers. Groups may have strong traditions not acceptable to some members. Pressure may be used to force conformity driving the person to conform or leave the group, which in church situations have spawned new individual churches or new denominations. In the case of society, at large, of course, proper traditions should be respected and continued; for example, honoring the flag because it is a symbol of our country and its ideals. (And honoring it is not worshipping it as some try to say. It is simply paying respect to a symbol identifying our country and its ideals.)

There are Dangers in Some Traditions and Practices - To begin with, any unthinking practice has potential dangers. So, any practice that becomes a tradition should be scrutinized to determine its real value and determine if it has lost its original good purpose. So, now we ask:

Does the tradition or practice reflect Christian values or standards? - If not, it should be replaced.

Are the traditions practiced thoughtlessly -Has repeated practice or the effect of time distorted or twisted the original purpose of the tradition or practice? Even worse:

Do these traditions or practices delay or prevent Christian growth? - For example, saying negate, even hurtful, things to children or youth which would prevent them from maturing because we want to control them even into adulthood? Let us always remember:

Truth Will Set Us Free! - Good traditions will always enable us to grow. They will serve to enhance, not degrade. They can be found in our work in our church, or in our recreation as we happily celebrate life knowing that:

God's demands are always fair - They promote freedom of the human spirit. Truth does not place us in bondage. Truth sets us free. Any practice or tradition that does not do this should be done away with.

God's laws exist for us. We do not exist for the law For example, Jesus said,

"The sabbath was made for man, not man for the sabbath."

God's laws lead us to experience love, peace, and joy, not bondage - How?

The apostle Paul explained it well, "Jesus Christ is our law of liberty."

So, we conclude that good traditions and good practices will always serve to enhance human life. And the correct biblical understandings that underpin these practices are vital to keep our faith journey on track, to elevate the human condition, never degrade it.

May we never take our salvation experience for granted. And may we never feel superior because we are Christians. Yes, we have been set free from the bondage of sin to experience new life in Jesus Christ. And yes, we practice certain biblical traditions like baptism and communion. However, let's us to be patient toward those who don't understand the Christian way.

Biblical understandings are vital, and their practices are important. And, as Christ's Church, we know how important it is to preserve correct biblical beliefs and practices, never allowing these to become twisted out of shape. True, some practices and traditions are born out of well-meaning ignorance. But beware!

Over the years, many influential persons and groups have distorted scriptural teachings, both of faith and practice, and led people astray, away from the simple, basic truths of the gospel.

I pray that we, as the Church of Jesus Christ, will never be led astray and ever remain true to the plain meaning of God's Word. May we never allow ourselves to become victims of twisted religion. As the writer of Hebrews tell us,

"Therefore, we must pay greater attention to what we have heard, so that we do not drift away from it. For if the message declared through angels was valid, and every violation and disobedience received its just punishment, how shall we escape if we neglect so great a salvation?"

Our response? We will never neglect our salvation, nor allow it to be twisted away from the truth of the gospel. We know God's truth is revealed in us. And it is God's truth, through Christ, that sets us free. And we are free. We are free, indeed! Christ has set us free!

Where Is Wisdom Found?

Scripture: Job 28:10-28; I Cor. 1:1-30; 2:1-7, 10.13 -14

Text: I Cor. 1:30

Knowledge without wisdom is a dangerous wasteland! Knowledge without implementation, with no purposeful use of it, has without the wisdom to properly utilize knowledge, no reason for being. And further we can categorically assert that knowledge without wisdom has potential without the energy needed for fulfillment. Standing alone, it does not say that we live in a moral universe. For example, scientific discovery having procedure, but without some kind some kind of moral purpose is therefore void of wisdom and is a disaster waiting to happen. Why? The person gaining knowledge must always ask the question why and the answer must always be, within the context of a moral universe. Plainly put, knowledge should exist for the highest good and should employ wisdom.

Renowned theoretical physicist, Stephen Hawking, when asked by Larry King in an interview, what is wrong with the world, curtly replied, "Greed and stupidity." I believe his answer to be largely true. Knowledge without wisdom is truly a wasteland. So, where is wisdom found? Let's take a look at Solomon.

Solomon, when only boy, looked heavenward and asked God for wisdom. His prayer was answered. And as king of Israel, he ruled with such wisdom that leaders from other lands and cultures came to him to try to learn the secret of his wisdom. Where did his wisdom come from? It was a gift from God. He asked for wisdom from God, "The Source." Wisdom was the answer to his prayer. It led him closer to the heart and mind of God where wisdom lay. With his God-gen wisdom, I believe, this is what inspired Solomon to write the books, Proverbs, Psalms, Ecclesiastes, and Song of Songs.

And considering Job we gain further insight into where wisdom is found? Job tells us:

I Wisdom is not found through the natural world We can observe the results of Divine wisdom that created and is sustaining the natural world. But wisdom, itself, and its origin, is only found at the "Source," which is God. This is why:

Job says that wisdom is not under the earth nor in the earth's treasures. It is not found in the beginnings or workings of things, nor in discoveries about the natural world. Strangely, new advances, and insights, often bring new problems and more new questions. For example, the amazing advances and discoveries in the electronic age have brought with them multiple new problems. Computers and automobiles are examples of this.

The natural world, while certainly intriguing, is but a result of the action and manifestation of "The Source." The natural world is the manifestation. It is not "The Source." God is the "The Source." So, it easily follows that the natural world is a manifestation of God. So, we can conclude that the only way it is possible to experience knowledge and wisdom is from our heavenly Father. He is "The Source." In fact, Divine revelation explains to us the inspiration that brought us the scriptures!

Is Wisdom An Unfathomable Mystery? - No, in the sense that we can ask for wisdom from God and receive it to become a part of our lives. On the other hand, yes, it is an unfathomable mystery because wisdom as part of the mystery of God, is beyond the natural senses. In fact, far beyond them. So, in that sense, it is hidden from mere human intellect because Divine wisdom transcends human intellect.

Now we have uncovered a major stumbling block in secular philosophy! You say, "What is that? Well, some philosophers, scientists, and others will say they recognize Deity, but declare that since only God knows the way of pure wisdom, it is unknowable and unreachable by human beings. This position denies spiritual reality, and especially the reality of salvation, which is the path of the agnostics who say, to me illogically, that humans can't really know anything. Why is this position illogical? If you say you can't know anything, then, you can't even know that you can't know anything!

As a Bible believing Christian, I will say emphatically that this is patently wrong. The Bible clearly informs us, "You will know the truth, and the truth will set you free." That is why, as Christians, we are set free because of the gospel. And further, we able to say that God has provided "The Way." It is the way of wisdom. How wonderful is this truth! After all, we are people of "The Way." This is our testimony to the world. Our lives are Christ centered, and because we are born again, we have an inner sense of Divine Truth, the confirmation of our salvation and Spirit led, way of life.

And since God created and is still creating the natural world, we know that God created time as a reality and, through Christ, has entered into our temporal space. So, if we seek him, he will lead us to his wisdom. Our authority for this?

Jeremiah 29: 13 is one reference, "You will seek me, and you will find me when you seek me with all your heart." In spite of what some ill- informed pundits say, God is not unknowable. Anyone who makes such a declaration is wrong! Christians know the truth and knowing the truth are set free, enabled to receive Divine wisdom. And, further, this frees us to be happy people! Hear these inspiring verses from Psalm 8:3-4,

"When I consider your heavens, the work of your fingers, the moon and the stars, which you have set in place, what is mankind that you are mindful of them, human beings that you care for them.

You have made them a little lower than the angels and crowned them with glory and honor. You made them rulers of the works of your hands, you put everything under their feet: all flocks and herds, and the animals of the wild, the birds in the sky, and the fish in the sea, all that swim the paths of the seas.

Lord, our Lord, how majestic is your name in all the earth! I will ge thanks to you, Lord, with all my heart, I will tell of your wonderful deeds. I will be glad and rejoice in you; I will sing praises of your name most high.

Now since God sees and knows his creation - the beginning to the end, the question may arise. How does wisdom begin its manifestation within us? The answer is:

Wisdom begins With a Divine Relationship Wisdom always seeks for the highest good. Its motives are always pure. In fact, wisdom and love are inseparable! They are Living water for us through Jesus Christ. And as we go to "The Source," we find real meaning in life. We learn that our very existence has meaning. This, we should always remember. You and I have value on this earth just because we are here. And our relationship with "The Source" (which is God, our heavenly Father, greatly expands that meaning. Coming to a keen awareness of God's holiness brings with it a profound sense of awe. Sometimes expressed as "the fear of God." The wonder of this is that we can really know God through Jesus, the One whom he sent, allowing us to experience the ultimate insight. What is that insight? We are loved and created to be eternal. And through believing on Jesus as our Savior, we are saved to eternal life. Our lives are made pure and whole through the saving grace and work of God. This marvelous transformation motivates us to seek what is good and shun what is evil. Let us be clear on this. "To shun evil is understanding," a gateway to wisdom. How? Well, understanding life on this level leads us to adopt values that point to "The Source" where wisdom resides. We learn in James' epistle, 3:13,

"Who is wise and understanding among you? Let them show it by their good life, by deeds done in the humility that comes from wisdom." And in verse 17, "But the wisdom that comes from heaven is first of all pure; then peace-loving, considerate, submissive, full of mercy and good fruit, impartial and sincere. Peacemakers who so in peace reap a harvest of righteousness.

So, if we ask. Where is wisdom found? We now see the obvious. Wisdom abides within the "Ultimate Source," which is God. Where does understanding dwell? It dwells within the "Ultimate Source." - the very mind of God. So, we can conclude true wisdom is the ultimate right decision that leads to the right action, that will lead to correcting evil and disorder. This is where it is helpful to read in Peter 3:13 "We are looking forward to a new heaven and a new earth, the home of righteousness".

Jesus, begotten of the Father, made the ultimate right decision, accomplished the ultimate right action, manifesting the greatest act of love the world has ever known and through it has overcome the world! So, we can say that:

True understanding is the ultimate insight into the meaning of life unified with Divine cause. Its resultant effect, and Divine process is within the context of God's eternalness. And it is amazing that being born again enables us to view our lives in this way because we experience spiritual transformation. The old life passes away and all things become new. This is genuine spiritual transformation- being spiritually born all over again! There is no other true salvation experience. (Everything else attempts to patch up the old garment, the old self, which remains the same old garment.) Authentic spiritual transformation points to the real meaning and purpose of our existence - "to glorify God and enjoy him forever."

True wisdom, then is found in "The Ultimate Good" - which is God. And the beginning of understanding is found in "The Ultimate Sacrifice" for humanity, Jesus the Christ, who is God's expression to us of the Ultimate Good. And Jesus Christ is our mediator enabling a life of spiritual insight. Jesus the Christ, the one who provides for us a life to be led joyfully within the context of beautiful, true enlightenment. The Buddha, who taught about enlightenment, was quoted as saying, "All is suffering," but Jesus taught, "If you obey my commands, you will remain in my love, just as I have obeyed my father's commands and remain in his love. I have told you this so that my joy may be in you and that your joy many be complete. My command is this; 'Love each other as I have loved you.'

Christianity is a joyful way of life! Embrace it! Don't let worldly conditions distract you from it. Jesus, revealer of "The Way" reveals to us the limitless love of God. It is love not bound by temporal experience. It is eternal!

This inspired the apostle Paul to write,

...We speak of God's secret wisdom ... revealed... to us by his Spirit, not the spirit of the world, but the Spirit who is from God that we may understand what God has freely given us ... in words taught by the Spirit, explaining spiritual truths in spiritual words."

How meaningful! These insightful words describe Jesus Christ as one "whom to know is life eternal," because bound up in this lovely promise is the ultimate decision, the ultimate action, and the ultimate good - God's expression in Jesus the Christ. And God's promise, sealed in the eternal covenant ratified on Calvary, and fulfilled in the resurrection reaches out to embrace the entire world!

We can indeed "glorify God and (through Christ) enjoy him forever." This is our eternal hope! This is wisdom!

The Challenge of Christian Tolerance

Scripture Reading: Romans 14: 1-23; 15:1-6

One of the most interesting facets of human nature is that, while we are more alike than we are different, we are, nevertheless, all different. Obviously, this helps us identify with each other and also marks us as individuals. If we all looked alike, we couldn't tell one from another. Even with twins, and multiple births, the mothers can always tell the differences.

This variety is good, of course. It adds much to the spice of life. To meet and know people who are different from us can greatly enrich our lives if we take the time to understand how their cultural and especially their religious practices have shaped their values.

However, these matters are often complex, requiring skill to handle these differences in social, political or religious thought and practice? On a national or international level many of these matters often seem out of our reach.

But on a local or personal level, we do well to ask. Are these differences worth destroying a friendship or splitting up a home? Or harming our community or hurting the church? It is good to pause and ask ourselves, "Are these differences permanent or transitory?" Are these differences in transition, as part of a group's simply seeking to solve a problem? Not having all the information that would properly lead to a solution and making a quick, premature decision is to be avoided?

Salespersons sometimes use pressure to get you to make a purchase before you have all the information you need. Where possible, we do well to take the pause and think approach before making a decision, especially when we are put under pressure. And it is important, when conflicts arise, to withhold judgment until all the facts are in so the situation can be properly dealt with. These kinds of problems are not new.

Considering Paul's writing to the Romans, the question was mainly over food and special days, considering whether one day was above another. Paul sums up these difficulties by promoting tolerance. And tolerance requires understanding before evaluation. Finally, he says, "Let everyone be persuaded in his own mind." Tolerance is a huge subject.

This leads us to think about how cultural influences can affect how we develop our own values. For example, here are some cultural mistakes I made over the years: While at L SU, I tried to eat lunch with students from other countries. And when I politely asked to sit at the table with the oriental students, they smiled, nodded affirmatively, and I seemed to be well received.

Perhaps I was, but when someone finally clued me in; he told me that what they really wanted was to talk with English speaking students just to practice speaking English. What an eye opener that was! I realized they

weren't just being friendly. They had motes. Nevertheless, I enjoyed their conversation. Here is another mistake I made:

One summer at LSU, as I enjoyed talking with Mideastern students over lunch, I saw a student eating alone. He looked to me like he was from Iran. I walked over and asked to join him. He nodded yes and, trying to be sociable, I asked, "What part of the Mideast are you from?' Looking somewhat startled, he said, "My name is Joe. I'm from the Bronx." I was embarrassed, but I didn't let on and we just continued a friendly conversation.

Here are some other mistakes I made:

When we moved to Jackson Louisiana, it was obvious that there were some militant black students there, and some band students wondering how I would treat them. I let them know up front that I didn't play favorites, and everyone would be treated fairly.

This approach was successful. There were no incidents, and in my fifth year there, when a black momma called me on the phone and said, "Dr. Boyd, we know you are fair with all our students." I was delighted since she was a spokesperson for the black community.

I taught there seven more years and then, seeking higher pay, we moved to Merryville, close to the Texas border, and got a large $10,000 raise. Bad decision. Many persons Living there, had crossed the Texas border to escape Texas law, and I was to teach their children. Some of the folks were fine, but it was obvious that some of them came from very troubled homes. I heard women in the lunchroom talking how their husbands beat them. Drugs were rampant. Fights were common. Biggest job seeking mistake I ever made. Money isn't everything. We then moved to Florien, Louisiana, a fine academic school, where I taught until I retired from public school teaching. The cut in pay was worth it.

So, thinking I would get off to a good start at Florien, I let the students know, as I did in Jackson, that I would be fair with all of them. Some students were insulted that I even mentioned that they were black. I quickly apologized and never made that mistake again. My problem was that I had misread the black culture in that area. A peaceful area and very different from Jackson.

It is obvious that the challenge of Christian tolerance requires empathy and understanding. Tolerance is an ongoing life-long learning experience. So, how do we deal with these challenges on a day-to-day basis, in a broad as well as a personal sense? Paul addresses these very questions concerning the

Church: He tells us:

We should accept and affirm fellow believers and other persons as persons of equal value in the sight of God.

He or she is, first and foremost, God's created child.

Their weakness requires empathy and consideration from stronger Christians.

Properly, our Christian Walk is a "journey of development," and our accepting one another is based on Christ- not upon our total agreement with that person. Jesus, in his entire ministry, never condemned anyone personally, only sinful practices.

Walking along a stream we can notice the many stones that are smooth. It took a long time for that to happen. As the current flows and the stones, being jostled around, are rubbed together, they become smooth over time. So, our association with other people can help to break down barriers and prejudices, and smoothen relationships, positively shaping our behavior. In dealing with everyday problems similar to what Paul describes, we learn that:

We should define problems clearly and in perspective.

Matters of food and religious ceremony

Matters of Holy Days.

The problem beneath the visible problems is often intolerance complicated by misunderstanding, especially of the Christian's relationship with Christ in relation to other people and other matters.

We should always consider our relationship as believers to the problem.

We belong to God.

God is the only judge.

We shall all face our God individually and ge an account of ourselves. Our goal is to hear, "Well done, thou good and faithful servant." Enter into the joys of the Lord forever.

Paul instructs that nothing is unclean in itself. This hearkens back to the creation when God pronounced his creation Good.

How we look at things may be in the mind, our individual prejudice, our personal weakness or our background. So, it is good to be tolerant of the other person as we seek to understand one another better.

At SMU I learned that the Mexican Christians were greatly offended if during a rehearsal or a program, secular and sacred music were mixed.

We must avoid hurting others, as Paul instructs. Though, sometimes difficult, our conduct should be guided by love, remembering that Christ also died for that weaker person.

We know that God's kingdom is about justice, peace and joy. It is certainly not based on mundane matters such as food.

So, let us continue to pursue peace and build up a common life. We may abstain if it causes someone to stumble.

In all this we are to be true to ourselves, remaining true to our own convictions, yet agreeing with one another after the manner of Christ who did not consider himself, but others.

"So, that with one mind and one voice we may praise the God and Father of our Lord Jesus Christ."

Let us allow trial matters to remain trial. Unity is a great testimony to any church. So may we stand together as a redeemed people - as one - one faith, one lord, one baptism and with one mind! - the mind of Christ! May we so le; then Christ lives through us!

The Keepers of the Vineyard

Scripture lesson: Matthew 21: 33-42 Text: Matt. 21: 42

This Parable of the Vineyard is full of symbolic meanings. It is different from most of the Kingdom of Heaven parables in that this one has several important themes. Told, in utter simplicity, using the natural beauty of a vineyard, Jesus reveals, the master plan to restore humanity's relationship with God, but also, alludes to mankind's responsibility to care for God's earth. This parable hearkens back to the account in Genesis (1:26) when God gave instructions to all mankind to care for the garden where he placed them. So, we see in this seemingly simple parable, Jesus begins by referring symbolically to the creation:

A Landowner Planted a Vineyard Nothing unusual here. However, the land, God's creation, represents potential. By itself, it is of little value until brought to good use. And, since it was his land to do as he saw fit, he decided to plant a vineyard. The vineyard here is symbolic of creation.

He put a wall around it. Like a hedge to protect the vineyard from wild boars and from thieves. (God protecting his creation.)

He dug a winepress. This illustrates work that had to be done to use the harvested grapes. Now, the winepress had two troughs. The upper one channeled into the lower one to collect the juice of the grapes. Obviously, with his careful planning, the owner expected a useful harvest. So, for further protection along the wall:

He built a watchtower The watchtower represents safety and comfort provided by the landowner, who in the parable represents God. The watchtower was placed high to provide time to warn of danger; it also served as housing and shelter for the tenants who worked in the vineyard. In this way the landowner cared for his workers' needs as well as caring for his vineyard. So, what did the landowner do with his vineyard?

The Landowner Rented His Vineyard This represents God sharing his creation and plan with mankind. He allowed workers to come and work in the vineyard. This shows a covenant relationship between the workers and the owner, where they would be useful, have gainful employment and he would benefit from their work. The key here is that the owner, who is God in the parable, trusted them. Like sharecroppers or tenant farmers they knew what to do to produce a good crop.

After the business transaction the owner went on a journey. Time passed, and then came the harvest. The trusted agreement was that the workers would receive earnings from their work and part of the crop earnings would go to the landowner. So,

The landowner sent servants, his workers, to collect his fruit. (The servants are symbolic of spiritual leaders and prophets, both past and present.) But alas, there was evil afoot. The servants who came to collect the owner's portion of the crop were beaten, stoned or killed. Tragedy! And the fruit still had to be harvested. So,

The landowner sent more servants. He spent even more than the first time in another attempt to obtain the fruit that was rightfully his. Again, the servants experienced violence and even death at the hands of the tenants.

Finally, the landowner sent his son - his greatest treasure. He was the one and only person who would one day inherit the entire vineyard; but pursuing with an evil impulse and entrenched in their own greed, the tenants thought they could somehow take the Son's inheritance from him. So, they killed him. This is Jesus predicting his own crucifixion, while, facing those who would want him crucified.

Jesus then asked, "Now, what will the landowner do to these selfish, evil tenants?" Looking steadfastly at the Chief Priests and Pharisees, Jesus forced them to face the truth about themselves. They are the tenants in this story, and they know it. In today's language they literally had a "Come to Jesus meeting." Jesus forced them to face the truth. Difficult for anyone, but much more so in this unique situation. Continuing the parable, Jesus asked them,

"When the owner of the vineyard comes, what will he do to those tenants?" They replied, "He will bring those wretches to a wretched end, and he will rent the vineyard to other tenants who will ge him his share of the crop at harvest time." Jesus said to them, have you never read in the Scriptures: 'The stone the builders rejected has become the cornerstone; the Lord has done this, and it is marvelous in our eyes.' "Therefore, I tell you that the kingdom of God will be taken away from you and gen to a people who will produce its fruit."

A shocking, but prophetical statement, and we learn that:

The original tenants, the original workers of the vineyard, lost their place of privilege. They are replaced. (This is prophetical of those who have accepted Christ.)

New people will be en1ployed and privileged to work the vineyard for the landowner.

New people will produce the landowner's fruit. (Christianity has become the largest religion in the world.) The happy continuation of the spread of Christianity.

There is a famous opera entitled Turandot. It is a very strange love story full of twisted intrigue about a cold-hearted Persian Princess trying to find love. As operas go, the tale was dramatized, with lots of singing, and strung out, making the listeners wonder if she would ever change to a nicer person and finally find love. Well, before she found love in the opera's story, the composer Giacomo Puccini died leaving the opera unfinished. In fact, it was first performed unfinished, though an ending had been written by Franco Alfano and was finally performed completed in 1926.

And at the premier performance of the completed opera, just before the end, conductor, Arturo Toscanini, abruptly stopped the music. Something never done. He turned to the stunned audience, and stepping forward, announced, "Here the master laid down his pen." Then, raising his baton, Maestro, Toscanini, conducted the rest of the opera to its strange, but happy conclusion.

Before this it was a great opera without an ending. Now it was complete, when, after Puccini's devoted student, Franco Alfano, wrote the last section of the music, it was completed to its happy ending.

How interesting to compare this story of Franco Alfano's, dedication to completion with today's parable and realize our dedication to carry on the work of Jesus, our great Master. It is for us to occupy him until he comes back to earth again. Yes, the harvest is great, but so are the rewards in rescued souls.

Jesus, relating this parable, is definitely playing hard ball. He deals with the ultimate truth about himself as Messiah. He deals with the punishment for the rebellious apostate and ultimate reward for those who are true disciples. And he deals with the importance of being faithful to our responsibilities. This parable, Keepers of the Vineyard, touches everyone.

On a broad, practical level, we are to care for the created earth and care for the needs of humanity. This includes governments and anyone with authority and the opportunity to do something about healing the environment.

On a personal practical level, by caring for our homes, our property and our loved ones, we are serving as keepers of God's vineyard, respecting what God has allowed us to possess and experience. And as Christians we also know we are to care about the spiritual welfare of others. All these things are important and, in the end, provide the most satisfying of life's experiences! You know the old saying that love isn't love until we ge it away.

Think of that good feeling we get when we share. It definitely is more blessed to ge than receive, though receiving is also a good thing and has its own blessing.

In today's setting, while facing the crowd, Jesus addressed who he was, "the stone that the builders rejected, who has become the chief cornerstone" of all that is. To accept him is to experience a wonderful spiritual transformation and have the spirit of selfish pride broken within us; but to purposefully reject Jesus, refusing God's love, and choosing the life of a rebellious apostate, leaves the person separated from God, with the most awful existence.

But what a blessing it is to accept the privilege of partnership with God and his plan. How incomprehensible to refuse it! We are now, at a crucial moment in the history of civilization as vital keepers of God's vineyard. May we continue to do God's will, not as drudgery, but as a point of privilege. May we continue to live our lives as keepers of the vineyard, by the power of the Father, and of the Son, and of the Holy Spirit. Amen!

Live to Please God

Scripture lesson: I Thessalonians 4:1-12

Today's Summary Text: for a comparison reading of I Thessalonians 4:12a, is from the New Revised Standard Version. Paul is instructing the Thessalonian Church concerning love for the brothers and sisters. He says:

"But we urge you beloved, to do so more and more, to aspire to live quietly. to mind your own affairs, and to work with your hands, as we directed you, so that you may behave properly toward outsiders and be dependent on no one."

He wrote this to the Thessalonians for several practical reasons, namely:

1. Make love of the brethren their first priority because it is essential.,

2. Avoid being boisterous stirring up the neighborhood because this fosters general unrest.

3. Avoid meddling in people's lives because this is often motivated by the need to control others.

4. Do the necessary work, not expecting others to do it, because sharing in work fosters compatibility and making our own way enables financial stability.

5. Doing these things gives a good Christian testimony to outsiders. The reasons for these admonishings are obvious. They are some of the important ingredients of a practical lifestyle that pleases God.

One of the most important things, when we decide to make something, is to begin with the best materials or ingredients. Though this is obvious, it is easily overlooked because no matter what our skills, the materials or ingredients are basic to any project. For instance, when working with wood I made small boxes and other items out of oak. Oak is a fine enduring wood, and a good varnish brings out beautiful grain. Some other woods are inferior, so are not useful for this purpose.

The same thing is true with cooking. The requirement for a good cook is to begin with the best food, the best spices and then combine them in a pleasing nutritious way. Of course, it takes care, lots of time and much skill. But isn't it amusing to hear a cook tell us how easy it is, while using as many as 14 different ingredients; and the TV cooks, after someone else has, beforehand, measured everything ahead of show time and placed them in separate dishes ready to be added by the cook. And, even, one bad ingredient can spoil everything. One time I got bad cottage cheese. Ugh! Another time I was given some kind of cleaning fluid for my drink. Tasting before I swallowed may have saved my life. It is sad to say, but to be around some people puts a bad taste in one's mouth. This is certainly not what the Lord wants of us. So, God's Word admonishes us:

Le a Holy Life -Because of Jesus and the presence of his Holy Spirit, we are enabled to live our lives separated from the sinful values of the unsaved world.

We are to be holy. This does not mean to merely act holy. Have you ever met someone who acted nice, but down underneath really wasn't nice? As soon as something doesn't go their way, they explode into the angry person they really are inside.

1. We are to avoid sexual immorality. Television and much of the media have tried to turn sexual immorality into a norm. Many situation comedies teach that it is cool to break moral law. We know the truth. Sexual immorality is a river of fire.

2. We are to learn and practice self-control in a way that is holy and honorable. This does not mean we should never be angry about anything. The Bible says, of course, for legitimate reasons, "Be angry and sin not." In the end, it is a matter of self-control measured to the situation that remains holy and honorable.

We are to accept and practice biblical instruction.

1. Rejecting this instruction is rejecting God's wisdom. (v8)

2. Rejecting this instruction is rejecting the wisdom of God's Holy Spirit.

We are to love the brethren this translates into seeing the needs of others and doing something about it. Since we know that love is a matter of the will:

1.Jesus commands us to love How do we do this? We allow God's love to flow through us radiating outward toward others.

2. We are admonished to increase our love for others. Paul's writing here is really an encouragement and is natural as we become more and more sensitive to other people's needs, not just our own.

Living a Quiet, Practical Life is a Living Testimony of Our Faith But what does this mean?

To lead a quiet life means we resolve problems - We don't seek to stir up issues.

To tend to our own affairs means we don't interfere in other people's lives. Of course, if we see a need that requires attention, or if anyone seeks our help we should offer to help.

To work with our hands simply means we should regard any honest work as noble and be willing to do it if we are needed. Illus. Cleaning the Band Room in Jackson.

We Are to live a Life of Stren1:th! - this means inner spiritual strength. And we are enabled by the Holy Spirit to do this.

It is important to win the respect of outsiders We may be the only Bible they will ever read!

It is important that we be as self-sustaining as is possible for us Paul is really addressing those who joined with the Christian community and were not doing their part to help by sharing in food and the workload. Yes, there were free loaders in the early Christian Church. There were those who were quite able to work but chose to leave it to others.

So, you might ask. Just what is a holy life? Is it a life that is perfect? No, only Jesus was able to do this. But a life that is holy is one that rejects the values of the secular world; it is a life that is moral and ethical, and it is a life that is quietly productive. And though we know that no life is perfect, the holy life is so led that it radiates a positive Christian influence.

Whether we are parents, grandparents, great grandparents or single, the positive impact we can have on our faith community and the community at large comes down to practical Christian Living with a special dash of love!

The Great Mystery of God's Will Revealed

Scripture: Ephesians 1:1-14 Text: Ephesians: 7:13

There are people today who never seem to question the purpose or value of their existence. They go through life wandering passively and aimlessly, without a real sense of purpose. Then, when things go badly and out of their control, they begin to question who they are and what life means to them. The question of meaning looms large and then they ask, "How do I fit in the scheme of things?" And it is important for all of us to take stock of our lives and try to see the big picture.

Today's message addresses these issues for us individually including the big picture; what is God's will for the human race. To begin with, atheism has no place in this discussion.

Why? Because it is foolish. How can we say this? We go to the scriptures and find that the foolishness of this position was made clear by the inspired writings of King David in Psalm 14: when he declared, "The fool has said in his heart, 'There is no God.'

Albert Einstein, world famous theoretical physicist said, "What I see in nature is a grand design that we can understand only imperfectly, on with which a responsible person must look at with humility." It has been observed that Einstein's belief in an intelligent designer was derived from his phenomenal insights into the Universe as the most brilliant scientist who ever led.

So, for our first premise concerning deity, we say without apology. There is God, that Jesus is deity and part of the Godhead, there is Father, Son and Holy Spirit. Certainly, as Christians we know this truth, but some folks do not. So, it will be beneficial to take a closer look at the remarkable scripture that declares God's will for the entire human race:

In Christ We were Chosen to be Holy and Blameless. This speaks of the universality of the gospel, an unfathomable mystery to the unsaved, but revealed to us. Jesus, the great Rabbi, sees value and potential in the entire human race and chooses to redeem all mankind if they will believe and trust in him.

Many great thinkers were and are in this search. The great scientist, Albert Einstein, accepted the premise of the grand design. This sounds plausible in the field of physics, which deals with material understandings of the universe; but if understood on a spiritual level, we can say that the Grand Design is found in Jesus Christ, who brought the Grand Design to earth to save humanity. This is the grand plan that reveals the need for salvation and that

God's love is boundless. In fact, we learn part of the grand plan that:

In Christ, we were actually chosen before the creation of the world It is for us to accept the great gift of Jesus as the final sacrifice for sin.

God, in love, also predestined us to be his adopted as sons and daughters. It is for us to believe in Jesus Christ as the Savior of the world. He is!

God, our Father, adopts us into his family through the saving work of Jesus It is for us to receive the greatest gift any human could receive.

In Christ We Are Redeemed

We Are Redeemed through his blood - which means that we have been brought back into a restored fellowship with God. The Jewish sacrificial system was God's plan as their schoolmaster teaching them the exceeding sinfulness of their sinful nature.

We are Redeemed Through His Blood -which means, though we were once lost, we have been found, like the lost sheep in Jesus' parable. In other words, we have not only been forgiven for all our sins but, in the process, we have been transformed. We are changed from sinner to saint. This is why the apostle Paul addresses the people in the various churches as saints and wrote, "All things are passed away and behold! All things have become new." This means that during our salvation experience, we become new creatures in Christ Jesus. Make no mistake. Our feeling of being so clean is real. We are indeed cleansed and made whole. We are saved, transformed, and justified- as if we had never sinned. So, let us rejoice in our salvation.

We are Redeemed through his blood We have had God's grace lavished upon us and we now have the hope of eternal life. "It is not of ourselves. It is the gift of God"

Through Christ, God Has Made Known the Mystery of His Ultimate Will What is God's will, hidden until Jesus came into the world? God's will be for every person who believes in Jesus as their Savior to be redeemed. And we are!

No more searching for truth as an unreachable entity. No more searching for eternal meaning in the material world. This kind of search is about eternal meanings that are beyond the material universe. Beyond the quest of secular philosophers who try by human logic to find truth or try to reduce truth with esoteric words or mathematical formulas.

True, such a search has value on a material level, but the kind of search which we are discussing is on a higher level. Why? Spiritual truth is more than words. It is higher than human logic confirmed deep within the human breast. We have an inner, inexpressible sense of knowing. As one philosopher at Dallas Seminary said, "You just know because you know." So, we need not seek truth as some unattainable essence. Our Bible says, "You will know the truth and the truth will set you free." We need not flounder, trying to find the real meaning of our existence with material understandings. These insights are good for what they are, but only for what they are, on a material level. Engaging in a spiritual quest on a material level is useless. Why? Because Jesus is the very essence of life's meaning.

He said, "I am the way, the truth and the life." So, we know, experiencing Jesus goes far beyond verbal or human expression, no matter how lofty. We just pray, "Lord may I feel your presence today?" And we will! And though it may be impossible to explain it to someone else, deep inside we know it is real. This is one reason why it is sometimes difficult to share our Christian testimony with those who are not born again. We find ourselves trying, without success, to describe our deepest feelings and our deepest thoughts with words.

believe this is one reason we have religious expression in the arts like music and dance because our experience with Jesus is so profound, so deep that it goes beyond our ability to describe or explain it. I remember a Black preacher once saying, to my delight, "It's better felt than telt." But we still try. And we should because some may see the light of gospel in spite of our meager efforts.

I remember reading the words of Saint Teresa, "God didn't call me to be successful. He called me to be faithful." I believe this applies to all Christians because we know that: Jesus is the way - He is the right spiritual path and direction that leads us to eternal life.

Jesus is the answer to purpose in our lives "to glorify God and enjoy him forever." And his love was shown by his coming to the earth to become the final sacrifice for our sins. This alone affirms our worth.

Jesus is the truth- He wants to establish within us that inner sense of spiritual knowing, so that we can say with conviction:

"I know in whom I have believed and am persuaded that he is able to keep that which I have committed unto him against that day."

His desire is for us to love him and be with him forever. No matter what our trials and tests are, we must never forget this.

And Jesus is the life eternal life. The ultimate reality, ultimate life revealed for all of us to experience. So, when we quote that wonderful scripture where Jesus said, "I am the way, the truth and the life," we know that it is God's ultimate will for us to experience eternal life with him This truth is not based on feeling. It is a fact. God loves us! And scripture tells us that these cosmic events will happen in God's appointed time. The apostle Paul writes these prophetic words:

Times must reach their fulfillment. This means that certain things must come to pass as recorded in the prophetical writings of both Old and New Testaments.

Then, total, unified, perfect order will be established All things will become new.

This means a total re-creation of the entire universe, and us as well.

This recreated, perfect, Divine order will be under one head - Jesus Christ! Then, Paul goes on to tell us of the most remarkable affirmations of our redemption in the entire New Testament. He declares:

In Christ We were Marked with a Seal How did this happen?

We heard the "Word of Truth." We heard the Good News, the Gospel and something stirred within our souls. We experienced what scripture teaches. "Faith comes by hearing and hearing by the Word of God." So, after hearing the gospel:

We believed -Acting on the stirring of the Holy Spirit within us we said, "I believe." And through the redemptive work of our Lord, we were changed. We were made new in Christ!

We Were Marked with a Seal by the Holy Spirit! - How did this happen? We were born again. We are now part of God's family. And to realize that God loves us as we are, is one of the greatest of all spiritual insights. WE can't redeem ourselves, but we don't have to. Jesus paid it all on Calvary!

God really does love us as we are, but he also knows what we can become as he enables us.

How great is God's plan for us! He chose us to be holy and blameless and provided the way through Jesus Christ. And He sealed it with his Holy Spirit. And someday he will return to finalize his great plan. Praise his holy name.

Who Is God's Family?

Scripture lesson: Mark 3: 13-35

I have heard people who are happily married use phrases like, "She understands me." or "She laughs at my jokes." "I feel comfortable around him." "He listens to me, and I feel understood." "We do things together." "We just enjoy being with each other." "We share life together." "We pray together."

Of course, no relationships are perfect, but this is marriage at its best and families at their best.

There is no substitute for these cherished relationships. Our family can ge us a sense of belonging, of being appreciated and feeling understood. This is important beyond words. To belong to a good family is very special and should never be taken for granted. After all, everyone wants to be loved and accepted. And nobody likes to be misunderstood.

In today's scripture lives on there are several important themes to deal with. First, Jesus chooses his apostles, his spiritual family. He is very careful in this, knowing the important challenges and tasks that lie ahead. Jesus needed loyal persons dedicated to him, able to do the necessary work to be required of them, and reliable. So, among the large number of followers that could be chosen, Jesus narrows his selection down to twelve.

Jesus Appoints Twelve Apostles Why twelve? Well, twelve is symbolic of the twelve tribes of Israel. And the apostles were going to be sent out to minister to the entire Jewish nation, to all twelve tribes as well as to the gentiles, no matter where they were scattered.

The selection process was very important. According to the renowned theologian, Dr. William Barklay, to be chosen as the student of a Rabbi was a great honor, longed for by many a Jewish boy. Why? Because only the best and the brightest were selected. So, it is nonsense to depict Jesus' careful selection of his Apostles as just a group of ignorant fishermen and low-class workers. Jesus knew their potential was far greater than this. They were selected to go out and change the world. Jesus chose his Apostles carefully, granting this honor not to just one person, but to twelve men carefully appointed by him:

To be with him because they needed to be taught. And because they didn't even know what they didn't know. He selected them:

To preach the good news to the world The apostles needed to be made ready to do this. Little did they know that they would travel to distant parts of the world, risking their lives to spread the gospel. So, Jesus also selected them:

To have authority over evil and its power His Apostles needed to receive power from on high to help usher in the Kingdom of God and the new Age of Grace. Did the religious authorities of the day grasp what was happening, with Jesus doing miraculous things and choosing his Apostles? No. They were blinded by the strictures and rules they imposed on themselves and on the people through their fastidious interpretations of Mosaic law.

Jesus Is Misunderstood Why? The people were looking for a military type of leader, not a shepherd. Jesus was much misunderstood because, though he represented the rugged individualism of a shepherd, he did not come with the military might of a dictator.

Jesus' family did not understand him, and they were embarrassed They thought he had gone mad; so, they called to him and just wanted to take him home.

The teachers of the law failed to recognize who he was and condemned him. True, they recognized his amazing intelligence, his unchallengeable interpretation of Old Testament scripture, but as to his miracle working power, they attributed it to Satan. So,

Jesus exposed their illogical, impossible conclusion and gave a stern warning that anyone who postures himself in total opposition to God, and ascribes the works of God to Satan, prevents God's forgiveness.

Jesus describes this sin as being unforgivable. Why so? Because persons attributing the works of God to Satan, place themselves in direct opposition to God. This is the mind of an apostate, one who totally refuses the saving grace and love of God.

Jesus Teaches a Great lives on About Family and Social Tyranny A very valuable insight because:

As wonderful as families and communities are when they are at their best, sometimes they make it difficult and quite painful for children and youth as they mature and enter adulthood.

How does this happen? By constantly reminding a person how they used to be as a child, treating the young adult or even an older adult like they were still immature children, when they are not; they've grown up and matured out of their former immature thinking and behavior. They have moved on, far beyond their childish ways.

And these positive changes should be respected and encouraged because they will help them mature even more. Most everyone has faced this kind of problem at one time or another.

I Corinthians 13: addresses the matter very well,

"When I was a child, I talked like a child, I thought like a child, I reasoned like a child. When I became a man, I put childish ways behind me."

Jesus' family was no exception. They misunderstood him in this new situation and likely saw him only as a family member or as the boy he used to be, not realizing he was now a man, to be publically confirmed by God as the Christ, the Messiah, at his baptism.

In today's terms, when a young person changes and matures for the better, it should be recognized and celebrated. How do we do this? It's really very simple, by saying things like, h My, you are becoming a fine young man or a fine young lady." Positive strokes are good when deserved and are helpful because we, too, may have experienced being treated as if we were still immature children. It is important to recognize growth and maturity and celebrate it when we see it. Put downs are a social dead end.

My father-in-law, who was a fine Christian man, knew me from the time I was fifteen, when I started to show an interest in his beautiful daughter. A hard-working man and a former marine, he always called me boy and he meant no harm by it. I knew this because he called his own son boy. At first it was tolerable and amusing, but as time went on, actually decades, it got to be a bit annoying. So, during our annual summer visit to PA, when I reached fifty years of age, I asked him "'Dad, How old does a fella have to be before you call him a man?' "Dad Snyder, sputtered defensively, "Well, you're still a boy to me." Josephine and I had a private laugh over that one. Fine Christian folks, and we got along well. But here is an example of being misperceived through the passage of time.

Another amusing incident happened one summer when Dad Snyder privately referred to his cranky neighbor as "'Old Geezer." Mom Snyder heard it and said, "Joe! You' re the same age as he is!" Josephine and I got another private laugh out of that one.

And my own dear father was, at times, also short sighted along this line. During my senior year at Central Bible College, I happened to mention one of my professors, whom I admired, Professor Nicholas Nikoloff, who had just received his doctorate from New York University, at that time, the largest university in the world.

Dad replied, seemingly unimpressed spouted, "Nick Nikoloff? I know Nick. I used to go to school with Nick." You see, Dad had graduated at the top of his class among the men and apparently outdid him in some of the courses. But dad no longer knew, the now, Dr. Nikoloff who had grown and matured beyond my own father intellectually. Yet dad still saw him as he knew him many years before in their undergraduate days.

I mention these examples because they are common experiences for all of us, especially for young people as they mature and progress in their careers. Granted, distance and the passing of time are sometimes important factors in this; when we don't see someone for a long time, we tend to remember that person as if we last saw him or her. However, the problem can still exist even when there is frequent contact with a person.

This same type of situation, that of being misunderstood, confronted. Jesus, now an adult, but misunderstood by his community and even by his own family. So,

His family disapproves - because they fail to see who he really is; they see him only as a family member, not as Jesus the Messiah, the Christ.

The community leaders disapprove The folks where he grew up thought they knew him; but they saw him only as a disruptor of the social and religious status quo challenging the influence of the local religious authorities.

His family, embarrassed, calls him to come home with them. They just wanted to get out of there. Apparently, blinded by only seeing him as a family member, they were confused by his Divine call. They didn't understand, and embarrassed, they just wanted to take him and go home, away from the disapproving crowd as though they needed to protect him. However, if Jesus were to go with them under these circumstances it would be like he was denying his very purpose for being here on the earth!

Jesus' family and the local community leaders, perhaps without realizing it, were tempting him to question his very purpose in life, get him to doubt his identity by showing their disapproval.

Families can exact great harm to a family member by unfair criticism and disapproval. It can affect them emotionally for a long time, sometimes for their entire lives.

However, Jesus knew who he was and was not influenced by family disapproval or the disapproval of the local religious leaders; he took command of the situation and:

Jesus gives an answer, including all of them, by asking a rhetorical question, "who is my mother and brother?" Then, he answers his own question in strongly declarative language, "Whoever does God's will is my brother and sister and mother." This concise answer, direct and seemingly so simple, is amazing in its scope because it includes the entire human race. Jesus does this by setting forth one vital criterion, "Whoever does God's will. And, in this case, God's will is accepting and believing in Jesus, the one God sent.

In this way Jesus' answer overrides human blood lines. It overrides all political and all other connections in favor of spiritual bonding with the family of God. This is huge because Jesus places the entire human race on a covenantal level, that we can all be as one as we do God's will, which begins with believing in him as our Lord and Savior as born-again believers we are all part of the family of God.

With so few words, Jesus explains the important covenantal relationship that transcends even the close ties of earthly family. So important because it enables missionaries and evangelists to deal with difficult situations, especially when they travel to remote parts of the earth.

And, of course, Jesus recognized that our earthly family is also important. When he was dying on the cross, he turned to his mother, Mary, and said to his disciple John,

"Dear woman, here is your son, and to John, "'Here is your mother." and from that time John took Jesus' mother into his house."

Biblical authorities tell us that Jesus' earthly father, Joseph, had probably died sometime before this, and since Jesus had been supporting the family, he wanted to be sure that his mother was being cared for. So, right up to the day of his crucifixion, Jesus also cared about his earthly mother and family.

And we know that the spiritual relationship concerning God's will, of which Jesus spoke at an earlier time, allows other matters to take their proper place in our lives, Doing God's will, enables to, unconditionally, love our neighbors as ourselves.

May God, through the presence of Christ, by the power of his Holy Spirit, help us to better understand others so that we may love unconditionally. And may our lives point to the source of Divine love our heavenly Father, through Jesus Christ, who loves every one of us as a father loves his children.

And so, having accepted Jesus Christ as our Savior and following him, which is God's will for us, "We are the family of God."

The Original Order of Things

Scripture lesson: Genesis 2:4-24; I Corinthians 15:22

Text: Genesis 3:15

'There is an old civilization that still exists in the high Sierra Mountains of the Bolia/Columbia region. These peoples, descendants of the ancient South American civilization, called the Tayrona, number about 45,000 today. They sought refuge from the Spanish Conquistadores high in a mountain paradise with peaks about 18,000 feet above the Caribbean coast of Colombia.

In the wake of the conquest, after having climbed to safety and settling there, they developed an utterly new dream of the earth. What is interesting is that they observed that there was a spiritual dimension in creation and in their own existence as well, and they also realized that things were out of balance., that their universe was out of balance. True, their insights were limited and not altogether accurate, but in their search for truth, they somehow sensed and concluded that balance was needed. So, with great effort they try to somehow balance the human mind and spirit with all the forces of nature. The Tayrona talk openly about the force of creation, or Se, which to them is the spiritual energy contained in all existence, and aliveness, what they understand to be human thought, soul and imagination.

What is fascinating about this and important to them is not what is measured and seen, but what are the many meanings and connections that lie beneath the tangible realities of the world. They see these intangible connections linking all things together. To the Tayrona every element is imbued with a higher significance; even the most modest of creatures can be seen as a teacher, and every feature of the world mirrors creation in a vast interconnection.

The Tayrona say that we are the younger brother who is poisoning the earth. And with other people and groups they are saying that civilization has departed from the original order of things, that we are destroying our environment, and along with it, ourselves.

The Tayrona have a point, perhaps somewhat overstated; but this line of reasoning does have value. It causes us to think seriously about the direction the world is going at various levels.

Consider our physical and emotional health, environmental concerns, political directions, economic stability in our country, freedom of speech and freedom of religion, all very important. And we know, of course, that these issues are complex, but reaching down deeper, as Christians, we ask, 'What is the root of the problem'?" And we conclude that it is the fallen nature of man, where man has pushed aside the good in order to follow selfish pursuits. The sin nature of man, the good creation of God, which has chosen to satisfy the self at the expense of others.

On the political front there has, for a long time, been talk of a new world order. And there is certainly a need for a new world order, but what kind? As promising as this might seem, world peace and the hope for mankind lies not in the secular world, but in a spiritual new world order. Here is the root of the problem. Humankind is in need of restoring the lost relationship, lost because of disobedience, with the One who has allowed us to be. In the book of Genesis, we learn several vital, very basic facts:

Physically, We Are Part of the Earth We are part of a giant ecosystem with an elaborate food chain and amazing systems that challenge yet sustain life. Some scientists say that the material universe is the result of a highly ordered chaos, partly described by the term fractals, which are unending, similar patterns. I disagree and prefer to perceive the material universe as the result of a highly ordered mind, the likes of which no one will ever really understand because it is the mind of God. It suffices to simply say:

God made us - Genesis says it in the very beginning of chapter one in the Bible. God made us from the dust of the earth. This is an undeniable fact concerning the physical part of our existence. But we are much more.

When we die, we know that our physical bodies return to the material of the earth, as does all physical life. This is part of the originally created order of things when God said that his creation was good, but we know that we are much more than our physical bodies. We are body, soul and spirit. Yes, we are good because God created us, but as free moral agents, we are capable of making decisions, even decisions that are not good. And listening to the evil one and following a path of rebellion and disobedience describes the fallen state of the human race. This was man's radical departure from the intended order of things, but thankfully, God provided hope in sending. Jesus to a fallen world.

Our breath is the breath of life- Our life is life that is God breathed and what a privilege it is! It is important that we recognize this. Life is a privilege, not a right. And by accepting God's provision of salvation through Jesus Christ we are now part of the restored relationship, part of the original order of things, because we are saved. Yes, we are much more than our physical bodies. We can say, as Christians, we are redeemed:

As Christians, We Are Part of a Glorious, Restored, Eternal Relationship with God God's original order is and has always been eternal. We must forever keep in mind that we are not just physical beings. We are body, soul and spirit. And the very fact that we can think of things that are eternal gives clue to the reality of the eternalness of our soul. And it is interesting to also consider that in the original order of things:

God made the first humans to be useful. That has not changed. In fact, psychologists say that one of the most stabilizing forces in a person's psyche is useful work and feeling useful.

God instituted marriage as a sacred bond. That has not changed. Marriage is sacred.

God desires an unbroken relationship with himself, based on obedience and a loving relationship with him. This has not changed. God wants us saved to eternity.

Jesus Has Restored the Order of Things and the original intent of man Having a beautiful relationship with his Creator fractured because of sin.

Looking for meaning in all this? First, it is important to realize that we are much more than Our body. We are body in that we are physical. We are soul and spirit integrated with our physical bodies that God has breathed into the breath of life, the elan vital. This is our mysterious eternal quality that gives us a God consciousness and the ability to recognize that. Jesus has conquered Satan's evil grip over fallen humanity. death, hell and the grave and made possible the return to the original order of things - that is, a perfect relationship with him.

He restores us to obedience And we now want to know and do God's will. He leads us from sinfulness to holiness. We are led from a life of confusion to a life of covenant. Through Christ the covenantal relationship is restored. He has conquered death that we might have eternal life with him now our sorrow is turned to hope and joy.

While it is obvious that physically we are a part of the earth and indeed, part of the earth's ecosystem, it is also true that we are much more than our physical body. God made us body soul and spirit. Our soul is the eternal seat of our consciousness, and our spirit is the life force, the elan vital, of the soul.

Jesus said, "I am come that you might have life and have it more abundantly." Jesus also teaches that the Kingdom of God is within us. In a world torn by war and hate there is a restoration that takes place within us through the guidance and presence of God's Holy spirit.

Let us be thankful for any good that is done in the world but let us also realize that there is a new spiritual world order coming. And that as the redeemed of the Lord, we are already a part of that new world order! Jesus Christ has made it so! Let us rejoice and be glad!

Jesus, the Giver of Living Water

Scripture lesson: John 4:7-15a; 25-26 Text: John 4:14

When space explorers analyze the properties of a planet, looking for life, the first thing they look for is the atmosphere. The single most important clue on their list is water.

Regardless of the minerals they might find and regardless of the terrain, locating water is primary because it is key to the possibility of life.

Water, the compound we know as H2O, flowing in our rivers, streams, lakes and oceans, is the hinge pin of life on the earth. All Living things need water, from the tiniest single cell to the African elephant to giant creatures of the sea. All Living things need water. And the human body, made of 40 -70 percent water according to the National Strength and Conditioning Association, needs a daily supply of water.

Research shows that we need to drink water or liquids containing water several times a day.

And many of us know why through painful experience. Not enough water in our bodies can cause leg cramps, low energy, a poor mood and even affect our ability to think clearly.

Drinking adequate amounts of water and going for a walk can help our overall health.

It's amusing when someone says to a person in a bad mood,

"Oh, go take a hike." Really, not bad advice, but it might be better to say, "Drink some water and go for a walk. You'll feel better." Water is precious. It is sustaining and it is vital.

Today's scripture narrate is about water and is most interesting because Jesus uses water as his venue to witness to this Samaritan woman who is in need of salvation. So, during their conversation, he uses the opportunity to reveal himself as the Messiah.

This interesting account begins with Jesus and his disciples travelling through the province of Samaria and coming to the town of Sychar, located near Jacob's well. Jesus was tired and thirsty from the journey. So, he stopped to get a drink from the well, while the disciples went into town for food. It was about noon. And while Jesus was resting at the well, a Samaritan woman came by to draw water. Being thirsty, Jesus asked her for a drink. To grant his request, a container with a rope was needed to get the water and the well was 100 feet deep.

Here is where Jesus' simple request gets complicated. This woman knows, that being a Samaritan woman, Jesus should not even speak to her. Why? Because of religious disagreements, the Samaritans only accepted the Pentateuch (the first fe books in the Old Testament as scripture); they worshipped only at their temple on Mount Gerizim, (not the required temple in Jerusalem); they intermarried with gentiles which was forbidden, and some mixed idol worship with worshipping the one true God. The situation was serious.

The Jews saw the Samaritans as traitors to their faith and hated the Samaritans to the point where they would not even use dishes the Samaritans used.

So, the Samaritan woman's response made sense. Why? It would be necessary for Jesus to use the forbidden Samaritan utensil, her container of water, to get a drink.

What would Jesus do? Ignoring her comment, he uses the situation to meet her spiritual need, telling her about the Living water he could ge to her. Her reply revealed the shallowness of her thinking, on a concrete level, so, she didn't understand that Jesus was instructing her on a spiritual level. (Often a communication problem today.)

However, since water was scarce and difficult to get, having a limitless supply of it appealed to her. So, she told Jesus she wanted the water he could ge, to never thirst again and not have to continue to draw water. (Remember, the well was 100 feet deep.) Unfortunately, at this juncture, the Samaritan woman missed the point!

But Jesus, wisely, doesn't address her misunderstanding. Instead, he goes directly to her immediate spiritual need. He recounts her fe husbands and she was Living with a man who was not her husband. Apparently startled, and realizing Jesus' amazing insight, she deflects the conversation away from her present immoral state saying, "Our ancestors worshipped on this mountain, and you say Jerusalem is the place we ought to worship." (She meant the Samaritan temple on Mount Gerizim.) Notice, she doesn't say that she worshipped there.

Was she trying to justify her religious position through the practices of her ancestors? And her defense comment brought up the old wound between the Jews and the Samaritans. But Jesus cleverly, deflected her comment predicted that a time would come when true worshippers would no longer worship at either temple. What did Jesus mean by his prediction? The coming of a new order, the coming of the Age-of-Grace that was open to the whole world!

Adroitly, after considering the value of natural water, Jesus, compared natural water to Living water with its eternal life giving and life sustaining properties.

Using this comparison, Jesus enlightened the Samaritan woman, by explaining that by partaking of the water he could ge her she would never thirst again. What was he explaining? The good news of salvation!

What a wonderful teaching tool! By comparing her natural thirst with her spiritual thirst and that he could permanently quench her spiritual thirst, the answer was clear; Jesus was leading her to salvation!

Digging deeper, you may still ask. What was Jesus really talking about? The thirst for truth? Yes. The yearning within all human beings to make sense of their lives? Yes. Is he addressing, by implication, that other religious paths offer no real quenching of spiritual thirst? Yes. Yes, to all of the above. The spiritual implications are there. And by addressing her spiritual condition directly, Jesus taught her about spiritual transformation, being born again and being forever changed, spiritual thirst forever quenched.

It is now obvious that Jesus had motes above and beyond the seeming simplicity of this situation, asking her for a drink. He led their conversation from a simple drink of water to meeting her spiritual need and reaching into the deep recesses of her soul.

Now, by taking another step by step look at this encounter we will gain more insights:

Jesus Revealed Her Spiritual Need to Her. Perhaps she was looking for happiness through her many marriages and was still struggling to make sense of her life. Jesus knew that she was a thirsty soul who needed the Living water that he could ge.

She needed to know who Jesus He is indeed the Christ, the Son of the Living God. She needed to know why he is who he is God's gift to her spiritual longings. She needed to know his mission on the earth. Her religion, steeped in tradition, blinded her to the truth. She needed to know God's grace and. Jesus the ger of life.

Jesus Revealed Her Need for Living Water She, like everyone else, was not able to live a life of purity, a life of holiness, without spiritual help.

She needed the water that could become a spring of Living water within her dry and thirsty soul. In short, she needed Jesus Christ in her life.

She needed the water of salvation, of eternal life - She needed salvation, being born again into a new covenant relationship where she would never thirst again.

She needed to spread the gospel, the good news to others of her experience with Jesus the Christ.

Jesus Revealed Himself to Her It is he who is the source of the Living water, of which he speaks, water that can quench spiritual thirst forever, because salvation is forever. This is no ordinary water. It is Living water, the answer to the spiritual longings within the Samaritan woman and of everyone. It bespeaks of the universality of salvation. Salvation is for everyone.

The Samaritan woman, at first, did not recognize Jesus as the Messiah Perhaps, an Old Testament prophecy explains this. Isaiah 53: 2b, says, "He had no beauty or majesty to attract us to him, nothing in his appearance that we should desire him." We're used to typing: Yul Brynner as Pharaoh or Charlton Heston as Moses.

Her eyes were opened, and she did recognize Jesus as Messiah - by his Wisdom and insights into her life. So, she responded positively by asking Jesus for the water he could provide. We're not told whether she gave the tired and thirsty Jesus a drink. Her spiritual need super-ceded his physical one.

She Ran to Her Village to Spread the Good News perhaps as the first missionary. When she realized, she was talking to her Messiah, she ran to spread the good news to others. We should do the same.

From a simple request for a drink of water, Jesus led the Samaritan woman to Living water, eternal life. And though we don't know her name. We do know that Jesus broke the barriers of social prejudice and led the Samaritan Woman to a knowledge of himself.

From natural water, that quenches thirst only temporarily, to the Living water of eternal life that Jesus gives, which enables us to live the most superior life on the face of the earth.

Beautifully, Jesus revealed himself to the Samaritan woman as her Messiah.

At first, she didn't understand; although she believed Messiah was to come. She said, "I know that Messiah is coming. When he comes, he will explain everything to us."

Then, Jesus told her plainly, 'I who speak to you am He." Upon hearing this, she left her water jar, went back to the town and told the people, "Come see a man who told me everything I ever did. Could this be the Christ?"

The townspeople then came to Jesus, and many believed in him because of the Samaritan woman's testimony. The towns people then asked Jesus to stay. So, he stayed for two days and many more became believers.

Then they said to the Samaritan woman, "We no longer believe just because of what you said; now we have heard for ourselves, and we know that this man really is the Savior of the world." And so, it is with us today. We know Jesus Christ is the Savior of the World!

Too Late for Tears

Scripture lesson: Hebrews 12:14-29 Text: Hebrews 12:28

Have you ever had anyone tell you, ""You're over the hill?" Well, while in my twenties, at the end of a visit with our family doctor, I asked him for some advice for keeping in shape. Instead of calmly suggesting some exercises, getting enough sleep and careful eating habits, he exclaimed, 'You're over the hill! You're over the hill! You are just trying to build big muscles." I was in my twenties at just around 140 pounds. So, I told him, "I'm not trying to build big muscles; I just want to know how to be more physically fit." He butted in, contradicted me, and blurted out again, ""Yes, you are. You are just trying to build big muscles. You're over the hill. You're over the hill!" (Back in the early nineteen sixties adult fitness was not emphasized as it is today.) Shocked at his response and feeling embarrassed for even asking his advice, it took a long time for me to get over the incident. Finally, I came to realize that he was the one out of line. He didn't know how to advise me in the area of physical fitness, in which he wasn't trained. In my twenties and over the hill? Nonsense! But this unpleasant experience did have value; it caused me to think more about the passage of time.

Sometime later, Josephine and I were on a shopping trip, walking on the streets in York, Pennsylvania. What an interesting city, with its large, old, brick row houses, many historic buildings, and some streets actually paved with brick. As we looked around, enjoying the walk, I suddenly realized that most of this was here long before I was born. Of course, we knew this from our history classes in high school; but, for some reason, now it seemed fresh, like a sudden insight. There is a vast difference between simply knowing about something compared with actually realizing it. So, while thinking about buildings and streets and other things that were here before we existed, I also realized that they, most likely, would be here a long time after we were gone, and that we were experiencing life in a small sliver of time.

These thoughts are valuable because they ge us more of a sense of our place in the scheme of things and help motivate us to live up to our potential by being usefully involved.

Reflecting on time and place, I realized more than ever the value of the sermon I heard in my youth by the evangelist, H. B. Kelshner. He strongly emphasized the importance of Living our lives in the light of eternity. I am very grateful for that spiritual insight and the sense of time it awakened in me. So, while walking the streets of York, Pennsylvania that afternoon we reflected on how important it is to make the most of our lives. We have tried to do this.

Thinking of the importance of the values we live by reminds me of the researcher, Louis Terman who did studies in intelligence. He developed the Stanford-Binet Intelligence Scales that are still in use today. Terman was especially interested in people who were very bright. His interest led him to do lifetime studies of 1528 persons who scored at the genius level.

The studies were continued by other researchers after he died. His study is the oldest, longest longitudinal study ever done in the field of psychology.

Sparked by the popular belief that gifted children were sickly, socially inept, and not well- rounded he was determined to get at the facts. His study, very accurate and complete, was originally based on data he collected in 1921-22. During the study, he found that gifted children were usually social, well-adjusted, did better than average in school and were even taller than average.

A follow-up study done in 1923-24 showed that the children had maintained their high IQ scores and were still above average overall as a group. Over half of them finished college, compared with 8% of the general population at the time. A relative few reached great prominence in their fields; but the majority of the participants' lives, by comparison with their potential for very high achievement, were more mundane. As adults they pursued common occupations that demanded far less of them than they were mentally capable of. Certainly, nothing wrong with that, but it led Terman to conclude, saying "At any rate, we have seen that intellect and achievement are far from perfectly correlated." What was missing? What was the missing ingredient? Motivation! And this leads to an interesting story.

Louis Terman, along with developing the Stanford-Binet Scales, also developed the Army Alpha test, designed to determine a person's aptitudes and predict success in various occupations. It was gen to the soldiers as they were mustered out of the army. Now, begins one of my favorite stories.

While teaching instrumental music in the Red Lion, Pennsylvania public schools, we gave fourth grade prospective band students the Selmer Music Aptitude test to help determine talent and which instruments they would most likely be successful in learning to play. We interviewed both parents and students.

Phil Burg's daughter wanted to play the French Horn but scored a little below the musical aptitude cutoff point for learning the difficult French horn. During the interview, after reviewing the results of the Selmer music aptitude test, I said to Phil, knowing his background, that I thought she would succeed, and we should ge her a chance.

Hearing the word of encouragement, Phil said, 'I'm glad you said that. When

I got out of the Army, I took the Army Alpha test and there were two main results. I should never go into music, and I should never go into business." Continuing, with a twinkle in his eye, Phil said, "There is one thing those tests can't measure and that is how hard a person can try. I have been in the insurance business for several years and I have played in the York Symphony Orchestra as a string bass player for ten years." It was thrilling to hear of his success!

But wait, the story gets even better. Several years later, after our family moved to Dayton, I got a phone call. Phil Burg's daughter, Kathy, went on to play professionally in the Spring Garden Band of York, Pennsylvania where I used to play. It was most exciting to hear this. She had seized the day, worked hard and succeeded. And on Nov. 5, 2023, when the band played my composition, "The. Journey," I was thrilled to learn that she was still playing in the band!

The point is obvious. You and I know of people who live their lives as though they had all the time in the world. They don't and we don't. They pass through their life phases seemingly oblivious to the passage of time. Biblical wisdom tells us to seize the day.

The writer of Hebrews gives us a close look at the practical side of the Christian life, leading us to consider our daily lives and our lifestyle as Christians. Life is precious and we should handle it with care. We want a sense of usefulness and minimize feelings and tears of regret because of bad decisions and missed opportunities. So, the writer of Hebrews tells us that:

We Have Great Personal Responsibility It is about personal covenant and putting to good use our talents and abilities. The mind and heart are awesome things to waste. In a world with so much turmoil, with so many angry, dishonest people and so much hate, we have a great personal responsibility to ourselves and to others.

We are to pursue peace with everyone especially in today's world when it is so easy to get involved in conflict and so challenging to maintain peace.

We are to pursue the holy life to literally, run after the holy life, which means to separate ourselves from the sinful life. So, we strive to live detached from the self-seeking, self-destroying values of the world, recognizing that we are, "in the world but not of the world." Why is this so important? God wants a special, eternal relationship with us, and to truly realize that this world is not our home. We're just passing through and because the time will come when it will be too late for change and too late for tears.

Thank God there is forgiveness now for our past indiscretions and opportunity still out there waiting to be seized. After all, 'Time is the measurement of our life." So, by Living our lives unto God, we will avoid the remorse and regret of bad decisions, when it is too late for tears. Now is the time to prayerfully live for the present and plan for the future. Now is the time to respond to the inner promptings of the Holy Spirit. Recognizing the gifts and graces within each of us, those special abilities and aptitudes we have in our possession:

We have a Great Social Responsibility. Individuals and society, at large, need Jesus Christ in their lives. And since we are a people redeemed, who know the love of God, who know the joy of salvation and know the importance of caring for others,

We are to look after the physical and spiritual welfare of others. As we practice loving our neighbor as ourselves. Jesus has commissioned us to care for the poor, the ill, the aged, the lonely and commissioned us to share the gospel with those who need Jesus in their lives. It is true. We affect people on many different levels, but most importantly on a spiritual level.

We are to help others, as we see the need and have the opportunity to guide them away from a sinful life. Why? Because the time will come when it will be too late for change and too late for tears. While there is opportunity, good advice and good examples can make all the difference. We should respond to the inner promptings of the Holy Spirit to share the gospel message that:

We have a Great Hope to Share with the World And, considering how the world is in turmoil, there is no better time to share the good news that, "Jesus is the hope of the world." Now is the time to teach spiritual values while it is not too late for change and too late for tears. We can share this hope because:

We are the people of a New Covenant. And because of the saving grace of Christ, a great change is coming. Our future is bright, eternally bright. As the redeemed of the Lord, we can say concerning our salvation, we have been forgiven, our sins are gone forever, lost in the sea of God's forgetfulness, and "behold all things have become new." Since we look at life through the eyes of a person redeemed, it is important that we live our lives by this great truth and share it with others. This realization has a positive, permanent effect on our values, on our vision for the future and on what is eternal. Scripture teaches that we have the promise that someday:

The entire order of creation will be changed. All things will pass away, and all things will become new including our newly created life.

What is eternal will remain eternal. God's Spirit and presence will remain forever because God is eternal. You may ask, "Why will these things happen?" The writer of Hebrews gives us the answer and inspires us with great hope for the present and for the future, saying:

"'Therefore, since we are receiving a kingdom that cannot be shaken, let us be thankful, and so worship God acceptably with reverence and awe."

"Therefore," is a decisive word that leads logically from previous statements to support the conclusion that something is absolutely true, in this case a wonderful promise; "Receiving a kingdom that cannot be shaken," the word receiving assumes that God is giving and that we are receiving and we will be part of God's kingdom, an eternal kingdom that promises eternal life with him; next comes the exhortation, "Let us be thankful," and notice that it says, "Let us," an incluse expression, and, of course, being thankful should be our natural response to God's great love for forever redeeming us; "and so worship God acceptably," implies, no more sacrifices for sin; Jesus was the final sacrifice for sin and pure worship is the right and grateful response, eliminating anything that would detract from the purity of its intent; "with reverence and awe;' happens during and after we are saved, after a true born again experience. Just as Jesus said to Nicodemus, we are born anew, cleansed, by God's Holy Spirit.

These are wonderful words for God's people because when our work on earth is done and our time on earth is completed, it will truly be a time of great rejoicing. There will be no reason for tears of remorse, only joy! Yes, it is true; it will be too late for tears of remorse, but shouts of victory and joy will be the order of the day. We are redeemed!

From the book of Revelation, written by St. John, hear these wonderful, inspiring words:

> "Then I saw a new heaven and a new earth, for the first heaven and the first earth had passed away, and there were no longer any seas, I saw the Holy City, the new Jerusalem, coming down out of heaven from God, prepared as a bride beautifully dressed for her husband. And I heard a loud voice from the throne saying, 'Now the dwelling of God is with men, and he will live with them. They will be his people, and God himself will be with them and be their God. He will wipe every tear from their eyes. There will be no more death or mourning or crying or pain, for the old order of things has passed away." He who was seated on the throne said, 'I am making everything new.'

So, may we remember these wonderful promises. God will wipe away all tears and the Saints of God, everywhere in the world who name the name of Jesus Christ, will sing the song of the redeemed! Will it be too late for tears? Yes, but now there will be shouts of victory and songs of joy that are the order of the day; and they will be right in tune and right on time!

Who Is He Who Is Called the Christ?

Scripture lesson: Hebrews 1:1-4; 2:9 Text: Hebrews 8:1-2

I believe that God wants us to be happy. The Bible makes this very clear in the gospel of John 10:10, when Jesus said,

"'I am the gate; whoever enters through me will be saved. He will come in and go out and find pasture. The thief comes only to steal and kill and destroy; I have come that they might have life and have it abundantly."

Jesus' proclamation to us is clear. The very essence of the abundant Christian life is for us to live our lives to the full, which allows us to enjoy abundant ling. You ask. What is Living our lives to the full? Of course, it means Living a useful life, but it also means to just enjoy being here, Living in the present moment.

Some folks become so wrapped up in their future and string to get ahead financially, that they don't enjoy the present. There is such wisdom in the scripture, "'This is the day the Lord has made! Let us rejoice and be glad in it!" Yes, for us to live in the present, the present moment.

So, living our lives to our fullest potential, with whatever abilities and capacities God has endowed us with, also means fully enjoying life, the life that God has given us.

It grieves me to think how some religious and political groups operate out of fear. Read the New Testament for yourself and you will find that God wants nothing but the best for everyone. Think of the power in John 3:16; and as we read it, do not add anything to it.

"For God so loved the world that he sent his only begotten Son that whosoever believes in him will not perish but have everlasting life."

Here is one of the most powerful, decisive, most incluse verses in the entire Bible and it is centered in love, beginning with, "'For God so loved the world." Obviously, God, our heavenly Father, wants the best for us and continues with an open offer that includes every human being on the face of the earth, "whosoever believes in him will not perish." Notice, the statement does not demand that one belongs to a certain group, as though that group is the privileged one to have eternal life. No! Here the scripture is clearly nonsectarian; it is a totally incluse statement of the truth of the gospel; no secret doubts have room to creep in, like; "Am I one of the privileged ones to have eternal life?" No! This kind of thinking is not scriptural and is totally wrong. The verse does not say, "may not perish." Deliberate, definite, and clear, all doubts are put to rest, with the words, "will not perish, but have everlasting life." So, we should smile, with a smile of inner joy because, along with this scripture, there are at least 20 more verses in the New Testament telling us that God wants us to live a joyful, happy life. Here are a few of them:

I John 1:1-4, "We declare to you what was from the beginning, what we have heard, what we have seen with our eyes, which we have looked at and our hands have touched - this we proclaim, concerning the Word of life. Life appeared; we have seen it and testify to it, and we proclaim to the eternal life, which was with the Father and has appeared to us. "We proclaim to you that we have seen and heard, so that you also may have fellowship with us. And our fellowship is with the Father and with his Son, Jesus Christ. We write this to make our joy complete."

In 2 John 1: 12, "I have much to write to you, but I do not want to use paper and ink. Instead, I hope to visit you and talk with you face to face, so that our joy may be complete."

In I Peter 1: 8, "Though you have not seen him, you love him; and even though you do not see him now, you believe in him and are filled with an inexpressible and glorious joy, for you are receiving the goal of your faith, the salvation of your souls."

So, still seeking, someone may still ask, "'who is he who is called the Christ?" Our answer!

He is the one who came that we might have eternal life, and live our lives joyfully, to the full.

I like the King James translation of John 10:10 where Jesus says, "I am come that they might have life and they might have it more abundantly."

All this talk about the American dream boils down to realizing that the good life is how we live out our faith journey. By being immersed in our relationship with Jesus, and shaped by the wisdom of the scriptures, we will begin to see beyond the superficial to life's deeper meanings; and that our walk with Jesus is truly Living the good life. And to realize that our life is important and meaningful, however small we think it is, in the great scheme of things. We are enabled to see ourselves as an important part of history because we are! And that we are an important part of our family, an important part of our local community and important to the community at large. We really are part of the big picture, important in our own unique way. And live our lives to the full.

Charles es (1874-1954) was one of the most noted of American composers. His father was the director of the Union Army Band and director of a local church choir. One Sunday after the choir had sung, someone complained about a certain person's voice in the choir. Answering the criticism, Mr. es said, "I think he is a very good singer. Listen and hear the song of the ages."

What an insightful remark! Only when we listen with our heart as well as our mind, can we feel the deep expressions of the soul and "hear the song of the ages," music that goes beyond the sound of the human voice and into our hearts as a pure expression of praise to God.

During ancient times and up to the present, many people have sought the good life through pleasure. So, is there anything wrong with pleasure, per se'! No, of course not, but the trap is when pleasure is not part of the broader life experience and becomes the end in itself.

A fine example of wholesome pleasure is commonly found in agrarian communities, where there is a celebration at the end of harvest, and often in some groups, a celebration at the end of each day's work. A beautiful cultural practice, where there is joy and satisfaction in doing the common work of life; genuine satisfaction in work well done is its own reward.

Since we know that seeking pleasure for its own sake is frowned on in the Bible, legitimate pleasure should not be confused with the satisfaction of doing something good, or pleasure in work accomplished.

The term pleasure has been so much abused and distorted that it is sometimes described with the ancient term, Hedonism. This belief says that since life has no meaning, anyway, you might as well just go and seek pleasure for its own sake. Very problematic because pleasure itself is so fleeting it leaves a person in a valueless vacuum.

A similar position, taken and declared at the beginning of Ecclesiastes, where the teacher, who is Solomon, taking on the role of a materialist, says, "Utterly meaningless! Everything is meaningless." Shocking until we read to the end of Ecclesiastes in chapter :8 when Solomon, still in the role of the teacher, says, "However many years a man may live, let him enjoy them." Then Solomon extols the importance of Living a good and useful life in verse 9,

"Be happy, young man, while you are young, and let your heart ge you joy in the days of your youth. Follow the ways of your heart and whatever your eyes see but know that for all these things God will bring you into judgment."

This was not the case with the Greek and Roman hedonists. They said you might as well spend your time wallowing in pleasure, since life has no real meaning anyway. How futile and purposeless is that! Living just for passing fantasies and pleasure for its own sake is wasting one's youth with fleeting illusions. So, misguided, the hedonists fail miserably, missing the satisfaction of Living a good life.

Our journey with Jesus Christ is light years beyond all of this. Jesus enables us to really live so that our joy may be full! - what God wants for you and me! And the wisdom we find in scripture leads us to live close to the Lord- This is the golden key to the good life!

Desiring to be happy is not new. Many folks in the past have sought meaning in the wrong places. For example, the ancient Greeks sought the good life by trying to grasp ultimate reality through pure thought. They figured that if they could free themselves from their bodies and elevate themselves into pure thought, they would somehow know ultimate good.

Psychological experiments have proven this wrong; emotion always accompanies thought. So, without science to guide them the Greeks seeking perfection in an imperfect universe, came up with the Theory of Forms - that says - For every object in this imperfect world there is a perfect object somewhere else. Where did this idea come from? Were they trying to find a perfect state of existence without knowing what it was, actually trying to find heaven?

Whatever they had in mind, the Theory of Forms, with its abstract spiritual dimension, greatly influenced the Greeks to seek perfect symmetry and balance in their art, architecture and even in their daily lives. It is amazing the length they went to, even in their sculptures. Their statues, idealistically depicting life forms, show both sides in relatively perfect symmetry, especially the human face. In their architecture they used mathematical balance and symmetry in what is called the golden proportion or golden mean. They even sought beauty, balance and symmetry in their ethics and morals, enacting laws concerning these and emphasizing education.

And - this is most amazing to me; the philosopher Plato (427-347 B.C.) in his writings on statecraft, predicted that a perfectly just person would be crucified. (Republic II, 361e - 362a). Astounding! Here great philosophical thought leads to the brink of great spiritual insight, but sadly, without a solution. Why? Human reasoning has its limits. But we know the answer!

The world needed the hand of God to lead it and then Jesus appeared on the stage of history at precisely the right time. The Greeks, Romans and others had reached their limit of understanding about knowledge beyond the physical universe. And the Jews were on a yearly merry-go-round of seasonal sacrifices for their sins. The sacrificial system, good in its time, had run its course.

Change was desperately needed.

Fortunately, the writer of Hebrews informs us that the New Covenant through Jesus is better than the old one. The New Covenant moved believers beyond mere law into the new Age, or dispensation, of Grace.

This New Covenant replaced the old one, where mankind, spiritually unfilled, was unable to keep the law perfectly. God's revelation led the human race to Jesus Christ, the perfect personification of the righteous person, that Plato mentioned in his Republic II. He said that because he was righteous, would be crucified. An amazing prediction. However, Plato didn't know the rest of the story. This righteous person he described would rise triumphantly as Savior of the world. An amazing prediction! Plato, without realizing the magnitude of his insight, actually predicted the coming of Jesus Christ.

And linked with this amazing insight, God sent his only Son, the Living Word, to dwell within us to become the final link that would restore man's lost relationship with God. Truly, as we read in Hebrews, Christ is greater than angels and is heir of all wisdom, wealth and glory.

Isaiah, speaks of the Messiah in chapter 53, and the writer of Hebrews connects with this and tells how God spoke through the prophets, about his covenant with Israel (beginning with Abraham) and about his revelation of the Redeemer (Jesus Christ.)

Further, we learn in Hebrews that Jesus is not only an agent in creation as part of the Godhead, but he is also the Divine energy of God radiating God's eternal glory through Jesus, the perfect form of all forms, the exact representation of God's being. Yes, we see God through Jesus Christ!

Who is he who is called the Christ? He is:

Sustainer- of all things by his Word.

He is the Creating God.

He is reason, wisdom and the Divine Word the Logos, the Divine Word!

So, here is the answer to mankind's search for meaning, Jesus Christ. Let the Greek philosophers like Plotinus, who sought purification from matter, or like Plato and the Stoics finally know Jesus as the end of their futile search for Divine reason, Divine law, and Divine order. Let Immanuel Kant and the transcendentalist philosophers, searching for the right action, the categorical imperative, find that the ultimate right action is to be seen in Jesus Christ through his life, death and resurrection. Let the logicians such as Charles Sanders Pierce find true meaning in the very works of Christ. Let them all learn that everything with meaning in this life and the next one is found in Jesus Christ, because he is the embodiment of truth.

Philo, the philosopher and Alexandrian Jew discovered the Logos (Word) to be God's first-born Son, God's image, God's ambassador and humanity's advocate and high priest. And further we read in Hebrews that Jesus Christ is:

Purifier - of all the sins of humankind. (Hebrews 2:9)

Jesus became the ultimate sacrifice for our sin.

No longer is sacrifice necessary- and Jesus is:

Our Heavenly High Priest - at God's right-hand interceding for us.

Jesus finished the work of atonement - which means that:

Jesus provided salvation - for all who believe.

Jesus is our High Priest forever after the eternal order of Melchizedek. He is at this very moment interceding for you and me before the Father.

We know that the good life is something we live, not something acquired. We know that the, so called, American dream is really a life well led unto God. Further, we know that Spiritual pattern and order are experienced in God's will and leading.

And we know that the ultimate action is the very life of Jesus, who is the Way, the truth and the life the answer to true happiness? - "Looking to Jesus, the author and finisher of our faith" "After he had provided purification for sins, he sat down." completing his work of redemption.

Listen, and hear the glorious song of the ages. Who is he who is called the Christ? He is our precious Lord and Savior!

Those who led by faith in God before Christ's coming stand as "a great cloud of witnesses" cheering us on, looking to the last chorus in that great song of the ages, the Song of Redemption.

So, "let us fix our eyes on Jesus, the author and perfecter of our faith, who for the joy set before him, endured the cross, scorning its shame and sat down at the right hand of the throne of God."

Who is he who is called the Christ? He is. Jesus our Savior! - "And the Word become flesh and dwelt among us." - Listen and hear the song of the ages!

Facing Our Responsibility

Scripture lesson: Ezekiel 18:1-9; Kings 24:3-4: Thessalonians 3:1-15

Have you ever resisted an inner prompting to do or say something you knew was right, but was difficult, even unpleasant? I have! And I suspect that you have experienced this inner prompting as well, since it often takes place in a common social setting with social implications.

Well, the prophet Ezekiel's situation was different. It wasn't so simple as a common social setting, but the challenge to do what was right in a difficult situation was quite the same.

Ezekiel received his surprise call in 593 B.C. and was of such magnitude that he sat overwhelmed for seven days. Why was he so overwhelmed? Well, think about it. Suppose you were being asked to do something extremely difficult at your job or at school and multiply it several times over. Would you or I be overwhelmed? Of course, you would, and so would I.

To begin with, the fact that God had manifested himself to Ezekiel was overwhelming enough. Just think for a moment of other times when God called people in the Old Testament and how they responded. When they were led to do or say something difficult, like Ezekiel, they were overwhelmed. Think of Noah being asked to build a giant ark in the desert, yet he built it. Think of Jonah. He tried to run away from God's call and got swallowed by a big fish. Think of Samuel. He was just a boy and had to be instructed how to respond to God's call. Think of ourselves and how we are to answer God's call, whatever it is.

Now, put yourself in Ezekiel's situation. Imagine that God called you to do a very difficult task, and you had no experience. Our response would likely be, "Why me? Why would God choose me for such a daunting task? And Ezekiel likely thought, ""I'm just a priest. I'm not a politician. I don't even have any experience in government. And besides, I'm happy with my life just as it is. Why me Lord?"

Have you ever asked yourself "Why me'!" I have, and I suspect you may have also. God's call gives our faith and determination a real workout.

And moreover, we might also be puzzled and ask concerning Ezekiel, "Why would God ge a simple priest, who only presided over sacrifices and rituals, the very public task of being a proclaiming prophet assigned to address a nation.

And a wayward nation at that?" Ezekiel's calling, being pastoral, made him responsible for the spiritual direction of his nation; no wonder he was overwhelmed.

Nevertheless, this was God's call to him; the person chosen for the work. His task? God commissioned him to speak to his fellow Israelites, the exiles at Tel Av.

Then, God became more specific and said to him, "Son of man, I have made you a watchman for the house of Israel." What! This was almost too much. What about his own future plans? He was likely quite satisfied with his life the way it was. Life was so predictable by just keeping things as they are. But this was not God's plan for Ezekiel. He was the one God called to address a wayward nation. And more specifically, called to be a watchman, to warn his fellow Israelites against their sinning and to guard their spiritual lives. Yes, it was difficult, but he answered God's call, and he did God's bidding.

And during his, some twenty-years of prophetic ministry as a watchman, Ezekiel was given amazing visions and words of warning to speak to Israel, words they didn't want to hear and didn't want to believe. It was very difficult. And Ezekiel's messages were misunderstood, in part, because he used unusual, symbolic acts to communicate his prophetic message, and though strange to his contemporaries, his prophecies were correct.

Only much later was his true greatness recognized, his writings, preserved for posterity, are now in our Bibles. There is a saying, "To be great is to be misunderstood." Ezekiel was more than misunderstood. He was largely ignored.

Nevertheless, Ezekiel was definitely called to be a watchman. His chief task was to warn the people of God's judgment against their sinning; and to bring Israel and the nations of the world to worship the true and Living God.

At this dark time in history, Israel and the surrounding nations were practicing animism, a kind of idolatry, where they worshipped objects made with their own hands as though these objects then took on magical powers. Not only were these worship practices useless, but they were also blasphemous.

Ezekiel's message brought with it a strong sense of God's sovereignty over his creation, and of God's activity in human history.

Along with Ezekiel warning Israel of God's impending punishment, he taught them to become moral and to worship the one true and Living God.

What happened as result of his warnings? His message was ignored. Years went by. And in 586 B.C. the temple was destroyed just as Ezekiel prophesied.

Perhaps, this tragedy was what caused a change in Ezekiel's message. It likely was because his message shifted to hope and salvation.

Ezekiel now tells Israel that God's glory is not tied to the temple in Jerusalem, nor is it limited to any location; he reminds them that God's glory traveled with them into their exile. Ezekiel was really telling them that God would go with them wherever they went. Further, with more encouraging words, Ezekiel tells the exiles that God himself would be their sanctuary until he would bring them back into their own land. And was willing to forge them, as penitent sinners, and restore them to life, even while they were in exile.

Then, n1ost amazing for its time in history, by proclaiming a theology of grace, Ezekiel prophecies that God will also renew them inwardly through the gracious bestowal of his Spirit. And, just as amazing, these prophetical words look forward to the coming of Jesus the Christ and the Age of Grace.

So, now we might ask; just why was Ezekiel's prophetical ministry so necessary at this time? First, we recognize that God's call is always necessary and on time.

Second, Ezekiel was aware of his country's dire circumstances being in exile. Third, he saw Israel's spiritual decline and that the new generation was blaming their misfortunes and present condition on their parents. They were not taking responsibility for their present situation, and they had caved in to the influences of pagan nations and their religions. They had regressed into immorality and idol worship in their rebellion against God.

It was true. When Jerusalem fell, it fell in part, because of the wrongful leadership of King Manasseh. He was an evil king of Judah, who actually promoted immorality and idol worship.

However, it is also true, that the people didn't have to follow him; but they

followed him anyway and were led into sin, like sheep who had gone astray. Now, they found themselves in a sinful state with only themselves to blame. But still avoiding personal responsibility, they blamed their parents. You heard it right. They blamed the past generation for their bad choices. Does that somehow sound familiar? They were at a spiritual impasse. And blaming wouldn't solve anything.

Seeing their refusal to face their responsibility, Ezekiel entered the scene. Led by God, he painfully pointed the way out of their dilemma, which was not easy, but he showed them the way, recognizing that, in spite of their waywardness, were still God's chosen people.

They just had to stop complaining and take responsibility for their own lives and that there was hope if they would listen to Ezekiel and act responsibly.

Ezekiel's basic message was universal; it addressed not only Israel, but it faces us today with our own present circumstances in:

Dealing with What is Right - which first means recognizing what a sinful lifestyle is and

Facing the fact of the sinfulness of fallen humanity - Humans have the impulse to sin and no one is exempt from this.

Facing our own fallen nature - All of humanity needs the saving grace of Jesus Christ and as Christians we have the responsibility to lift up those who have fallen or who arc weak or in need of our support.

Looking toward a bright future - This is a walk of faith.

Doing What Is Right - even when it is difficult or unpopular to do the right thing. "We are not slaves to our past unless we allow ourselves to be." We have the power to choose what is right, the power to make choices and the power to take a new direction in our lives if we need to. How does this happen?

It happens as God reveals himself to us on our spiritual journey through his revealed Word, using our ability to reason, applying spiritual wisdom gained with our own experiences with God.

It happens in the light of our acting positively - through a sense of community, a sense of belonging and by embracing our fellow human beings with love and care.

It happens by reaching out to our community - beginning within our family, continuing within the Church community, and reaching out into the local and world community. This is done in part, by:

Living a Righteous Life in an Unrighteous, sinful World

Of course, everyone's spiritual journey begins with repentance which begins with recognizing our spiritual need as much more than feeling remorse for any sins in our life. It means a change of direction, a complete turning around, not merely talking about it, really making an effort to do it. It involves self-appraisal as to where our lives are going and where we need to change, allowing the Holy Spirit to lead and redirect our lives.

We enter a new life of faith important because a person not Living a life of faith is Living outside of spiritual reality. That person is headed toward despair and will never know the joy of the truly spiritual life.

It is like the little boy pressing his nose against the window of the candy shop. The candy looks good, but he will never really know until he experiences it. He will never realize it until he tastes it. Scripture describes this well, 'Taste and see that the Lord is good." The realization is in experience. We must enter God's candy shop and taste for ourselves. Then, we will have the spiritual knowing that passes all understanding. Inside of your being you will know because you know! God has put a spiritual sense of knowing there. Trust it! No one can ever take it away. The change that manifests itself ·within you is because of God's presence and is the very armor of God. This presence enables us to deal with life spiritually empowered and moving forward toward greater maturity, being more Christ-like. It empowers us because we recognize that life has a spiritual dimension. We can now prayerfully, scripturally better use our ability to reason and live our lives truly unto God. We can lead others to follow the spiritually enlightening path that Jesus trod - like the two disciples walking with Jesus to Emmaus, this too, is our spiritual walk, becoming more and more conformed to the image of Christ. So then, as Christians, being a people of scripture, a people of reason, and a people with a genuine spiritual experience, we are ever moving forward toward the city of God.

In our walk with Christ, we perceive life more and more in light of spiritual realities. We are more enabled to grow in righteousness and take responsibility for our thoughts and actions, realizing that our spiritual life is between us and God. We now recognize the importance of God's Holy Spirit with us to lead us on our journey - like the disciples we walk with the Lord to Emmaus.

Living for God on Our Daily Walk

Scripture lesson: Hebrews 13: 1-8 Text Heb. 13:6

During the horse and buggy days, a story was told of a man who with his wife, led at the top of a mountain, perhaps North Carolina, and being in their mature years, needed someone to take them for groceries and other supplies.

So, they advertised for a chauffeur in the local newspaper. Several people applied. And as the story goes, the first driver, a young man, determined and overly confident, drove the carriage down the mountain at a dangerously high speed; no accident, but what if? Frightened at the thought, the carriage owner turned the reins over to the next applicant. He drove too fast as well but did stay on the narrow path better than the first driver.

However, when the third driver came to take his turn at the reins he said, "Sir, I do need this job and I would like to have it. I have had considerable experience driving my own carriage. But your road is quite dangerous, and I would need to drive slowly, staying close to the mountain side of the road to maintain control. Frankly sir, if you need a fast driver, I'm not your man. But if speed is not an issue, I would like to be your chauffeur." Surprised at the man's openness and honesty, the owner thought for a moment; then he said, "I need someone to take us up and down the mountain safely. You're hired."

The lesson is obvious, as we apply it here, is to live carefully and on the side of caution. Dring schools instruct their students to drive carefully, cautiously and defensively. Why? It is a well- known statistic, confirmed by higher insurance rates, that young drivers, especially young men, up to the age of twenty- fe have more accidents than the rest of the population.

The sign for us to remember is, "Life is fragile. Handle with care," a reminder to live our lives with wisdom and caution. True, sometimes we are caught where we have to take a calculated risk, but like the carriage driver, caution is the way we need to proceed. A few minutes of careful thought can often prevent miles of misery.

I remember, with sadness, a high-strung young lady who played trumpet in the Jackson High School band when I was the director. Her dad let her have a car to drive; she drove too fast, wouldn't listen to reason and wound up in an accident. Rushed by ambulance to Baton Rouge to the hospital, where she lingered for several days and finally died. What a waste! Here was a bright, talented young lady whose life was cut short because she wouldn't drive cautiously and listen to reason.

In 1953, the year Josephine and I graduated from high school, some young men in our senior class decided to have chicken races in the dark, going down a winding mountain road outside of town. One of the cars hit a tree at high speed and they were all instantly killed just several days before they were to graduate.

And there was no excuse for us boys, while hiking in the woods outside of the town, Moosic, PA., we explored an abandoned coal mine, ignoring the warning sign, Do Not Enter. We went in anyway, but frightened when we heard a cracking sound, we quickly retreated just in time to see large rocks fall behind us near the entrance.

We never tried that again. It took a close call with possible death to learn that not only is life fragile, abandoned mines are taboo!

Today, we have road rage problems, drug problems, shootings and the often-unnecessary bitter conflicts in social relations; all so unnecessary and nonproductive.

Life, indeed, is fragile, including our spiritual lives, to be handled with care, and should never be neglected. It seems so easy to travel life's path, throwing caution to the winds, oblivious to its dangers. But the mountain path of life can be treacherous. Caution, not carelessness, is the watchword. So, it is also wise for us to guard our spiritual lives carefully, remembering that life is not just about the destination, it is also about the journey. And living a fulfilled life, as a Christian, is a vital part of our personal journey.

We certainly don't want our lives to be summed up like the ancient king Belshazzar, king of the Chaldeans, found in the book of Daniel. This pagan king gave a great feast to a thousand of his lords; and as they drank wine, lifting their goblets, they praised the gods of gold, silver, brass, iron, wood, and stone. So misguided and hedonistic, they were Living for pleasure and revelry.

But God was watching. And during the feast an amazing thing happened, there appeared fingers like that of a man's handwriting words on the wall," Mene, Mene Tekel Ulharsin," words that summed up Belshazzar's life.

"Thou art weighed in the balances and found wanting." And history records that this was the very night Belshazzar died.

As we well know, living our lives as Christians is challenging because spiritual values are like climbing a mountain that leads us upward, to be the best spiritually that we can be. So, it is wise to avoid Living our lives on the edge, like the carriage driver who, tried to see what he could get away with. Instead, we should determine, like the careful carriage driver, to live as close to God as we can. There is no mystery in this. And it is doable. The important thing is for us to keep our lives close to the Lord. The writer of Hebrews exhorts us in practical Christian Living to:

Keep on Loving Each Other - It may not seem to pay off in the short term, but in the long-term love always wins. And:

We are to be hospitable remembering that the culmination of God's grace in our lives is graciousness. And that affirming the other person's worth; words and notes of encouragement and acknowledgement are ministry.

The Writer of Hebrews tells us to remember those in prison. They are too easily forgotten, especially those suffering for the gospel, as many are today.

There is so much persecution of Christians in the world today that much prayer and care is needed. The answer is clear. If people everywhere would follow the scripture, "Do unto others as you would have them do unto you," there would be no more war. Further:

The Writer of Hebrews exhorts us to honor marriage and keep it pure.

This means:

1. Keep the sacred marriage vows while building a bond of trust through faithfulness,

2. Show respect for one another; lack of respect means a lack of love. And remember love is caring! And we should:

3. Make every effort to solve problems quickly.

Allowing a problem to fester only makes the wound worse. The scripture,

"Let not the sun go down on vous wrath," is great wisdom.

And, be assured, in any marriage, fidelity is the only option, with

trust as its close cousin. If you don't have trust, you don't have anything.

Live with Values Higher Than the Materialistic World.

Keep free from the love of money. We should learn to use money wisely and not let money use us. The world is literally loaded with dishonest business schemes and advertising lies. Don't fall for them. Laugh and walk away.

Be content with what you have Avoid greed for greed has no end. It is never satisfied and like a fatal disease, it devours its victim.

Remember that we live with the highest value within us Our bodies are the temple of the Holy Spirit; the very kingdom of God is within us.

Remember Your Leaders and Remember who Jesus Christ is

True leaders will speak the Word of God to us. And in the past, they have done this. True leaders have led the life of faith Consider the outcome of their lives they are in God's hands.

True leaders lead a life so close to God that they imitate Jesus Christ. Therefore, imitate their faith. Their faith is in Jesus Christ who "is the same yesterday, today and forever."

There is no greater life to be led than the life that is led unto God. For we who are Christians, love has a spiritual dimension beyond this world.

As for values, we know that eternal values have the most meaning. And in a world whose values are constantly changing, we have great stability in our lives knowing that "Jesus Christ is the same yesterday, today and forever."

Yes, the search to know God in a deeper, fuller way is a lifelong adventure as we remind ourselves to handle our spiritual lives as well as our natural lives with great care. May we be ever mindful that it is in Christ, "Whom to know is life eternal."

Godliness With Contentment

Scripture lesson: I Timothy 6:3-2 Text: I Timothy 6:12

Let's begin by asking. What is Godliness? Is Godliness simply abstaining from things which are wrong? Certainly, we should try to do this. But will that make a person Godly? Some sincere people sincerely believe that the way to be godly or holy is to simply avoid every wrong action or thought. To pursue this some persons, decide to become monks and live in Monasteries.

When Josephine and I were Living in Missouri, during my undergraduate years, we visited the Trappist monastic order in Ava Missouri. Upon entering we were greeted by a young monk, who, in his first year was allowed to talk, told us in our conversation with him, "I am not saying that I am holy, but I am trying awfully hard."

The daily routine of the monks is 3:15 A.M. Rise, the Office of Vigils; 6:30 Morning Prayer and Eucharist; 9:00 Mid-Morning Prayer, Work until :30; :45 Mid-Day Prayer, Dinner in common, Dishes; 2:00 Mid-Afternoon Prayer, Work till 4:30; 5:45 Evening Prayer, Meditation; 7:45 Compline; last of the canonical hours) and Retire. On Sundays, no work. Throughout the day are several periods of time for personal prayer, reading and study, walks and creating activities. A light breakfast and a light evening meal are available. A siesta afternoon meal is optional.

The monks make a promise, they say is not a vow, of not speaking unless necessary. Then, after making their commitment to silence, the monks communicate with sign language. Also, Ascetics may even isolate themselves, attempting to totally separate themselves from evil. If they enter monasteries for this reason, they are perhaps shocked to find temptations are also there.

In the early days of our nation, there were groups who settled in the Felicianas, near Baton Rouge, Louisiana, and formed isolated communities attempting to be free from the corruption of the world. Their attempts failed because problems erupted in these communities just like everywhere else because the impulse to sin is in everybody. The evidence confirms that the human race needs redemption, and that a negate definition of godliness is self-defeating. However, after thinking about the way the world is today, we exclaim, "'Godliness with contentment!" What is that'? Is it even possible'?"

It does seem so impossible that persons sometimes shy away from becoming Christians because they know they couldn't live the life of perfection they think scriptures demand. We, of course, realize that nobody can do this. So, what does the scripture mean by Godliness? And what is godliness with contentment? And where do love and grace fit into all of this?

To begin with, Godliness cannot be defined negatively; its earliest definition meant. "'set apart." And it is true; godliness involves adopting values separate from the secular world. And certainly, what is immoral, unethical or selfish should be avoided; but this is not the definition of Godliness. So, what is Godliness? Godliness is putting a genuine spiritual relationship with God into practice. Further, you may ask. What about doing positive things to help others? Does this define holiness? No, as fine as this is, the definition of Godliness is more than this.

Godliness is being born again with the natural outflow of good works. Next, still puzzled, we probe with the next question, "What is real contentment?" Is it sitting under a tree with a cold drink on a warm spring day? No, it runs deeper than that. Is it looking at a beautiful vista, framed by trees, at the top of a mountain? No, this is a pleasure for the moment. Could it be singing, "'Happy Trails to You'?" while we stroll in the woods? No, though the song attempts to reach toward contentment, it does not address real contentment.

What about sitting on your front porch gently scratching your dog's ears? An amusing scene Josephine and I saw many times while going to and from work and we would mutter to ourselves, "Doesn't he have more to do than that?"

So, to be clear, contentment doesn't mean inactivity. We can be quite content while being busy. Then, what constitutes "'godliness with contentment'!" Be assured, it cannot be properly understood on a superficial level.

The key is in the word "with" because pursuing a life of Godliness is inextricably woven into our relationship with Jesus Christ. And whatever our stage of spiritual development may be, as maturing Christians, we are safe in God's loving hands. where there enters into our souls a wonderful, deep settled peace; this is the "godliness with contentment' we so earnestly desire.

Sounds too simple. In this technological age, it might be for some folks, but scripture confirms it. The apostle Paul, writing his first letter to the younger Timothy, addresses him as "my true son in the faith," and then he makes this profound statement:

"But godliness with contentment is great gain. For we brought nothing into the world, and we can take nothing out of it. But if we have food and clothing, we will be content with that. People who want to get rich fall into temptation and a trap and into many foolish and harmful desires that plunge men into ruin and destruction. For the love of money is a root of all kinds of evil."

This is Paul, the teaching evangelist, wisely helping Timothy to consider the human condition, and its weaknesses and reminding him of his new responsibilities.

He charges the young pastor/evangelist:

"'But you, man of God, flee from all this and pursue righteousness, godliness, faith, love, endurance and gentleness. Fight the good fight of faith. Take hold of the eternal life to which you were called when you made your good confession in the presence of many witnesses."

Why does Paul talk to Timothy like this? Didn't he just describe him as, "'My true son in the faith?" It is because Timothy, like the congregation he is to pastor, is also subject to the same temptations that they face, true of everyone, including Christian leaders.

Continuing, Paul advises Timothy concerning his preaching ministry, ending with a positive, uplifting note. He says:

"'Command those who are rich in this present world not to be arrogant nor to put their hope in wealth, which is so uncertain, but to put their hope in God, who provides us with everything for our enjoyment."

"'Everything for our enjoyment!" What is this he just said? You heard it right. God wants us to be happy. All through the New Testament there are statements like, "that your joy may be full" and "it is unspeakable joy" and "'at his right hand are pleasures forevermore." There is this emphasis about joy and happiness in the scriptures because our heavenly Father wants us to be happy. The Christian life is meant to be full of "joy unspeakable and full of glory." You heard it right. Our heavenly Father wants us to be happy, free from the burden of guilt everyone struggles with and free to live the joyful life of faith. And free from fighting the burden of sin, trying to escape the dark feeling with hedonistic pleasure and living in denial.

Further, Paul says, "that they may take hold of life that is truly life." Why is he implying that some people, though physically ale, are not really living? He wants them to realize a true spiritual existence and know that "Godliness with contentment is great gain." That is really living!

You see, in spite of the dim view taken by some purists in physical science, there is such a thing as spiritual knowing. A spiritual sense that transcends the bounds of science and leads us to be able to declare with the apostle Paul,

"I know whom I have believed and am convinced that he is able to guard what I have entrusted to him for that day."

In our world today, with so many agnostics, don't be afraid to say "'I know." Don't allow anyone to dictate against what you know in your spirit to be true. Go ahead and say it and say it with conviction, "I know whom I have believed and am convinced that he is able to guard what I have entrusted to him for that day." Dare to say that you know. Remember, your inner spiritual sense of knowing goes beyond anyone's materialistic thinking. It baffles the carnal mind because it is spiritually discerned. Don't be baffled because herein lies the secret of contentment. What is it? It is a settled faith that has experienced redemption through Christ and a faith that pursues godliness as spiritual development and growth.

So, in today's scripture we see the apostle Paul giving instructions to Timothy, telling him how he should properly pastor his flock. (By the way, sheep in the holy land have a poor sense of direction and need to stay with the flock to keep from getting lost. Another reason for the parable of the lost sheep.)

Continuing our narration, Paul is firm and direct. He has to be. Early Christians, like today, were surrounded by many clever, false ideas about Jesus Christ and what it meant to be a Christian. Often having their roots in pagan religions, the Greeks believed their body was nothing but a tomb and agnosticism that says you can't really know anything and concurrently, a rise in the belief that only what is material exists. Sadly, this had led to a higher suicide rate and the seeking of pleasure for its own sake, since to them, nothing else matters. You may ask, "How did all this get started'? We owe this to the negate side of Eighteenth-Century Enlightenment and many of these same problems also existed in apostolic times, So, Paul says to Timothy:

Let Your Faith! - Have a firm grounding in what you believe. Pray much and stay with solid doctrine - especially important today in such uncertain times. Know your Bible. Stay firmly with its truth, which is the plain, clear message of the gospel, found in the plain meaning of the text," as John Wesley wisely advised. And don't devote time to religious speculations.

Why? Because they lead to useless arguments.

The people Paul is referring to are the sophists, dispute-loving Greeks and Jewish Hellenists who seek to gain a reputation through their devious, self-serving arguments; and some even got paid for this. These practices of disputation so often emphasize the wrong things. They don't consider that life has a spiritual dimension. They ignore genuine spiritual experiences and try to lower Christianity to their level, the level of argument. Christianity is not an argument. It is an experience, a spiritual experience. The Christian life is only properly understood in the sunshine of a genuine spiritual experience with Jesus Christ, undergirded by sound biblical doctrine.

So, Paul instructs Timothy:

Don't lose sight of the practical, physical essentials such as food and water; but still keep your focus on what is really important-your spiritual life.

Le by the spiritual essential truth - 'Godliness with contentment is great gain."

Be proactive in your faith Fight the good fight of faith and "Take hold of eternal life to which you were called." - This is also necessary for us, especially today, since there is such a lack of true spiritual faith in the world.

Teach the Faith Remember your own public confession of faith!

Teach the limitations and traps of seeking material wealth knowing what we have does not define who we are, and we should never let it even appear to define us.

Teach believers to fix their hope in God and if they have wealth, use it for good. Teach Christians to be rich in good works that they may grasp real life values which are spiritual values.

To the Magi, Jesus was Royalty. They somehow recognized that he was born a king. To the Magi, this unusual child was worth travelling a great distance, over rough terrain, risking hardships and danger just to see him and pay tribute to him. Somehow, they were drawn to him, and it only seemed proper to pay him tribute.

The Magi, themselves royalty, recognized Jesus' special royal status to the point, that they humbly bowed down to him and gave him gifts of tribute and respect.

The Magi observed an unusual heavenly body they interpreted as Jesus' personal star and followed its direction. It became their personal witness of this special event - the birth of the king of the Jews.

The Magi brought the Christ child tribute gifts, as kings did, recognizing another king. What caused the Magi to recognize Jesus as Dine? Why would they worship a child, whose origin they really didn't know? What is the significance of their gifts? These are legitimate questions and I believe God revealed these things to them. As to their gifts: Gold - represents royalty. They recognized his royal status.

Frankincense - represents the priesthood; they also recognized Jesus' priestly status. Myrrh - represents preparation for burial. The gift lovingly recognized the importance for preparing for the end of life and was prophetic in nature, symbolic of Jesus' future death on the cross for the sins of the world.

How singularly interesting is this that the Magi somehow knew who the Christ child was, recognized his importance in coming into the world and so giving him gifts, bowed before him, recognizing him as king of the Jews before most people knew he was born. But what about Herod?

To King Herod, Jesus was a Threat Another king to potentially challenge his own kingship. The Magi didn't know this and innocently went to Herod seeking Jesus' location. Herod was not happy to hear the news.

Herod was disturbed along with the city of Jerusalem Why? It was not uncommon in the East to crown children as kings. Herod certainly didn't want a child king taking his throne.

Herod's council verified the prophecy of a Messiah. They knew the Old Testament scriptures, respected their authenticity and they told of the coming of a Messiah. Herod's council interpreted this as the coming of a king to liberate the Jews from being under Roman rule. Herod saw this as a threat to his rule.

Herod sought to kill Jesus. However, Joseph was warned in a dream of the danger, so they fled to Egypt and escaped his wrath.

Next, we ask: Who was the Christ child to Simeon and Anna? They were among the faithful believers looking for the Messiah, burdened for their people under tyrannical Roman rule. They knew the promise, as does every orthodox Jew today. The difference? We recognize the coming of the Messiah. They don't believe he has come yet. We should pray for our Jewish brothers and sisters that their eyes will be opened, as has already happened to some, to the great revelation that awaits them. We should love them and pray for those who have not as yet seen the light.

So, now we ask again. Who was the Christ child to Simeon and Anna?

To Simeon and Anna, Jesus was, "The salvation of the Lord."

Simeon waited in anticipation for the Messiah.

Simeon was obedient to the Holy Spirit's direction.

Simeon saw the salvation of the Lord. His prayer was answered.

Anna, too, gave thanks to the Lord.

What Does Jesus Christ's birth mean to you today? - to all of us.

It means, by accepting Christ into our lives, we have "new life in him." Free from the nagging burden of sin, we can, by faith, live life to its fullest. We can experience spiritual fulfillment as well as human fulfillment. They are different you know. To have the satisfaction of a life well led unto God, there is nothing better than this!

It means we can experience "the deepest meaning of love." -Christ's unconditional love and cleansing. Through experiencing God's call on our lives, and he calls us all, we can experience our own personal, spiritual fulfillment. No one can do this for us. We must embrace God's love for ourselves.

It means that true Christians are enabled to help change the world- one soul at a time.

What does Christmas mean to you? To the Magi, Jesus was royalty. To King

Herod, Jesus was a threat. To the Council of Herod, Jesus was the fulfillment of prophecy. To Simeon and Anna, Jesus is the salvation of the Lord.

Over seven hundred years before the birth of Christ, the prophet Isaiah spoke in: (Isa. 9:6-9 "For unto us a child is born, unto us a son is gen, and the government will be on his

shoulders. And he will; be called wonderful Counselor, Mighty God, Everlasting Father, Prince of Peace. If the increase of his government, there will be no end. He will reign on David's throne and over his kingdom, establishing it and upholding it with justice and righteousness from that time on and forever." - God's eternal kingdom!

Who was he who was born in Bethlehem? He is Jesus, the Messiah, - God with us, prophet, priest and king - our blessed Lord and Savior who gives "joy to the world!"

The Good Example of the Shepherds

Scripture lesson: Luke 2:1-20 Text: Luke 2

Just as we take a census in our country, the ancient Roman Empire would take a census to find persons to conscript for the Roman army. And for tax purposes a census was taken of every person every 14 years.

Although exempt from military service, the Jewish community was, nevertheless, required to pay taxes. Remember when Jesus said, "Render unto Caesar what is Caesar's and unto God what is God's." In times past scholars raised some doubt about the record of the census described during the birth of Christ; but census documents from A.O. 20 to around A.D. 270 have established that the practice was common and that a census was also taken in Egypt and Syria verifying the statement that all the world was to be taxed, meaning, of course, the then known world.

Now, Judea was part of the larger province of Syria. The little town called Bethlehem was located in Judea, which we might liken to a county. And Judea was located within the larger province of Syria which we might liken to a state.

At any rate, the journey Joseph and Mary were to take for the required census for tax purposes was from the town of Nazareth to Bethlehem. The distance of the journey was about 80 miles. And it was over rough terrain. Of course, there were no motels like we have today. The eastern khan (or inn) was like a series of stalls that opened into a common courtyard. As a traveler you must bring your own food, but the innkeeper did provide fodder for the animals and a fire to cook the food. Since there was no room for Mary and Joseph in one of the stalls, described as the inn (what we today call motel rooms), they had to stay in the common courtyard. This is where Jesus was born. He was placed in a limestone food trough, called a manger.

The night of his birth was likely a relatively quiet night with a few sounds from the animals.

But the quiet was interrupted by a burst of song from high in the heavens. Something amazing had just happened. The most wondrous birth ever. Jesus was born!

And who was the first person to hear this great news and witness the celebration of the heavenly hosts? Shepherds - located in the fields just outside of Bethlehem.

Shepherds -those rugged, ruddy faced men who, day after day, year after year, withstood the sweltering heat of a midday sun and survived the chilling cold of the desert nights. They spent so much time looking out in the distance after their flocks they typically became far sighted.

Shepherds - those men who were looked down on by the strict orthodox Jews because they were not able to keep all the details of ceremonial law. Yet it was from their flocks that the altar sacrifices for the sins of the people were made. All this was made possible because of their faithful work.

Shepherds - those men whose limited wealth and very livelihoods were constantly threatened by weather, by lions, bears, wolves, snakes and by thieves.

Shepherds - those faithful men who constantly guarded their flock every day of their lives to protect it from danger. Yes. it was to these shepherds, representatives of the common people, that the first news of the gospel was gen.

Prophecies concerning the coming of the Messiah, like a long unbroken filament, stretched from Genesis to Malachi and from Malachi to the New Testament. And it finally happened.

Jesus - the Long-Awaited Messiah is Born! - He was born near the shepherds, in the little town of Bethlehem. Jesus - the Desire of Ages. the One, who is God, incarnate, God in human flesh, is finally here, born of a virgin, come to save all those who would believe in him.

Born into humble circumstances - with earthly humility - but, coming from the realms of glory, Jesus became one of us.

Raised in a difficult environment, (as one person quipped, "Can anything good come out of Nazareth?") Jesus who, from the beginning, was one with his Father, remained one with his Father even declared for all to know, "I and the Father are one." So,

Jesus Revealed, by the Heavenly Hosts, Is the Long-Awaited Messiah.

Jesus' birth is revealed first to shepherds Although these were people of low social standing, they were of high ethical standing. They were men of vigilant watchfulness; they were men who cared, men who knew hard work and sacrifice; they were men who in the midst of their work, were also looking for the Messiah. And they were the first ones to hear the grand announcement by the heavenly hosts.

Jesus is proclaimed as Savior - the eternal answer to the soul that seeks redemption. The eternal answer to all who seek God, the one who is all in all; the one who is eternal.

Jesus is Proclaimed by the Shepherds - Who would believe them? Men of such low social standing. How could they possibly be the ones chosen to bear the message? Would they become a laughingstock? Would people believe their story? They proclaimed the message anyway. Would anyone challenge their right to bear such a message? That was not their concern. They would proclaim the truth!

They joined In With the heavenly hosts and glorified God. And they should; it was the most important message of their lives. They had their moment and they seized it. How wonderful it all was! - The shepherds both experienced history and made history that amazing night.

Joining in with the hosts of heaven they glorified God. There was no concern whether they could make the choir. They just felt they, too, should praise God, so they joined in and became part of the celebration and spread the good news that Jesus Christ - Messiah had come into the world.

Yes, there was much they didn't understand, as it still is today, but no matter; they knew that the Messiah had come - that the Savior was born. That was all they needed to know, and they proclaimed the message - as we should do today.

May the good word of the faithful shepherds reach the hearts of men and women, boys and girls everywhere! And may we also spread the truth of the gospel, hot from our hearts into the hearts of others, with our lives as well as by our testimony.

Indeed. the Savior is born! This is news that never gets old. True joy, eternal peace, new spiritual meaning and new hope has come into the world. It is now revealed in the person Jesus Christ our Lord!

Since he is the only one for whom Christmas exists, our Christmas celebration is like a birthday party for Jesus who brings joy to the world for all who believe in him.

Jesus is Born a King

Scripture Reading: Luke 2: 1-20 Text: Luke 2:

It seems that 2017 has just flown by and here we are once again in the Christmas season. In the midst of all our activity and responsibilities, we know that it is much more than a cultural celebration. If we were to ask, "What does it really mean?" The answer is that Christmas is important enough to be celebrated worldwide and though it means many things, they all hinge on the birth of Jesus Christ. Jesus certainly is, as the oft quoted saying, "the reason for the season." But it is easy to become so taken up with the activities surrounding the celebration that the activities and responsibilities seem to diminish the real reason. God, in human form, has come to the earth. And it is such a happy time.

Consider the bright, beautiful colors we use to celebrate Christmas. How beautiful is the message of these bright, happy colors splashed on store windows, banners and billboards and filling greeting cards with words of love and caring.

Then, there is the music. Such meaningful and beautiful music of the Christmas and Easter season is unsurpassed anywhere in the world. We feel inspired to say that the composers themselves certainly must have been divinely inspired. George Frederick Handel, after he wrote his oratorio, "The Messiah," stopped writing operas and he conducted "The Messiah" every year after that for the rest of his life.

We have the lovely traditions of gift giving among family and friends that remind us of Jesus, the greatest gift of all. Included in the celebration, there are the family visits and visits with friends who, with busy work schedules, may not have seen each other in many months, sometimes years, who make the extra effort to visit during the holidays.

And those precious photographs we take to capture the memorable moments, knowing that we may not be able to have the opportunity to get the pictures in quite the same way again.

And, of course, we look forward to the super good food, often taken from favorite family recipes. Extra effort is made, and extra time is spent, usually by the ladies, in planning to make the meals very special. And special they are.

Last, but not least, is the fellowship that accompanies these celebrations. It is great fun getting to see people we love, catch up on the news and happenings. And with this come the stories. Oh, those stories, how important they are.

They are an important part of our visiting time. They help us relate to each other and gain a better sense of who we are! Do you remember those, remember when, stories? Or the, can you believe what happened, stories.

Not to mention the can you believe what somebody did, stories? In our family, sometimes, the stories are outlandish; sometimes they are improbable and often just plain funny. These stories can be very important, especially for children and grandchildren. They help them learn about their roots. who their kinfolk is and their humanness. With these stories we all get a better picture of who we are. They help us to know and understand each other better.

Ah! Those stories. We must share the stories. We must remember to tell the stories.

And for the times when we have had, or others have had, difficult circumstances during the past year or even during the Christmas season there can be painful memories. It is especially important that we deal with those difficult times with care and understanding, and especially prayer. When we make an effort to do this, we can help fill the bad memories with good ones. Prayer. Caring and understanding can do a lot to help promote healing. The difficult times can become a special time to remember when family and friends showed comfort and support.

And it is important to remind ourselves that folks with little no spiritual understandings view Christmas through a different lens. Christmas, to them, is a celebration seen through materialistic eyes. Sadly, these dear folks miss the true wonder and joy of it all. We should be gracious and pray for them and pray for ourselves, as we determine to keep Christ in Christmas. It is good to remind ourselves the importance of meaning and ask us, in the middle of all the activity:

What does Jesus' birth really mean to us today? Have we allowed ourselves to become distracted from the true meaning of Christmas? And what did Jesus' birth mean to the people who led in the Mideast during that time?

Sadly, there are some who don't celebrate Christmas. They say that Jesus didn't celebrate his own birthday, so why should they. I speak. Well, why not? The Biblical Record tells us that the very heavens rejoiced at Jesus' birth. If that's not a celebration I don't know what is!

Further, we might ask, "What was the importance of Jesus' birth to the Magi?" Of course, we know the answer, but it is good to think about it and ask a few questions. For example, how did the Magi come to their conclusion about the importance of Jesus' birth? What inspired them to make the long, difficult journey across the desert and into a strange and possibly dangerous land? What prompted them, when they found Jesus, to ge him gifts?

And why did they choose the particular gifts they gave him? And when they arrived, why did they bow down before him? As far as I can tell, I don't know anyone who told them to do this. Nevertheless:

To the Magi, Jesus Was Royalty These mysterious men from the east somehow recognized that Jesus was born a king! Apparently, their mathematical knowledge of the stars and planets gave them such a firm sense of knowledge that it led them to their amazing conclusion. This birth was no ordinary birth; it was the birth of a Divine King, and it was worth travelling a great distance, over rough terrain, risking hardships and danger just to see him and pay tribute to him. And, as incredible as it seems, at this point they didn't even know his name! Does Christmas mean as much to us today as it did to the Magi? those mysterious wise men from the East? It should mean even more. I love that bumper sticker that says, "Wise men still seek him."

The Magi recognized Christ's Kingship Somehow, they knew that something amazing had occurred, a Divine King was born. Their knowledge is the kind that baffles science. It reminds me of the introduction of acupuncture to the United States. The American scientific community wouldn't accept it as a legitimate treatment at first because they couldn't figure how it worked. The oriental community didn't seem to care about how. They just knew it worked and had practiced it for many hundreds of years. Nowadays, acupuncture is commonly accepted, and I have not read whether anyone has yet figured out how it works, but it works. Perhaps, this was like the mentality of the Magi? They reached conclusions after studying the skies and weren't worried about the details they didn't understand. They figured they knew enough to authenticate their historic journey.

They observed a strange heavenly body, perhaps a star, and followed its direction.

- It became their motivation to follow its lead. It became their personal witness to a mysterious truth, a Divine intervention into human affairs. So, they endured the long difficult journey to find the truth for themselves. We must do the same, find Christ for ourselves.

They brought the Christ child tribute gifts, as kings commonly did in those days, recognizing another king, but the Wise Men did something more, they worshipped the King. Again, we question. What caused the Magi to recognize this child as Dine? Why would they worship a child they didn't even know? What was the significance of their gifts? Legitimate questions, these. I believe God somehow revealed these things to them. As to their gifts:

Gold - represents royalty; The Magi recognized his royal status.

Frankincense - represents the priesthood; They also recognized his priestly status.

Myrrh - was ointment for burial. The gift recognizes the end of natural life.

How singularly interesting is the fact that the Magi, somehow knew the importance of the Christ child coming into the world and bowed before him, giving him gifts of tribute, gifts befitting a king. This is who Jesus was to the Magi. But, what about Herod?

To King Herod, Jesus Was a Threat another king to potentially challenge his authority to rule. Herod wasn't about to pay tribute to the Christ child as the Magi did, although he pretended that he would do it. He, then, had hundreds of babies killed to eliminate any possible rival to his power. This definitely happened. (There is still a marked graveyard in Bethlehem as clear evidence of this.) Herod had little doubt of the importance of the coming of the Christ child.

Herod was disturbed along with the city of Jerusalem. (Matt. 2:3) - This is where it became political in the eyes of the general population.

Herod's Council checked the Old Testament and verified the prophecy of a coming Messiah (Matt. 2:5-6) This was a threat he couldn't bear and so he took the despicable action of having hundreds of male babies killed to secure his position of power.

Herod sought to kill Jesus But Joseph was warned in a dream so, they fled to Egypt were apparently there for some time.

Next, we ask: Who was the Christ child to Simeon and Anna? Important here is the fact that they were among the faithful looking for the Messiah. They were burdened for their people under tyrannical Roman rule. They knew the promise, as does every orthodox Jew, even today. The difference? We recognize the coming of the Messiah; they don't believe He has come yet. We should pray for our Jewish brothers and sisters that their eyes will be opened to the great revelation that awaits them. Some have already accepted Christ. We should continue to pray for those who have not yet seen the light.

So, who was the Christ child to Simeon and Anna?

To Simeon and Anna, Jesus was, "The Salvation of the Lord." - Jesus was to them the hope of the ages, though they didn't understand fully the meaning of all this.

Simeon waited in anticipation for the Messiah (Luke 2:25) "Moved by the Spirit he went into the temple courts. When the parents brought in the Child Jesus to do for him what the custom of the Law required. Simeon took him in his arms and praised "God, saying, "Sovereign Lord. As you have promised, you now dismiss your servant in peace. For my eyes have seen your salvation, which you have prepared in the sight of all people, a light for revelation to the Gentiles and for glory to your people Israel."

Simeon was obedient to the Holy Spirit's direction (v27).

Simeon saw the salvation of the Lord (v30) His prayer was answered.

Anna, too, gave thanks to the Lord (v38) Her prayer was answered.

To Us, What Does Christ's Birth mean Today? - He never changes:

It means - we have "new life in him." We can live life to its fullest. We can experience spiritual fulfillment as well as human fulfillment.

It means - we experience "the deepest meaning of love." - to really experience unconditional love. It means to experience God's all-embracing love and experience this same love through other Christians.

It means - we realize where the hope of this world is; it is in Jesus, the one we celebrate today - Jesus the Christ, God's only Son.

It means - that as Spirit filled believers, we have the power to help change the world - one soul at a time.

So, we repeat the question. What does Christmas mean? To the Magi, Jesus is royalty. To King Herod, Jesus was a threat. To the Council, even of Herod, Jesus was the fulfillment of prophecy. To Simeon and Anna, he is the salvation of the Lord.

Over 700 years before the birth of Christ, the prophet Isaiah spoke:(Isa. 9:6-7)

"For unto us a child is born, unto us a son is gen, and the government will be on his shoulders. And he will be called Wonderful Counselor, Mighty God, Everlasting Father, Prince of Peace. If the increase of his government, there will be no end. He will reign on David's throne and over his kingdom, establishing it and upholding it with justice and righteousness from that time on and forever."

Who is he who was born in Bethlehem? He is Jesus the Messiah God with us. He is prophet, priest and king our blessed Savior!

The crowd praised God for the miracle They saw Jesus as the channel through which God restored the man back to life. And we should take note that Jesus did say, on other occasions, that everything he said and did came from his Father in heaven. So,

The crowd exclaimed, "'A great prophet has risen among us." and "God has come to help his people. So, could there be another reason for this miracle? Yes, for every miracle that Jesus did, there were broader, more far-reaching implications than the miracle itself. Remember, that during this same time John the Baptist was in prison. He was isolated, inside prison walls, wondering what was happening to Jesus and the events surrounding him.

Scripture does tell us.

"John's disciples had told him about all these things; so, John sent two of his disciples to the Lord asking, 'Are you he who is to come, or are we to look for another'!"

It appears that, under the strain of prison with its uncertainty, John had doubts. He needed some affirmation. Was Jesus really the Messiah as he had previously declared at Jesus' baptism? What would Jesus say? Would he, with reasoning, try to defend who he was? No. Instead, he recounted his many miracles and ended his remarks by showing keen insight into the minds of the people he was trying to reach. He told John:

"The poor have the Good News told to them; and blessed is he who does not find a stumbling -block in me." - It appears Jesus is confirming his Messiahship to John.

Todays scripture began with a deceased young man, his desperate mother and a large crowd in mourning, but it ended with a miracle and an amazed crowd. There were, without a doubt, mixed in the crowd, unbelieving Stoics, Greek Hellenists and other nonbelievers, who viewed life fatalistically and without hope of eternal life. Here, they witnessed a miracle and it totally upset their fatalistic thinking. They were forced to rethink their feeling of hopelessness.

Here, right in front of them, was hope. Jesus had the power over death and life.

And with great power, as is this miracle, Jesus sent his Holy Spirit to live within us, to be among us and to transform us daily. Be assured, spiritual growth is, itself, a great miracle. It changes us to become more like Christ!

God loves us. He cares about us which is why he gives life amidst despair. We know this because he sent his Son to the cross for our sins, to literally love us into the kingdom; he taught us the power of prayer, and to experience him in our own lives.

We experience answers to prayer, miracles in our own lives and in the lives of others. And we experience the wonder of personal transformation as we grow in faith, praying, living in the Spirit and rejoicing as we go from glory unto glory! Isn't salvation grand!

Jesus Calls a Tax Collector to Follow Him

Scripture lesson: Luke 5: 27-35 Text: Luke 6:32

Social stratification is a reality! Circumstances, such as the family into which we were born, economic situations, government regulations or oppression, religious ideas and other factors, affect us. Positive or negative circumstances can affect our self- esteem and can even keep us from bettering ourselves. In America we have the, so called, 'American Dream," the belief that we can better ourselves through education, careful planning and hard work. And many people have done this, but the opportunities that exist in a free society don't always exist in other countries. For example:

In India there is a caste system that, at birth, places a person into a certain caste or excludes that person from any caste, being an outcast, at birth, and it is that person's status for life. The ancient custom dictates that the person is not to socialize or even talk to someone of a lower caste. And even worse, if born so low as to not even being in a caste, that person is known as an outcast and is an outcast for life. Some people have come to America to be free from this kind of fixed social stratification.

In American culture, this same term, outcast, is also common in our language and it means that the person so identified is generally cast out from society. Thankfully, in America citizens are not doomed to live within a certain caste or be forever considered an outcast. In our country, normally, a person, through education, an improved socially accepted level of lying, or through accomplishment in the workplace, is able to enter into the mainstream of society. We know of some people in our own community who have done this.

However, various levels of social, economic, and intellectual status are found, in cultures all over the world. Even in a free society, such as ours, Ye find social stratification everywhere, based on wealth, political power, family status, social connections, academic achievement, or achievement in the workplace. Some people even carry a sense of status because of where they live and may view their status as giving them a kind of entitlement.

I remember, with amusement, an old western movie where a young girl saddled up to a stranger and threatened him in no uncertain terms, 'My daddy is mayor in this here town and you had better do what he says." The young girl felt powerful through the position of her mayor daddy and so she felt entitled. However, as amusing as this is, on a serious note, we ask ourselves. What place does social stratification have in the Church of Jesus Christ? And the answer is that it has no place in the Church of Jesus Christ because we are all of equal value in the eyes of God. The highly educated, apostle Paul leveled the field when he wrote in Corinthians 3:9, "We are God's fellow workers; you are God's field, God's building." Today's scripture lesson gives us an excellent example of the renowned Rabbi, Jesus honoring a social outcast by selecting him to follow him. Unusual because of the social barriers in their society, yet:

Jesus Calls a Social Outcast, a Tax Collector, to Follow Him. A tax collector? Yes. Why would Jesus call a social outcast, someone hated by his fellow Jews, and not even allowed in the synagogues to worship with them, to follow him? Why would Jesus' call Levi from his workplace while he was collecting taxes from fellow Jews who hated him. Why would Jesus honor this hated man by even speaking to him, as was forbidden by the Pharisees? And everyone knew it was an honor to be selected and called by a Rabbi. So, why would Jesus call this social outcast Jew, seen as a traitor because he worked for the Roman government, to follow him?

And would Levi, the tax collector actually follows Jesus? There was a lot for him to consider. Would he ge up his lucrative job, that of collecting taxes to follow Jesus? Would he ge up his allegiance and employment benefits of Rome to now ge allegiance to Jesus? Yes! In front of those standing there he made his decision. The call was simple. His decision was immediate and life transforming. Jesus simply said, "Follow me." And Levi got up immediately, left everything, and followed him.

Then, Levi did a beautiful thing; after receiving the honor of being called by Jesus, Levi, in turn, wants to honor. Jesus. How would he do this? He chose to have a great banquet in his house, not an ordinary meal, a great banquet. Why would he do this? Levi understood the magnitude of his call and wanted to celebrate it at the level he saw it. He understood that Jesus calling him was an honor.

So, who were invited to this great banquet to celebrate with him? His friends, and among his friends were his fellow tax collectors. There was a large crowd of tax collectors and others sitting at the table with them and apparently the Pharisees and their scribes were also there. (An important clue here is that during this period of time, important figures took scribes with them to record important events, which explains, in part, how some scriptures were recorded.) Important to recognize that here,

The Pharisees and Scribes (teachers of the law) saw Levi's life change a change of allegiance away from Rome to that of allegiance to Jesus. Did they celebrate with him? No, of course not, their own religious authority was diminished since Levi was now following Jesus, his new religious authority. Not understanding what had happened, they complained, seeing the situation through narrow legalistic eyes, blinded by their own social customs, they didn't approve of Jesus eating with sinners. Perhaps, they tried to imply guilt by association. But whatever their reason, instead of rejoicing with Levi, honored to be called by a Rabbi, they shifted the celebration to criticism about Jesus. They asked,

"Why do you eat and drink with the tax collectors and sinners?" - We know the scribes and pharisees wouldn't break their social codes and do what Jesus did, eat and drink with tax collectors and sinners. So, instead of trying to understand, they criticized Jesus by questioning, what was to them, a liberal lifestyle. It was like they were asking:

Why have you crossed over the social line? - Why would you dare to cross the social taboo, probably inferring that, by doing this, Jesus was contaminating himself.

Why are you allowing yourself to be numbered with the outcasts of society? - We don't do this. It is forbidden. How does Jesus answer their critical questioning?

www.ingramcontent.com/pod-product-compliance
Lightning Source LLC
Chambersburg PA
CBHW051004140626
46546CB00016B/330